Praise for *Interventions*

"[A] resolute, detailed, and unflinching re... hours . . . No one ever came closer to being the voice of 'we the peoples' and no one paid a higher price for it. The world still needs such a voice, but the next person who tries to fill that role will want to reflect long and hard on the lessons of this candid, courageous, and unsparing memoir."

—Michael Ignatieff, *The New York Review of Books*

"[A] taut and timely memoir . . . a treatise on the doctrine that has defined and scarred the post–cold war years: interventionism. It is part reflection, part stricture, and part call to arms. No one is better suited to address this, for it has also defined and scarred Annan himself." —*Financial Times*

"Only after reading his recently published book, *Interventions: A Life in War and Peace*, did I get a true sense of how difficult a job he had. As a voluntary organization of 192 states, it's easy to criticize the effectiveness of the UN, but without it, we would be substantially further behind on issues of global health and development. . . . For anybody who wants to understand the complexities of the role of the Secretary General, this book is an illuminating read."

—Bill Gates, *The Gates Notes*

"[A] fluent, compelling account . . . clear-eyed and honest . . . Annan emerges as an effective and charismatic embodiment of the UN's ideals. His softly spoken manner and astute diplomacy have tended to mask his sharp judgments, pragmatic assessments, contempt for villains, and disdain of the modish and self-serving tosh spoken by the politically correct, the vainglorious Third World champions, the corrupt, and the compromised." —*The Times* (London)

"Annan doesn't shy away from admitting that he made mistakes, or that the UN needs to reform its outdated administrative structures. Yet he mounts a passionate, impressive defence of the organization. . . . The UN may be imperfect, but this powerful memoir shows that it is vital." —*The Sunday Times* (London)

"This is a good, lucid book by a wise and compassionate man who, despite having spent much of his life in the political stratosphere, never loses sight of the plight of the little man." —*The Daily Telegraph* (London)

"Avoiding the nebulous rhetoric of many political memoirs, Annan instead provides a peacemaker's invaluable perspective on those crises as well as insight into the daunting challenges facing international diplomats in today's strife-ridden world." —*Booklist*

"[An] interesting memoir . . . The accounts related by Annan . . . are worth every minute spent reading them. Nobody alive can quite match what he has heard and seen. As a bonus, he names names of national rulers and less well-known diplomats. For readers who want to identify heroes and villains, the book provides plenty of material. . . . With his book as his legacy, perhaps [Annan] will inspire younger individuals to make inroads against incredible cruelty around the world."
—*The Christian Science Monitor*

"An insider's personal account based on lessons drawn from long experience."
—*Kirkus Reviews*

"In this thought-provoking new memoir, Kofi Annan describes the peaceful and more equitable world that is within our grasp and offers his candid perspective on the challenges we must overcome to get there. *Interventions* is a powerful reminder that the United Nations still matters—and must continue to matter if we want our new century to be more free, peaceful, and prosperous than the last."
—President William J. Clinton

"Kofi Annan has been a powerful voice for the poor and a tireless advocate for peace. As a catalyst for international security and human rights, Annan reminds us that we, as a global community, are more alike than different. His life's work demonstrates what is possible when we focus on the universal values of equality, tolerance, and human dignity."
—Bill Gates

"Kofi Annan is a great global leader of our time. This wonderful book gives the readers a lucid and enjoyable understanding of the kind of reasoning and commitment that has made Annan such a force for good in the troubled world in which we live."
—Amartya Sen

"Behind the velvet tones of Kofi Annan's dulcet Ghanaian voice, there's a fearsome and fearless iron will, intent on finding solutions to some of the world's biggest problems."
—Bono

"An insightful and candid account of the most defining and complex conflicts and peace deals of the last decades of the twentieth century intertwined with the vision and the life journey of one of the most outstanding global leaders of our times. Kofi Annan marks his footprint in history with leadership values in which truth, humility, and dignity are the weaving threads."
—Graça Machel, founder of the Graça Machel Trust

"Kofi Annan gives a candid, clear, and thoughtful account of his successes and failures in one of the world's most challenging and thankless jobs."
—Lee Kuan Yew, former prime minister of the Republic of Singapore

PENGUIN BOOKS

INTERVENTIONS

Kofi Annan was the seventh secretary-general of the United Nations serving two terms from January 1, 1997, to December 31, 2006—and was the first to emerge from the ranks of United Nations staff. Annan has served the United Nations in various capacities since 1962, including working as the under-secretary-general for peacekeeping operations and the special representative of the secretary-general to the former Yugoslavia. Born in Ghana in 1938, Annan is the first sub-Saharan African to hold the post of secretary-general. In 2001, Kofi Annan and the United Nations were jointly awarded the Nobel Peace Prize with the citation praising Annan's leadership for "bringing new life to the organization."

Nader Mousavizadeh is the chief executive officer of Oxford Analytica, a global analysis and advisory firm. Previously, Mousavizadeh served at the United Nations in the office of the secretary-general from 1997 to 2003 and was an investment banker at Goldman Sachs. A Rhodes Scholar and a graduate of Harvard College, he received his MBA from the Massachusetts Institute of Technology as a Sloan Fellow. He is a foreign affairs columnist for Reuters and the editor of *The Black Book of Bosnia*.

INTERVENTIONS

A Life in War and Peace

KOFI ANNAN

WITH

NADER MOUSAVIZADEH

PENGUIN BOOKS

PENGUIN BOOKS
Published by the Penguin Group
Penguin Group (USA), 375 Hudson Street,
New York, New York 10014, USA

USA | Canada | UK | Ireland | Australia | New Zealand | India | South Africa | China
Penguin Books Ltd, Registered Offices: 80 Strand, London WC2R 0RL, England
For more information about the Penguin Group visit penguin.com

First published in the United States of America by The Penguin Press,
a member of Penguin Group (USA) Inc., 2012
Published in Penguin Books 2013

THE LIBRARY OF CONGRESS HAS CATALOGED
THE HARDCOVER EDITION AS FOLLOWS:
Annan, Kofi A. (Kofi Atta)
Interventions : a life in war and peace / Kofi Annan with Nader Mousavizadeh.
p. cm.
Includes index.
ISBN 978-1-59420-420-3 (hc.)
ISBN 978-0-14-312395-8 (pbk.)
1. Annan, Kofi A. (Kofi Atta) 2. World politics—1989- 3. United Nations—
Biography. 4. Statesmen—Ghana—Biography. I. Mousavizadeh, Nader. II. Title.
D839.7.A56A3 2012
341.23092—dc23
[B]
2012008173

Printed in the United States of America
1 3 5 7 9 10 8 6 4 2

DESIGNED BY AMANDA DEWEY

Penguin is committed to publishing works of quality and integrity.
In that spirit, we are proud to offer this book to our readers; however,
the story, the experiences, and the words are the author's alone.

I dedicate this book to my wife
and partner, Nane; my daughter, Ama;
my son, Kojo, and my stepdaughter, Nina.
I will always be grateful for their
love, patience, and support.

CONTENTS

Preface

THE ARC OF
INTERVENTION

What do we stand for as a global community? What are the responsibilities for our common fate in a world that is simultaneously coming together and coming apart—and how do we exercise those responsibilities? How do we strike the balance between growth and development, equality and opportunity, human rights and human security? And where does the United Nations—an organization founded nearly seventy years ago in San Francisco to prevent another world war—fit into a world transformed by forces of globalization and technology that are not defined by boundaries of nation or ideology?

We stand at the crossroads of a global realignment as momentous as the one faced by the UN's founders in 1945. While the past quarter century has witnessed an extraordinary escape from poverty on the part of hundreds of millions in Asia, Africa, and Latin America, the scourges of war, terror, and weapons of mass destruction still remain as present as ever. What has changed is the power of individuals—men and women in every part of the world emboldened by education and rising expectations of a better life in larger freedom—to demand a say in how they are governed, and by whom. The empowerment of the individual—from Tahrir Square to Silicon Valley to Chengdu to Juba—presents an unprecedented opportunity for advancing human dignity. At the same time, this shift is challenging established centers of power—from presidential palaces to corporate executive suites—to restore the breach in public trust that is the condition for the successful development of any just society.

In my four decades of service to the United Nations, I was privileged to work with an extraordinarily committed and talented group of diplomats, development experts, and humanitarians for whom these questions were at the center of all we sought to achieve. It was rarely an easy journey. As often as we succeeded in alleviating suffering or halting a conflict, we found ourselves powerless to do so before far too great a toll had already been taken. As the first secretary-general elected from the ranks of the organization, I came into office with a hard-won appreciation for the limits of our powers, but equally determined that we would not simply give up in the face of setbacks—that we could do better, and would do so in the name of the peoples for whom the Charter of the United Nations was written.

I sought to catalyze action across a wide range of issues—from the struggle against HIV/AIDS to girls' education, development in Africa to post-tsunami relief work, advancing human rights and the rule of law to insisting that sovereignty must be a matter of both rights and responsibilities. I dedicated my efforts toward achieving a United Nations that would step up rather than stand by; rise to the demands of a new century rather than recoil from them; and be guided by a purpose greater than protecting the interests of states.

This is the arc of intervention that frames my account of the principal challenges facing the international community today. It also reflects my conviction that while humanitarian intervention is a moral and strategic imperative when the alternative is genocide or gross violations of human rights, military action pursued for narrower purposes without global legitimacy or foresight about the consequences—as in the case of Iraq—can be as destructive as the evils it purports to confront. The emerging global convention of a "Responsibility to Protect" was conceived as a universal principle of protecting fundamental human rights—not as a license to make war in the name of peace.

This book appears fifty years after I first joined the United Nations in the World Health Organization's offices in Geneva—a half century that has seen the United Nations achieve considerable progress on some of the highest aims of its founders, and encountered failures and disappointments that mirror the worst of man's cruelty to man. My mission as secretary-general was built around a vision of bringing the organization closer to the peoples whom it was founded to serve, and to place each individual's aspirations for security, development, health, and human rights at the center of everything we did. I reached out to new constituencies among nongovernmental organizations, businesses, and citizens from every continent in order to shift our priorities from the United Nations in its conventional form to a more united world—one where every nation and community, faith and organization embraces the responsibilities of global citizenship.

This book tells the story of my mission through the prism of some of the most consequential crises and questions I confronted as secretary-general—and the way they illustrate the wider implications of the challenges facing the global community of nations. By necessity, a measure of selection and priority has been given to those issues that I believe best illuminate the recent history of international affairs, and help provide a path to addressing the coming threats and opportunities facing nations as well as individuals. The book does not, therefore, hew to a strict chronology of events or exhaustively examine every item on the agenda of the United Nations. Rather it addresses each of the key themes of my tenure as illustrated by my engagement with the global leaders at the center of the many conflicts and crises of the past two decades.

This is a personal account of my service to the United Nations and my efforts to address the major diplomatic, development, and humanitarian challenges facing the international community. Throughout this immensely rewarding and challenging journey, my wife, Nane, was a tireless companion. As we traveled together, she visited schools, refugee camps, and people living with HIV/AIDS across the world, thereby grounding our work in the needs of the most vulnerable, as well as supporting the UN's efforts on women's empowerment. Little that I achieved over more than four decades of service to the United Nations would have been possible, however, without the professionalism, creativity, and loyalty of the teams I was privileged to lead. During a career that included service with a wide range of UN agencies and offices, I was fortunate to work with a great many dedicated international civil servants and diplomats from around the world.

A number of individuals merit particular mention for their singular contributions to the causes at the center of this book. From my period as head of the United Nations Department of Peacekeeping Operations, I brought with me to the office of the secretary-general a small circle of close aides, among whom Iqbal Riza, my chef de cabinet, was my most trusted confidant through every significant challenge and success of my time in leadership. Wagaye Assebe, Tasa Delenda, Fred Eckhard, Elisabeth Lindenmayer, Lamin Sise, and Shashi Tharoor complete the group whose resourcefulness and commitment I relied on for more than a decade to advance our agenda.

As secretary-general, I was privileged to call on the leadership skills of a remarkable group of experienced idealists who never wavered from their commitment to the UN's mission: K. Y. Amoako, Hedi Annabi, Louise Arbour, Alicia Bárcena, Yves Bertholet, Lakhdar Brahimi, Sammy Buo, Patrizio Civili, Joseph Connor, Hans Corell, Antonio Maria Costa, Robert Dann, Álvaro de Soto, Nitin Desai, Michael Doyle, Jan Egeland, Ibrahim Fall, Ahmad Fawzi, Louise Frechette, Ibrahim Gambari, Victor Gbeho, Jean-Marie Guehenno, J. P. Halbwachs, Peter Hansen, Patrick

Hayford, Noeleen Heyzer, Abdoulie Janneh, Bruce Jones, Soren Jessen-Petersen, Tuliameni Kalomoh, Georg Kell, Angela King, Rolf Knutsson, Stephen Lewis, Carlos Lopes, Rachel Mayanja, Haile Menkarios, Nicolas Michel, Bernard Miyet, Michael Moller, Edward Mortimer, Nader Mousavizadeh, Jose Antonio Ocampo, Hisham Omayad, Robert Orr, Kieran Prendergast, Terje Roed-Larsen, Gert Rosenthal, John Ruggie, Warren Sach, Jeffrey Sachs, Mohamed Sahnoun, Stephen Stedman, Gillian Sorensen, Danilo Turk, Sergio Vieira de Mello, Margareta Wahlström, Nadia Younes, and Ralph Zacklin. Among the heads of the UN agencies and programs and other organizations who worked on the front lines of every battle we fought: Carol Bellamy, Catherine Bertini, Hans Blix, Mark Malloch Brown, Gro Harlem Brundtland, Michel Camdessus, Jacques Diouf, Mohamed ElBaradei, Thoraya Obaid, Sadako Ogata, Peter Piot, Mary Robinson, Nafis Sadik, Juan Somavia, Gus Speth, Anna Tibaijuka, Klaus Topfer, Hans Van Winkle, and James Wolfensohn all played a vital role in renewing our purpose.

Many of these individuals also gave generously of their time to read parts or all of the manuscript, and I am grateful for their comments and insights.

In deciding to cast my memoirs in the broader context of the ideas and practice of global statecraft in the twenty-first century, I asked Nader Mousavizadeh to collaborate with me on an endeavor that would draw on his remarkable understanding of the emerging architecture of international affairs.

Writing a book that seeks to address such a wide range of global issues over such a long period requires the work of many hands. We benefited from the assistance and encouragement of numerous friends and collaborators. One individual among them stands out, without whom this project could not have been completed: Tom Hill, a brilliant and immensely resourceful young scholar from the Department of War Studies, King's College London, devoted countless hours of research and contributed to every aspect of our account. Mats Berdal provided us with his unmatched insights into the perils and possibilities of UN peacekeeping, and Robert Dann offered us his profound understanding of the Arab-Israeli conflict and its wider implications for the Middle East. Simon Chesterman gave us valuable insights into the questions of global governance and the rule of law. Anthony Appiah and Kwame Pianim read the chapter on my early years in Ghana and provided greatly appreciated comments.

Finally, we were privileged to embark on this journey with two preeminent figures in publishing at our side—our agent Andrew Wylie and editor Ann Godoff. Throughout a complex and demanding process, they provided us with a degree of patience, attention to detail, and penetrating literary judgment that any author would be fortunate to have. Any errors or inaccuracies, of course, are solely our responsibility.

It is my hope that this book will leave readers of all generations with a deeper understanding of the forces transforming our world, the calamitous cost of conflict, and the still-great promise of global cooperation in fighting poverty and disease. Above all, I wish for a world in which men and women of every nation achieve a measure of dignity and opportunity in their individual lives that allows each of them to serve others, and to stand up to the forces of injustice and inequality wherever they exist—in other words, to *intervene*. And so, in the words of the poet,

"to act, that each to-morrow / Find us farther than to-day."

KOFI ANNAN
Accra and Geneva
May 2012

Prologue

PEACEKEEPER, PEACEMAKER

K ofi, they've made an honest man of me," Colin Powell said, with a huge smile across his face. The relief—and the exhaustion—was palpable. I could not help but smile along with my friend, and wanted to share in his comfort. The U.S. secretary of state had called and asked to come see me in New York six weeks after the U.S. invasion of Iraq, and with his typical confidence appeared on the thirty-eighth floor of UN headquarters by himself, with no aides and without the U.S. ambassador at his side. I could only be impressed by the resilience of this man, who had endured so much to argue for a war he clearly did not believe in. "They've found the mobile labs, and while we're not prepared to make the announcement yet, you'll see the news reports tomorrow." U.S. forces in Iraq had discovered what they thought were mobile labs for the production of weapons of mass destruction (WMD), and Powell was emphatic that this time it was real. The war had been justified; the cause affirmed.

While I did not have any reason to doubt Powell's sincerity, I was not convinced that this was, in fact, the hard evidence of WMD that U.S. forces with increasing desperation were searching for in Iraq. I had been down this road before—most vividly six months earlier when John Negroponte, the U.S. ambassador to the United Nations, had asked to see me privately in order to show me some of the evidence that the United States had accumulated about Saddam Hussein's illicit weapons program.

As Negroponte and the senior CIA officer accompanying him flipped through image after image—explaining in solemn tones the gravity of the evidence—a disturbing pattern emerged: it was all circumstantial. They would show an image of a building from five years ago, and then show another image of the same building two years later, immediately after a U.S. strike, but now rebuilt with a new roof and trucks entering and exiting. One of my aides then remarked: "But this doesn't really show us anything except that a building was built, then bombed, then rebuilt. How do you know what's in those buildings? It could be anything!" This was not what Negroponte had expected. As the CIA officer sat silently collecting his images, I asked a few more questions to which they had less than complete answers.

What had been presented to me by Negroponte as a unique opportunity to realize the severity of the threat managed only to do the opposite. As we entered my private office following the meeting, another one of my aides wondered aloud: "Why would they promise such definitive revelations only to bring at best highly circumstantial evidence? Is it because they think we can be convinced so easily, or is it because this is all they have, and that we're asking the basic questions that they're avoiding?"

We would soon learn the answer.

After September 11, following an initial outpouring of support for America, a heavy curtain soon fell between America and the rest of the world. To many Americans, and the Bush administration in particular, a global response was eminently justified by the barbarism visited upon the country and two of its greatest cities. For much of the global community in those days—shocking though this seemed to many Americans—the greatest threat to world peace came not from Saddam, but from an enraged and vengeful United States. Tragically, the chaotic, bloody aftermath of the subsequent invasion of Iraq did little to change this perception.

If 9/11 changed the world, the consequences of the Iraq War were of a similarly dramatic magnitude—from the Arab nations, appalled by the mayhem unleashed following the fall of Saddam, to the deep distrust among Security Council members bruised by the torturous negotiations in the run-up to the war to the growing isolation of a United States no longer as feared or respected. What the United States had lost, as a consequence of the invasion, was the benefit of the doubt. This pained me deeply. Throughout my years as secretary-general, I had often found myself in the role of global interpreter, explaining the United States to the world, and the world to the United States. Despite the singular contribution of the United States to the UN's founding and its mission in the decades that followed, after Iraq, America was too often unwilling to listen, and the world unable to speak its true mind.

On the ground in Iraq, the costs of the war could be measured in the more than one hundred thousand civilian lives lost in the turmoil following the invasion. Internationally, the war resulted in broken relations and hardened animosities, but also in the damage to the personal integrity and the standing of some of the principal players involved. No one endured this passage more painfully or publicly than Colin Powell, who would ultimately resign after the Bush administration had exploited, and exhausted, his stature. And no leader would carry with him the consequences of the Iraq War more lastingly than Tony Blair.

"Yo, Blair, how're you doing?" As soon as I read these first words of the exchange between U.S. president George W. Bush and UK prime minister Tony Blair captured by a rogue microphone at the July 2006 G8 summit in St. Petersburg, I thought of Blair, and knew he had to be cringing. Offering to travel to the Middle East, he told Bush that he was happy to leave immediately to try to reduce tensions. When Bush replied that his secretary of state Condoleezza Rice would be going soon, Blair remarked that he could prepare the way for her diplomacy. The aide who handed me the transcript of the exchange said I should read on. They had been speaking about me, it turned out—and not in flattering terms.

I arrived at the G8 summit four days into the raging war between Israel and Hizbollah. Hizbollah had triggered the war when it fired rockets at Israeli border towns before crossing the Lebanese border to attack an Israeli patrol, taking two of its personnel hostage. This provoked a heavy military response by Israel against the militant group, as well as against the Lebanese state and the country's infrastructure as a whole. I was determined to press for a cessation of hostilities and argue the case for the deployment of an international force as a condition for a durable peace. I knew I had annoyed at least one of the leaders there by asking Russian president Vladimir Putin to change the agenda and allow me to address the key session of the summit. As Bush and I engaged in a charged and pointed debate about my argument in front of the other leaders— with only France's president Jacques Chirac joining in at the very end of the session—it was clear that Bush saw this as a simple matter of good versus evil. He was blunter still with Blair. "What about Kofi?" Bush had continued, according to the transcript. "I don't like his cease-fire plan . . . His attitude is basically cease fire and everything sorts out . . . What they need to do is get Syria to get Hizbollah to stop doing this shit and it's all over . . . I felt like telling Kofi to call, to get on the phone with Assad and make something happen."

Now I wish that I—or anyone—could simply "make something happen" with just a phone call. And while the U.S. policy of isolating Syria meant that I was one of few global leaders communicating with the Syrian leadership, getting a solution would take more than just a conversation. Given the complex set of interests and motivations in Syria—and among its neighbors, including Israel—this was a three-dimensional chess game played between the wiliest and most mutually distrustful of powers.

In fact, the Lebanon war was not just a wrenching tragedy for the Lebanese and Israelis. It was—in its tangled and bloody roots, its complex regional character, and its carefully UN-negotiated conclusion—a reflection of those forces of global order and disorder that I had been wrestling with throughout my decade as UN secretary-general. Intervention in long-standing conflicts; the rights and responsibilities of sovereignty; the role of peacekeeping; the place of the UN in the era of American dominance; the emergence of nonstate actors engaged in asymmetric conflict; the personal shuttle-diplomacy of a UN secretary-general in a fragmenting world—each of these was at stake in the Lebanon war. A simple battle between good and evil it was not.

For Blair, however, this conflict—no less than Iraq—was refracted through his lens of a meta-conflict between modernity and the medieval, between tolerant secularism and radical Islam. We had met privately in St. Petersburg before the formal summit session, and when I told him that the G8 statement had been too weak and too vague to make any difference on the ground, he replied coolly that the question was not whether Israel could be convinced to cease fire today, but rather in "ten days or two weeks." Two weeks? I gave him an astonished look. His only response was that the conditions for a cessation of hostilities were not yet in place. This was not the Blair with whom I had agreed so passionately about the moral necessity of a humanitarian intervention to halt the Serbian attacks on the Kosovar Albanians in 1999—a stand that compelled me to override my own commitment to Security Council authorization of the use of force, and which cost me greatly with major powers, including Russia and China. Something had changed in Blair, and with it, I felt, his ability to act as a credible mediator in this conflict.

I was concerned with the scale and scope of Israel's retaliation from the outset. Of course, the Israelis were justified in responding. Any nation, when attacked, has a right to defend itself. Israeli positions had been raided across an internationally recognized border. And I had personally certified the Blue Line in 2000 after working closely with Israeli prime minister Ehud Barak to enable his withdrawal of Israeli forces from Lebanon after an eighteen-year occupation. But Israel's justified defense of its borders rapidly became about something far greater, and far more difficult to achieve—namely, the destruction of a popular guerrilla organization with ample means of survival and retaliation.

On the day of the attack, I told Condoleeza Rice that I feared Israel would soon discover the limits to what could be achieved by force. There had to be a political agreement, a political understanding, I argued. Hizbollah was an organization with deep roots in Lebanese society and represented many long-standing, popular local grievances. It could not be disarmed by military means alone. But Israeli leader Ehud Olmert would have none of it. In my call with the prime minister the next day, he said that Israel was "not going to stop any military operation against Hizbollah," but rather was going to "intensify it."

Olmert's demands were, in principle, legitimate: a release of the Israeli soldiers captured in the raid, withdrawal from the border, and the complete disarmament of Hizbollah as called for in UN Security Council resolution 1559. That did not mean, however, that they were obtainable through war. Indeed, everything we knew about the history of guerrilla warfare—in the region and around the world—suggested that there would ultimately have to be a negotiated solution, no matter how long or relentlessly Israel struck Lebanese targets.

Insisting on these conditions being met even before agreeing to a cessation of hostilities was a recipe for war without end. This much I knew from the first hours of the conflict, and over the next three weeks I took this message to anyone with power to influence the parties. Ten years of painful, drawn-out negotiations with the Palestinians and Israelis had taught me a grim lesson about the futility of killing off the first stages of a settlement between mortal foes.

Israel was already under siege on a second front, Gaza, where

Hamas had attacked an Israeli border post two weeks earlier, killing two soldiers and kidnapping a young corporal, Gilad Shalit. An Israeli leader without a military background, Olmert needed to demonstrate decisiveness and strength. And ample license was given. The United States, along with the United Kingdom, took the view that Hizbollah had given the Israelis a unique opportunity to crush what had become a state within a state in Lebanon. Washington appeared to have decided that its primary responsibility in the early stages of the conflict was to buy time for the Israeli Air Force to inflict what it hoped would be a strategic defeat on the movement.

For an organization like Hizbollah, mere survival means victory. Ever since its founding in response to the 1982 Israeli invasion of Lebanon, Hizbollah had become part of the fabric of Lebanese society—whether one liked it or not. And I made clear my own disapproval when I spoke to the Security Council one week into the conflict and condemned Hizbollah's "deliberate targeting of Israeli population centers with hundreds of indiscriminate weapons." I concluded that "whatever other agendas they may serve, Hizbollah's actions, which it portrays as defending Palestinian and Lebanese interests, in fact do neither. On the contrary, they hold an entire nation hostage."

By not losing, Hizbollah was winning. And for Israel, much more than another battlefield victory had been gambled. The essential myth of Israel's invincibility—its strategic deterrence of its Arab neighbors—was now at risk. As its military commanders and political leadership came to recognize their miscalculation, their tactics became ever more desperate. Over the following three weeks, Israel carried out a widespread air campaign stretching from suspected Hizbollah positions in the south to the suburbs of Beirut and every major infrastructure artery, including bridges, roads, and air and sea ports. The state of Lebanon was being crippled, and more than one thousand civilians were killed—without, however, putting a halt to Hizbollah's indiscriminate rocket attacks. During the same period, the group fired thousands of rockets, hitting targets as far as Haifa, and forced more than a million Israelis into shelters night after terrifying night.

I n Lebanon, Israeli and U.S. policymakers had attempted to change the country's politics through military force. I had, in my own way, been disabused of the notion that the international community could fully understand the forces at play in such societies. In 2000, I was visiting Islamabad on a long-planned trip to Pakistan that coincided with the Taliban's destruction of the Bamiyan Buddhas. There I met with the man who represented the Taliban to outsiders as its foreign minister, Wakil Ahmad Mutawakil. I was staying at the Marriott Hotel (which, in 2008, was destroyed in an al Qaeda bombing), and as the Taliban delegation entered my suite, I knew that we were dealing with an entirely new phenomenon in international affairs.

Six young men, several of them barely out of their twenties, bearded and wearing traditional Afghan robes, walked in, seemingly engaging in their first meeting with a diplomat of any kind. A few appeared barely to understand even the translation of the conversation, and Mutawakil himself had only one, tellingly bizarre, reply to my different appeals for a halt to the destruction of the Buddhas: "Under our laws, nothing we do can be considered illegal." And when I warned them that their behavior could lead to further sanctions, including a ban on international travel by their leaders, Mutawakil looked puzzled and responded: "Travel? Why would we travel? We don't want to go anywhere."

The Buddhas were only an element of our meeting, however. Having long played a critical role in providing humanitarian assistance to the Afghan population, the UN needed assurances that we could continue our work without being attacked. Mutawakil, in this case, pledged his support, and this gave me the opening to raise what I knew would be a sensitive issue—just how sensitive I was about to discover.

I had been asked—in a highly confidential request—to inquire of Mutawakil about the presence in Afghanistan of a man still in those days referred to as UBL—Osama bin Laden. Were there any circumstances under which the Taliban leadership would agree to an exchange involving this individual? I made clear that this was a high priority and that meaningful goodwill would accrue to the Taliban if such an arrangement could be arrived at. From Mutawakil's response—and a look that combined fear and outrage in equal measure—the extent of UBL's influence in Afghanistan became clear. There was no question whatsoever of an exchange involving their "honored guest," he said, as directly as he could manage. The meeting came to an abrupt end, but the memory stayed with me until that fateful day in September 2001 when UBL changed the world.

The United Nations played a critical role in the Lebanon conflict from the outset. The raid that triggered the hostilities was across a UN-delineated and UN-sanctioned border. UN Security Council resolutions 1559 and 1680 had previously mandated the central conditions for peace in Lebanon: withdrawal of Syrian forces, disarming of Hizbollah, and government control over all Lebanese territory. Once fighting erupted anew, it was clear that any solution required the authority of the Security Council and the means to impose its will.

To provide the Israelis with confidence that their withdrawal would not simply be followed by a return of Hizbollah forces to their prior positions, I needed to create a new, strengthened peacekeeping force that could end the attacks across the border. Rice—caught between Washington's intent to buy Israel further time for its bombing campaign and her recognition of the damage done to the position of the United States by continuing to stand by while Lebanon was being hit—called me to suggest a two-stage deployment of forces. First, she argued, one could have a "humanitarian stage" with relief workers deployed alongside Israeli forces as Hizbollah withdrew. Then, one could have the international force come in to boost the United Nations Interim Force in Lebanon (UNIFIL).

This was yet another attempt at conditioning a halt to the violence, a sequencing that I knew from long experience would not work. Citing the history of the UN's efforts in Africa and the Balkans, I told Rice that all sides would have to move in parallel—Israel, Hizbollah, and the international forces all taking new, mutually acceptable positions simultaneously.

I had not come to this conclusion lightly. I knew the cost of sending peacekeepers into the field without the mandate, resources, leadership, or moral confidence to succeed. I had seen with my own eyes what failure looked like in lives destroyed and hopes shattered. On my watch as under-secretary-general for Peacekeeping Operations, the UN lived through some of the most traumatic experiences in its history.

In one case, Bosnia, three years of brutally intimate civil war challenged the UN to see beyond its traditional notions of neutrality to distinguish good from evil, aggressor from victim. We failed, and the massacre at Srebrenica became an indelible stain. In another case, Rwanda, a lone voice on the ground—one of our own commanders—warned of a calamity to come, but at headquarters in New York the memory of Somalia defined our decision making, and three months later, *after* the genocide had started, the UN's key member states withdrew the few forces left in the country.

But for the UN, especially, this was only part of the picture. Entering any arena of conflict, with its blue helmets and white vehicles and a flag symbolizing far more powerfully than any words shelter from the storm, the UN was making a solemn pledge: we have come to keep the peace. This was our commitment, and perhaps our greatest failure was never fully to grasp the enormity of this obligation. To a man, woman, or child for whom the presence of a blue helmet is all that lies between safety and certain death, talk of limited mandates, inadequate means, and under-resourced missions—however accurate—is, at best, beside the point, at worst, a betrayal.

As secretary-general, I was determined that we would acknowledge these realities. This was not only a moral necessity. I was convinced that we, as an institution, could not claim a future role for peacekeeping unless we demonstrated, in word and deed, a recognition of our moral and military failures. For a UN secretary-general, what he says—or fails to say—is often as important as what he does.

The first test of my commitment as secretary-general came with the 1999 Serbian campaign against the Kosovar Albanians. As Slobodan Milošević's onslaught grew in ferocity, I spoke in increasingly direct terms about the international community's obligation to prevent another Bosnia—by force if necessary. And so when NATO decided to act against Serbia without Security Council authorization, I expressed regret but said that "there are times when the use of force is legitimate in the pursuit of peace."

No secretary-general of the United Nations had ever before endorsed a military action that did not enjoy the blessing of the Security Council. I struggled greatly with this decision, but I believed that our experience in Rwanda, as well as Bosnia, had left us without easy answers. If, as I asked the General Assembly of the United Nations later that year in reference to Rwanda, "in those dark days and hours leading up to the genocide, a coalition of states had been prepared to act in defense of the Tutsi population, but did not receive prompt Council authorization, should such a coalition have stood aside and allowed the horror to unfold?" I suspected that few leaders in the audience would wish to be purists in retrospect.

At the same time, I warned of the danger of a world without rules for intervention: "To those for whom the Kosovo action heralded a new era when states and groups of states can take military action outside the established mechanisms for enforcing international law, one might ask: Is there not a danger of such interventions undermining the imperfect, yet resilient, security system created after the Second World War, and of setting dangerous precedents for future interventions without a clear criterion to decide who might invoke these precedents, and in what circumstances?" Four years later, Iraq provided the tragic answer to this part of my question.

Throughout my time as secretary-general, I sought to match the unique authority of the United Nations as the sole, truly universal organization of states with the credibility of seeing that rights were defended, suffering alleviated, and lives saved. In an increasingly fragmented twenty-first century populated by a growing number of private and public actors, abstract claims to legitimacy would simply not be enough. After all, what good was the UN's unique legitimacy to the men and boys of Srebrenica, or to the Rwandans, in their hour of desperate need—all of whom were abandoned to their fate by a United Nations Security Council acting in perfect unity? If we were to win a primary role for the UN in the new era, we would have to acknowledge our past failures and set out a vision for how we would act differently in the future.

For far too long, the UN had been considered the sole prerogative of states and their representatives. And it showed. Nongovernmental organizations (NGOs) and young people on every continent were challenging with passion and effectiveness outdated dogmas and unjust practices, but were deemed unworthy of serious engagement. The dynamism of the private sector that was revolutionizing business in the developed world and markets throughout the developing world was rarely to be seen. Instead, stepping into a UN hall often felt like entering a time machine to the most arid North-South debates of the 1970s about power and justice, capitalism and development.

From my first days in office, I reminded the heads of state that the first words of the UN Charter did not refer to them—indeed, they were written in the voice of "We the Peoples." From the Millennium Development Goals (MDGs) to revitalizing the struggle against HIV/AIDS, from disarmament and humanitarian assistance to engaging the private sector and business through the Global Compact, I wanted to bring the UN closer to the people we were there to serve. Instead of leading an organization dedicated to the governments of the world, I would put the individual at the center of everything we did.

A United Nations for the twenty-first century would have to create new partnerships, respond to the needs of individuals, and stand for the principle that national sovereignty could never be used as a shield for genocide or gross violations of human rights. It would have to advance a much broader view of security that integrated peace, development, women's empowerment, and human rights if it were to address successfully the challenges of a global age. It would have to make a difference in the four key challenges of the twenty-first century: peace and security, growth with development, respect for human rights, and the rule of law.

All this I knew to be fundamental to the UN's future relevance and effectiveness. But even as I fought to maintain our focus on these long-term aims, I found myself time and again as secretary-general drawn back into the vortex of conflicts that threatened entire societies with destruction. If the United Nations truly was to reflect a humanity that cared more, not less, for the suffering in its midst, and would do more, and not less, to end it, the organization had to be an agent of intervention in every sphere of human security.

INDEPENDENCE

African Beginnings

My father, Henry Reginald Annan, was not a rebel by nature. A Ghanaian executive of a European trading company, a Freemason, and a devout Anglican in a culture of tribes and ancestral worship, a hereditary chief in a time of radical change, he was not one to make a point. And yet he gave each of his children African names, a signal departure for a man of his background and position in the Gold Coast of the 1930s and 1940s. To him there was no contradiction in being African in identity and European in outlook, a nationalist as well as a traditionalist, a proponent of political change and an upholder of those values of respect, dignity, discipline, and hard work that had sustained his own life and career. But by naming his five children Nana Essie, Essie, Kofi Atta, Efua Atta, and Kobina, he made an unmistakable wager on behalf of a proud and independent African future for his children.

To H.R., as he was known to friends and associates, crossing over— and back again—was inherent to his life, heritage, and political outlook. H.R. refused to choose—between radical change and the status quo, traditional and modern, tribal and national, Fante and Ashanti, African and European. Instead, he insisted that the only sustainable kind of change toward self-government was one that would honor the proud heritage of Ghana's people and ensure a balanced society able to stand on its own feet and make of independence a success. He managed to be both a pillar of society and a builder of multiple constituencies across tribe, class, and profession.

A business executive who went to work in a dark suit and broken collar every day alongside European managers, he was also a traditionalist in his home, with his base being my grandmother's extended family in Kumasi. In a society where people identified closely with tribe and village, he was himself a product of a marriage between a Fante and an Ashanti, and among his wives were both Fante and Ashanti women. H.R. had four wives who bore him five children, including my twin sister, Efua, and myself.

My father worked as an executive of the United Africa Company, a subsidiary of Lever Brothers, the Anglo-Dutch multinational corporation that later became known globally as Unilever. His job kept us moving from city to city, town to town, throughout my childhood—from Kumasi to Accra and Bekwai, from Koforidua to Nsawan and Nkakaw—and in this shifting panorama of home and belonging, no part of Ghana was foreign to us. My own mother, Rose, lived in Cape Coast with my half-sister, Ewura Efua. My twin sister, Efua Atta, and I saw very little of her growing up, until we went to boarding school in Cape Coast in our early teens. Instead, a vital constant throughout this nomadic period was the family home in Kumasi to which we would always return, meeting with three generations of aunts and uncles. At the many precarious moments of childhood, there would always be somebody to go to for guidance and love, when the subtle messages of traditional proverbs would be used. "You don't hit somebody on the head when you have your fingers between his teeth" was one such proverb, a concept that reminded us that even when in dispute we remain bound to each other.

Every day would bring a new face, a different language or tribal tra-dition into our home, and teach us a life lesson about the richness of the mix and mash of cultures and peoples. As a consequence, we were raised nontribal in a tribal society, political moderates in an era of radical activ-ism, conciliators in a time of choosing sides.

This was the Gold Coast in the late 1930s and 1940s where a small British colony in West Africa became consumed with the prospect of independence. Growing up in the twilight years of the Gold Coast—destined to become the first independent country in sub-Saharan Af-rica and to be renamed Ghana—was to experience a complete change in culture and society. By the time I was ten, in 1948, the independence movement was in full force, and as I came of age, so did Ghana as a free republic, in the vanguard of an African emancipation that would bring sixteen new African nations into the United Nations within two short years.

For Ghanaians, these were days of extraordinary hope and promise, the expectation that Africa was about to take off, and that we finally had an opportunity to create for ourselves all that we had accused the colonial power of denying us. For me, the personal coming-of-age was indistin-guishable from the independence struggle. Politics had a meaning and purpose above and beyond tribe or ideology or the division of spoils that in so many other African societies since has become the norm. There was a complete mobilization of society as everybody joined the struggle in his own way to bring independence to life. Leaders of the movement would end up in jail only to emerge as future prime ministers and judges and military chiefs.

In Ghana, the process of decolonization was defined more by a struggle among different groups within the country than one of blacks against whites. The mosquito saw to that. Although the slave trade thrived over many centuries, there were very few white settlers because of malaria and yellow fever. Instead, the struggle was between Ghanaians—radicals and gradualists—and my father became a prominent figure among those who sought change through a process of steady, measured transformation.

Ghana's independence struggle was defined by this duality of the traditional and the modern, the educated and the working class, the Ashanti and the coastal tribes. As in many other African colonies, it was soldiers returning from the Second World War, who had served in the British army, who began to question more fundamentally the iniquities of colonial practices. They witnessed white British soldiers alongside whom they had fought and bled receive generous pensions, land, and other benefits in Africa—none of which were available to Africans. Together with leading members of Ghana's professional classes—lawyers, doctors, and engineers—these veterans began a campaign for independence. As conservative members of society—by definition, those who had status and assets and privileges even under colonial rule—they were looking for a cautious, methodical change of regime. Their independence slogan was—tellingly—"Step by Step."

This was the group that formed the United Gold Coast Convention (UGCC) as their party, and decided to appoint as secretary a fiery, courageous activist, Kwame Nkrumah. A member of one of Ghana's smaller tribes, and the son of a village goldsmith who had gone on to educate himself in the United States and Britain, Nkrumah brought to the cause an impatience and a passion that could not, in the end, abide the gradualist tempo of Ghana's elite. Tired of their condescension toward him and their dismissive attitude to what they considered his rabble-rousing supporters, he broke away from the UGCC to found the Convention People's Party. Nkrumah possessed more than just impatience, however; he had a keen strategic mind and an ability to organize people that far surpassed that of his former colleagues. He soon became the indisputable driver of Ghana's independence.

For my father—one of the few African trading executives of a European company, a leading member of the UGCC, and a close friend of the Ashanti king, the Asantehene—this was a time of careful balancing. Our house in these days became a gathering point for senior members of the UGCC—to the point where Nkrumah activists would hold rallies in the park across the street. As a young man, I was deeply influenced by the discussions going on at home with my father and his friends. At the same time, I was emotionally drawn to the passion and urgency of Nkrumah's calls for "independence now." Some of the statements that he was making—that we must stand on our own, that we must have our destiny in our own hands—resonated deeply with me.

All this taught me, in the way only a lived experience can, that peaceful change—even transformational change—is possible. After watching the first-ever Ghanaian police commissioner, or first Ghanaian head of the army, being sworn in, suddenly nothing seemed impossible. A sense of pride and, most of all, opportunity filled everyone of my generation. As I embarked on an education that would take me to the United States and Europe, and an early career that included working for the World Health Organization (WHO) in Geneva, the UN Economic Commission in Addis Ababa, the UN headquarters in New York, the United Nations Emergency Force based in Cairo, and the Ghana Tourist Development Company, this belief in transformational change remained constant.

In Ghana, as in other African countries at the threshold to freedom, the struggle for independence led to the creation of a national movement, as opposed to political parties in the more traditional sense. After independence, leaders would argue that the people should unite behind a single national organization, with the inevitable result of a one-party state. The UGCC represented more than just a contrast to Nkrumah's view on the timing and manner of independence, but a deeper-seated belief in more traditional values and practices with strong roots among ordinary Ghanaians. A blessing for Ghana was that both sides sought the widest possible constituencies and therefore never based their appeal on tribe, protecting the country from the traumas of tribal conflict, which has bedeviled so many of its neighbors on the continent.

This difference in outlook and experience was reflected within Ghana, too—between those tribes concentrated at the coast and the northern region, and the Ashanti in the center of the country with their capital of Kumasi. Though my family was a mix of Fante and Ashanti, I was born in Kumasi, and the Ashanti heartland was my father's principal area of influence and economic activity. Because the Ashanti had long enjoyed an extensive degree of autonomy—and not experienced the daily interaction with European traders and soldiers familiar from the coast— they had to a far lesser degree than other Ghanaian tribes internalized the prejudices and presumptions of a racist Europe in its dealings with Africans.

In Kumasi, there was no sense of being subservient or inferior to the European traders, and little taste of the racial discrimination experienced by people in Accra. There was, rather, great pride in the achievements of the kingdom and its warrior ethos that had fought the British a full generation longer than the coastal communities before surrendering in 1902 and being annexed into the colony. Unlike the coastal tribes of Ghana— and, even more so, the people of East Africa, who were dominated by large European settler populations—the Ashanti did not grow up with any sense of limits as to what they could do.

Even as the Ashanti were known as a warrior people able to stand up to the British and dominate other tribes, among Ashantis themselves there was an important priority placed on compromise and negotiation. Indeed, the Ashanti king did not have his own army, but had to convince tribes and subtribes to provide troops in times of war and crisis.

This tradition of political persuasion and contribution to a broader cause through dialogue and negotiation has set deep roots in Ghana's society and informed greatly the traditions of peaceful coexistence. Later on, after independence, when my father was appointed regional minister of the Ashanti region, he was able to further this tradition in managing carefully the balance between the interests of the state and those of the Ashanti king with whom he had developed a long and trusting friendship. Modern ways of republican government had to be fused with traditional structures of authority. As someone who had always believed in the coexistence of these strands of life, he was in his element.

My father in many ways embodied the possibilities and conflicts that this status permitted. As a leading professional of his community, he was deeply involved with Freemasonry and the Anglican Church. Working alongside European executives of the United Africa Company—and treated with complete equality as a fellow professional—he represented the African businessman to Europeans set in a tradition of dominance and superiority that was only slowly beginning to realize the dimensions of the change on the horizon.

To be able to do both—to take part in his country's struggle for independence as a leading member of the UGCC and also maintain his professional commitment to a colonial company—required patience, a calm disposition, and an ability to see value and merit in different contexts. With British managers on one side and Ghanaian revolutionaries on the other, he had to be very careful to balance his values and his responsibilities without ever compromising his dignity. It made of him a disciplined man with little patience for weakness or cowardice.

In this respect, my father was representative of a deeper cultural tradition of patience, negotiation, and reconciliation. For Ghanaians, the concept of the African palaver tree has always been a tangible part of our heritage, and a source of the relative peace and harmony among myriad tribes and religions. A place to meet and talk, to seek compromise and settle disputes, to bridge differences and foster unity—this was the meaning of the palaver tree. Of course, this tradition coexisted with centuries of warfare between the Ashanti and other tribes, when compromise was elusive and force deployed. More recently, in the first decades of the republic, a series of military coups that scarred the character of the country and set back its development demonstrated our capacity to fail our heritage.

Nonetheless, the act of talking under the figurative palaver tree has resonance even today, in twenty-first-century Ghana. If you have a problem and you can't find a solution, you meet again tomorrow and you keep talking until you find a solution. You can disagree with behavior or a particular position, but you do not resort to calling an opponent worthless. This notion extends to the relationship between traditional chiefs and their tribes, where there is accountability in the case of abuse or arrogance, including providing for the removal of chiefs who have lost the trust and respect of their people.

By the age of thirteen, when I went away to boarding school, I had been exposed to a wide range of events and influences that would form a foundation of confidence, tolerance, and discipline. From my father I learned that it was possible to keep an independent mind even at a historical crossroads as defining as the country's independence, and that a critical perspective amid supposed certainties and absolutes was essential. He taught me that when others insisted that sides must be chosen, and that it had to be either/or, there was another way that was truer to the reality of a complex world. His own life had been defined by the coexistence of tribe and language, place and purpose—the mix of heritage and hope that could bring Africa a new beginning, with dignity at its core.

I was a member of Ghana's "independence class" of 1957 at my boarding school, Mfantsipim, in the city of Cape Coast, and to me and my peers, politics and the fate of our country were never far from our minds. If the greatest legacy of Mfantsipim was to bring together boys from every tribe and region of Ghana and to make of us all young citizens of the nascent state, the life of the school, nevertheless, reflected the broader division then playing out in our society between the more fiery nationalists and the gradualists, then known as the "democrats."

Ghana's oldest school for boys, Mfantsipim was founded by Methodists, and though it followed a standard British curriculum, the school was already run by Africans. We wore khaki uniforms, shorts, but no tie, except on Sundays, when we also wore a white suit. Every morning we gathered for prayer in a stark hall; on Sundays prayers went on longer. Everything was spartan: small wooden desks, stone floors, bare walls, corrugated iron roofs. Stoicism was prized, along with learning and character.

Much as our teachers tried to keep our focus on our studies, the struggle for independence seeped into every lesson, every discussion, every playground argument. A favorite pastime was role playing, mimicking the debates of our elders about the manner and timing of independence, with factions forming on each side of the argument. We even held mock parliamentary elections, and as "deputy leader of the opposition," I argued the gradualist case in debates with fiery nationalists on the other side. I quickly earned the nickname "Annan-Domo" reflecting my allegiance with the democratic side, which, of course, was the position my father was very publicly identified with.

It was not always an easy place to be, among young men impatient to show their power and authority, and I certainly shared their admiration for Nkrumah's courage and persistence. During those years we saw huge changes taking place. Suddenly the British governor-general was gone. A Ghanaian soon became the president, and so we grew up believing change is possible, even monumental change.

As I left the challenging but intimate surroundings of Mfantsipim to attend the University of Science and Technology in Kumasi, I took with me, above all, the passion for politics and debate at a time of dramatic—and to many of us unimaginable—change. At Kumasi, I joined the National Union of Ghanaian Students and soon after, as its vice president, received an invitation to a conference in Sierra Leone to represent the

Ghanaian students' movement. Young men and women from the entire region were engaging in passionate discussions about the future of their nations, the struggle for independence, and what happens the day after.

In the audience was a representative from the Ford Foundation's foreign student leadership project. The program was designed to identify students in the developing world with leadership potential and offer them a chance to study in the United States before returning home to help develop independent states. For me, this led to an offer of a scholarship to attend Macalester College in Minnesota—a state whose climate, social environment, and racial makeup could not have been more different from my native Ghana's. My family imagined my returning with my U.S. education to do great things for my new nation. I had the same idea. Education was linked in my mind to service. I never dreamed, any more than my parents, that my departure from Ghana would be near-permanent or that America would challenge my thinking in so many ways.

Privileged as I had been to grow up in a stable and secure family and attend a school that opened my eyes to the power of knowledge and understanding, I was not immune from the poisonous legacy of colonialism and its hierarchy based on race. One experience came from my father's employer—and triggered our first significant disagreement as father and son. Early in my professional career, while working with the World Health Organization in Geneva, I was approached by Unilever—at my father's request, I suspect—and recruited to work for them in Africa. Rather than post me to Ghana, however, they suggested that I begin my work for them in Nigeria, which would not, in principle, have been an issue. The devil, though, was in the details.

Whereas other expats would have been provided special contracts with domestic and other arrangements handled by the company, I would be treated as a local employee, as I was, in their words, "from the region." Neither my American education nor my Ghanaian upbringing or my international experience working with the WHO had prepared me to accept such unequal treatment. I was to be an expat, a Ghanaian in Nigeria.

But to the company, I was a "local." So I declined their offer of a position. This was not how I was going to start my career as an African professional. For my father, however, my rejection was a great disappointment. He said, "Accept the job and fight from within for equal treatment." I replied that doing so would give them every reason to continue to treat me as second class.

By this point, I had already spent two years in Geneva, first at the Graduate Institute of International Studies, and then, with the WHO, starting as a P-1, Step 1 (the lowest professional rank within the United Nations system). In Geneva, I found a worldly and engaging environment, and as someone who by the age of twenty-four had lived in three different cultures—African, American, and European—I began to realize that community for me would mean something different from what it had meant to my father's generation.

Nevertheless, the desire to make a contribution to my continent's future was a recurring theme of my life and career. In 1965, after three years with the WHO in Geneva, I joined the Economic Commission for Africa, a UN agency with the responsibility of promoting regional integration and economic cooperation. Addis in those days reminded me of the Ghanaian independence struggle of my adolescence—a place consumed with the cause of African unity, energized by convening a new generation of African leaders. This was the first era of African unity, one very much driven by the vision of Kwame Nkrumah.

In 1963, when the Organization of African Unity (OAU) was founded, the initial membership comprised thirty-three countries. This number grew as more and more countries became independent and joined the organization. In 1960 alone, seventeen countries gained their independence, and the number continued to grow to the current fifty-four. During that period, I witnessed the comings and goings not only of new presidents and prime ministers, but also of leaders of liberation movements and freedom fighters. All these leaders came together, trying to map the future of Africa and to ensure that the entire continent was fully liberated. One could feel the electricity in the air, and for a young man these were heady days and made a lasting impression on me.

On the other side of town we in the UN Economic Commission for Africa (ECA) were focusing on research and proposing ideas for economic development of the African continent, including regional and sub-regional integration or at least cooperation. I remember our conversations within the ECA focused on improving infrastructure, energy, building roads, and expanding the railway systems so that trains could flow across borders unimpeded. I had no doubt then that with the right leadership and management Africa could take off.

In a telling—if tragic—sign of Africa's many false starts on the path to development, it is widely recognized today that the two principal obstacles to African development are energy and infrastructure. To recall how clearly this was understood forty years ago is to realize the price that Africans have paid for bad governance ever since. It is one thing for young and idealistic professionals to identify the obstacles to progress and the ways they can be addressed; it is quite another for leaders to see beyond their own personal interests to marshal the resources of their society to the advancement of the common good.

After completing my master's degree in 1971 at the Massachusetts Institute of Technology as a Sloan fellow during a sabbatical leave, I returned to the United Nations in Geneva but continued to seek an opportunity go back to Africa. Soon after, I received an offer to manage the Ghana Tourist Development Company within the Ministry of Tourism, a post I took up in November 1974. The aim was to boost tourism to Ghana by encouraging investment, establishing hotels along the coast, and creating duty-free shops to attract tourists to visit and shop. What I found, instead, was a Ghana transformed by military coups. The country was now living under the heavy shadow of military rule—and defined by a debilitating combination of stultifying corruption and bureaucratic inefficiency.

If it had been just a matter of bureaucratic obstacles, I suspect I would have stayed in Ghana and sought to change the system from within. The biggest constraint in any bureaucracy is the one bureaucrats put on themselves—and Ghana was no different. I returned home with my first wife, Titi Alakija, and my two small children, Ama and Kojo, and enjoyed the embrace of family and friends in the endeavor to help build a prosperous economy. The military, however, began to impose itself on every aspect of life—in the public and private sectors, in the media, and in culture. As a consequence, the economy was grinding to a halt. The work ethic and the cumbersome decision making conspired to frustrate any attempt at entrepreneurial activity.

Between the forces of bureaucratic inertia, bad governance, and military rule, I saw little possibility of advancing the kind of change that was so necessary to Ghana's—and Africa's—progress. Today, forty years later, as a new generation is rebelling against this conspiracy of corrupt rule across the continent, I recognize that frustration and the power of such ideals in our own feelings from a generation ago.

In my own case, faced with forces I could not change, I reluctantly concluded that I would have to pursue my career outside my home country. My experience in Ghana reinforced my commitment to serving an international organization, which I knew my country—and others in the developing world—would rely on for support and advice. I realized that, for me, working for the UN was the best way to serve my country and my continent. The United Nations would from then on become my home.

PROMISES TO KEEP

Somalia, Rwanda, Bosnia, and the Trials
of Peacekeeping in a World of Civil War

Three decades after I joined the UN, I found myself squeezed between four U.S. soldiers, alert and poised with heavy machine guns. Now a UN under-secretary-general for peacekeeping, I was seated in the hot confines of a U.S. military helicopter flying over the Somali terrain. There had been a dramatic recent change in world affairs.

The year was 1993, and below lay a venture into the unknown, UNOSOM II, the United Nations peacekeeping mission in Somalia—and things were not going well. The troops, deployed under the mantle of a UN peacekeeping operation, had no peace to keep and were being drawn into a complex and shifting civil war. The previous certainties of UN peacekeeping were now being pitilessly tested in the most hostile of environments. Not long before, on September 25, 1993, a U.S. helicopter had been shot down in Somalia. Attacks against UN troops in the country had ebbed and flowed in the previous months, and they were growing again, with intelligence reports of hundreds of additional fighters loyal to the Somali warlord Mohamed Farrah Aidid now flooding into the capital city of Mogadishu.

Land mine explosions, small-arms fire, and rocket-propelled grenade attacks had become frequent against UN troops. It was one such rocket-propelled grenade that had clipped the U.S. helicopter and brought it down. We had been told that the aircraft had burned on the ground while Somalis cheered around it. Later that same day, reports emerged of Somalis parading through the main Bakara Market with an object in a white food-aid sack. They claimed it was the torso of one of the three U.S. soldiers killed in the crash. This was a single attack that foreshadowed a far bigger disaster that would hit the operation a few days later, in October.

This was a long way from my first field experience of UN peacekeeping in 1973. I had been sent to Egypt as chief administrative officer for civilian personnel serving in the peacekeeping operation that was under way. The UN Emergency Force in Egypt (known as UNEF II) was stationed to supervise the withdrawal of forces from the Sinai Peninsula after the 1973 Arab-Israeli War. The job of the force was to demarcate the cease-fire line between the Egyptians and Israelis, and reinforce both parties' confidence in the other's commitment to the "line in the sand." The mission was beset with complications, as all peacekeeping operations were, which affected my work every single day: there were administrative and logistical challenges arising from a force made up of multiple troop-contributing nations, including Finland, Sweden, Peru, Ireland, Canada, Poland, Panama, and others. This meant multiple lines of command and logistics chains, numerous languages, clashes in military and administrative cultures, and irregular fluctuations in the size of the force, as different countries provided and withdrew troops at different times.

But UNEF II was a largely safe and peaceful mission for its participants, as almost all peacekeeping operations were before the end of the Cold War. Now, in 1993 on the ground in Somalia, we were encountering all the same old complications of UN peacekeeping that we had suffered from in Egypt in the 1970s—but in a totally different arena. This was one of violent instability, where troops were not keeping any peace. They were often *fighting* through the country. Whatever the politicians, UN officials, and media commentators called the operation in Somalia, this was a highly complicated form of war fighting the troops were now engaged in.

"The UN should move in there and take over the administration of the Mogadishu population, surely?" the reporter asked. "Don't you agree that's the only way this thing's going to get resolved?"

"That will take an enormous number of troops. And troops that can take the kinds of risks necessary. It would be a war," I replied. It was several months earlier, in September 1992, when I was assistant secretary-general and deputy chief of the UN Department of Peacekeeping Operations (DPKO). The reporter's question reflected the bold and uncritical naïveté accompanying the international community's new interest in humanitarian action. Many wanted something done quickly in response to the terrible scenes they were witnessing in news reports in Somalia, but without fully accepting the implications—particularly the political will required to fulfill these ambitions. The result of this disconnect, between the international community's professed goals and the resources and risks it was willing to commit to achieve them, would be the prime driver of the peacekeeping trials to come.

It was at this time that peacekeeping was just beginning an explosion in the scale, number, and ambitions of operations worldwide, transforming its role in global security. Between 1987 and 1992, most operations (except for stark exceptions, such as the relatively large operation in Namibia) had involved one hundred observers or fewer in missions involving comparatively little risk to peacekeepers. By early 1994, there would be a total of eighty thousand peacekeeping forces deployed in seventeen operations worldwide, the vast majority of these begun after January 1992—and in operations that now saw many peacekeepers suddenly placed in harm's way. Furthermore, in a break with the past of almost all peacekeeping operations, excluding one or two historical exceptions, all these new missions were deployed to the turmoil of territories torn by civil war. These were huge quantitative and qualitative changes, and a complicated array of factors had come together to set the UN on course for some of its toughest-ever crises—and greatest of failures.

The first would be in the collapse of the UN peacekeeping mission in Somalia in 1993; the second, in 1994, in the descent of Rwanda into genocide, all under the gaze of a UN peacekeeping operation; and, finally, the third, in the massacre of eight thousand Bosnian men and boys at Srebrenica in 1995 in, of all places, a UN-designated "safe area."

The roots of the disasters in peacekeeping in the early 1990s, resulting from the misuse of this crucial instrument, extend to its origins. Peacekeeping emerged soon after the UN's founding as a set of practical responses to the global security environment. The rapid retreat from empire by the colonial powers after the Second World War saw fresh struggles emerge between newly formed, independent countries, such as between Israel and its neighbors or between India and Pakistan. But with the onset of the Cold War, such conflicts gained a new international salience. The hostility between the United States and the Soviet Union meant local wars between countries had the potential to draw in the rival interests of the superpowers—a dynamic that threatened escalation to a global confrontation.

With this concern explicitly in mind, and the heightened sense of global insecurity brought about by the invention of nuclear weapons, the second secretary-general of the UN, Dag Hammarskjöld, institutionalized a practice called "peacekeeping." Hammarskjöld recognized the need to contain the threat posed by these local conflicts and to stabilize them as quickly as possible, to insulate the risk of escalation to a global crisis, or worse, nuclear war. International, neutral troops were to be used to supervise the cease-fire lines between former belligerents following cessations in hostilities, enhancing trust across the divide and so defusing tensions between previously warring parties. It was a form of "preventive diplomacy," as he called it, to keep "newly arising conflicts outside the sphere of bloc differences."

Building on the experience of the very first UN field missions in the late 1940s—during which observers were sent to supervise the truce in Palestine and to oversee the cease-fire between Pakistan and India in Kashmir—the concept of peacekeeping operations was created and its basic principles and rules laid down by Hammarskjöld in the late 1950s. This use of international troops to act as a buffer zone to reinforce confidence in and stabilize cease-fire lines became recognized as a distinct contribution by the UN to international peace and security. It was a remarkable innovation in the service of world peace and international order within the tight constraints of the Cold War politics at the United Nations.

Following Hammarskjöld's lead, the principles of peacekeeping were later formally codified in 1973:

- Peacekeeping troops could be deployed only with the consent of the parties to the dispute.
- Peacekeepers had to be strictly impartial in their deployment and activities.
- Peacekeepers could use force only in self-defense.
- Peacekeepers should be mandated and supported by the Security Council in their activities.
- Peacekeeping operations had to rely on the voluntary contributions of member states for military personnel, equipment, and logistics.

A custom also emerged that the permanent five members of the Security Council would not contribute troops to these missions, given the potential for this to escalate rather than reduce Cold War rivalries.

On December 7, 1988, however, Mikhail Gorbachev, the general secretary of the Soviet Union, gave a speech to the UN General Assembly announcing a dramatic reduction in size of the Soviet military, particularly in its presence in Eastern Europe. This signaled the end of the Cold War, with profound implications for the UN's role in the world. The Security Council, envisaged by the UN's founders as the prime body for international peace and security, had been in a state of near-constant deadlock for forty years due to the superpower rivalry of its two most powerful members, the United States and the Soviet Union. But Gorbachev's speech heralded an end to this confrontation and the paralysis it had caused within the Security Council.

For the Department of Peacekeeping Operations, at first, the consequences of this change were significant, but manageable. Before 1988, only a dozen peacekeeping operations were launched in all of the UN's forty-three years. But in the brief period between 1988 and 1992, the Council created another ten. The Council was now able to agree, in a way that they had not been able to before, on its response to crises suitable for the intervention of peacekeepers. UN peacekeepers were now deployed, for example, to monitor cease-fires between Iraq and Iran, to supervise the political transition in Nicaragua and the withdrawal of Cuban troops from Angola, as well as other operations elsewhere.

What then followed from 1992 was an explosion in operations. This was driven not by a peacekeeping mission but by Operation Desert Storm. In response to the Iraqi invasion of Kuwait in 1990, the Council, in complete unity, passed a resolution mandating the full use of military force as provided for under Chapter VII of the UN Charter. This led to the deployment of 956,600 men and women from 34 countries, resulting in the successful liberation of Kuwait in 1991. It was a UN-authorized, U.S.-led coalition that reversed an overt act of war and conquest by one member state against another—precisely the task for which the UN had been founded.

The full potency of this new and active Security Council was now exposed, stirring a desire among the Council's members to sustain the

Council's central importance in world affairs. As a result, in January 1992, the first-ever meeting of the Security Council at the level of heads of state and government was held to consider how to take forward this ambition. They commissioned Secretary-General Boutros Boutros-Ghali to report on how the UN might be utilized in the transformed geopolitical climate. In the resulting document, *An Agenda for Peace*, Boutros-Ghali focused on the civil wars gripping different parts of the world. He noted that these conflicts were now receiving an unprecedented level of international attention and stressed the need for the Council to take the lead in responding to them.

But *An Agenda for Peace*, crucially, also encouraged the Council to consider peacekeeping—with its long-standing history—as a well-tested instrument for carrying this agenda forward. It suggested moving away from a previous crucial condition for almost all peacekeeping operations: specifically, that henceforth peacekeepers might not necessarily be deployed with the full consent of all the parties to the conflict. This was a small change on the page of peacekeeping principles, but one with potentially huge implications regarding what peacekeepers might be tasked to do.

Even as *An Agenda for Peace* was released, a new range of major operations in response to civil wars—in the former Yugoslavia, in Somalia, and in Cambodia—had already been launched by the Security Council under the rubric of UN peacekeeping. Managing this task was in the hands of the new United Nations Department of Peacekeeping Operations, founded that year to take over the responsibilities of the office of Special Political Affairs led over many years by Sir Brian Urquhart. Yet the department—then led by Under-Secretary-General Marrack Goulding—had barely increased in staff size while managing a gargantuan increase in operations and the numbers of peacekeepers deployed on them worldwide, as well as an acute escalation in the operations' complexity. It was at this time that I was transferred to the UN peacekeeping office at the UN's New York headquarters. I came from my previous post as controller of the UN, in the Department of Management, before which I had served as head of UN Human Resources and director of the Budget. I was to support Marrack Goulding from the newly created post of deputy head of the department.

The possibility of deploying field missions without the full consent of all belligerent parties meant there was a need to be prepared, if necessary, to use force. This simple fact meant that peacekeeping troops would be in need of a very different range of capabilities than usual if they faced armed factions opposed to the aims of the mission's mandate. This also meant troop-contributing countries might need to accept very different levels of risk, as well as to provide much higher levels of political commitment, attention, and responsiveness alongside the Security Council. This, however, was poorly recognized. The gulf between ends and means began to widen fatefully.

In 1992, the Security Council neglected to consciously create or review the possibilities of a distinctive new set of governing principles and structures for UN peacekeeping. Instead, all the legacy structures and doctrine of UN peacekeeping from the Cold War were carried into this new era.

This meant that the old and creaking Cold War machinery of peacekeeping was being turned to situations for which it was never intended. Peacekeeping had been cobbled together out of the limited possibilities presented within the political constraints of the UN system during the Cold War. The idea that the UN should have its own troops, commanded entirely by its Secretariat, was never accepted by the UN's member states. As a result, UN peacekeeping operated under a tripartite governing structure, among which relationships and authority over operations were unclear at the best of times. First, there was the Security Council, which had the power to bring into force a UN field operation, and was responsible for determining its mandate, objectives, and parameters as part of an ongoing supervisory role. Second, there was the UN Secretariat, the administrative body of the UN, which had responsibility for overseeing the day-to-day management of these operations, particularly through DPKO and the office of the secretary-general. And third, there were the troop-contributing countries, which retained authority over the forces they deployed on UN missions, and in practice remained in ultimate command of their own troops.

Peacekeeping was therefore reliant upon an often conflicted intergovernmental body for its political master, in the form of the Security Council, while its logistics and administration were run by a UN department whose authority was unclear. And, worse, missions were entirely dependent upon multiple troop-contributing countries whose troops took decisive orders only from their own governments. The chain of command was confused and decision-making responsibility fragmented, with unity of purpose often absent between these three parts.

In traditional peacekeeping during the Cold War, this had often led to slow and disorganized deployments, problems in the direction of troops, and great difficulty in equipping and sustaining the force. But most of these problems had been in field missions in relatively stable environments involving the monitoring of clearly delineated boundaries between warring countries, as I witnessed personally in 1973 in Egypt. The inherent weaknesses in the system of peacekeeping operations were never exposed in such missions in so serious a manner as to produce any momentum for reform. The system was sufficient to allow the deployment of peacekeeping forces, regardless of any shortcomings along the way.

The new interest in civil wars made things very different. Due to their greater complexity and the number of factions and subfactions involved—but particularly the unclear boundaries between belligerents due to the typical involvement of irregular forces—such wars are far more fluid, unstable, and prone to rapid changes on the ground than those of wars between countries. With the new ambitions of peacekeeping missions in civil war zones around the world, the situation was set for those weaknesses, contradictions, and strains in the governing structures of UN peacekeeping to be tested as never before.

Compounding this problem was the style of management embraced by Boutros-Ghali as secretary-general. He took great pains, in particular, to control and restrict the flow of information to and from the Security Council. Almost all information for the Council was conveyed through his personal representative, Chinmaya Gharekhan. Troop commanders were very rarely allowed to brief the Council directly, nor were officials at DPKO, including its head, the under-secretary-general. Boutros-Ghali maintained strict, private control over his own personal communications with representatives and leaders of member states, as well as special representatives of the secretary-general (SRSGs), who run the political side of the operations on the ground. This meant that, at any stage, we in DPKO could never be sure who knew what, or what had been agreed to in the day-to-day running and direction of operations. DPKO sat within a chain of command, below the office of the secretary-general and the instructions of the Security Council, while in support of troop contributors who retained priority of command.

Underlying the management challenges of peacekeeping in those years was the opportunism of some member states. They had seized on the instrument of peacekeeping to carry forward their humanitarian ambitions, deploying troops under the UN to be managed by DPKO, but in a manner that often abdicated their responsibilities. In the very short term, they took credit for acting in the face of humanitarian crises, but simultaneously avoided reckoning with the tough realities of the situation. They took few steps to prepare their populations and parliaments for the tasks—and risks—their troops would be required to face. At DPKO we realized that these missions required force, and were encouraging others to understand this, too. But UN peacekeeping had long been perceived as a task that traditionally involved almost no risk to the troops involved.

And it was still in this style that peacekeepers were deployed. Hiding behind the label of "peacekeeping," governments sent troops into civil wars whose conditions were fundamentally different to traditional peace-keeping.

SOMALIA: FAMINE AND CIVIL WAR

"When you drop a vase and it breaks into three pieces, you take the pieces and put it back together. But what do you do when it breaks into a thousand pieces?" This was how Mohamed Sahnoun, the UN SRSG to Somalia, described the dilemma the country had come to pose by 1992. It had not taken long for Somalia to shatter. In January 1991, President Siad Barre had fallen from power in Somalia. This caused a power struggle that swiftly saw the unraveling of the country's densely knit structure of clans and kinship networks. By November 1991, hostilities had escalated and violence gripped the capital, Mogadishu, with fighting between factions supporting, respectively, the interim president Ali Mahdi Mohamed and the chairman of the United Somali Congress, General Mohamed Farrah Aidid. From then on, the country's authority structures disintegrated in a proliferation of armed factions and gangs that saw the war—or, rather, a series of multiple and ever-shifting mini-wars that made up the larger conflict—engulf the whole of Somalia.

UN humanitarian relief agencies were fully engaged in Somalia from March 1991, shortly after the fall of Barre. But with the spreading contagion of the conflict and its accompanying fundamental breakdown of Somali society, the UN presence was not enough to stall terrible consequences for the population. Services and systems of trade and food distribution disappeared as the months rolled past. Over half of the population, 4.5 million people, became threatened with severe malnutrition, and an estimated 1.5 million were considered at immediate risk of death.

The images on the news programs and reports on the television in 1992 were some of the worst I have ever seen. Somalia seemed to be a landscape of emaciated bodies—some dead, others barely alive—men, women, and children alike. Hundreds of thousands of Somalis were dying.

However, the problem was that simply delivering supplies had little decisive effect. This was not a famine created by the weather and an inept food-distribution system that could be remedied in the short term through humanitarian relief alone. While a devastating drought had created the initial food shortage, this famine was one created by armed men willfully obstructing the most basic means of survival to entire sections of a population. Delivering humanitarian aid was not enough to deal with a famine born from a brutal civil war.

It would have been immensely difficult for any force to just move in and stop such a major and complicated civil war, nor was there any precedent for such action. In UN culture and experience, negotiation and a deal between factions was seen as the only feasible manner through which the UN could try to create a secure environment for humanitarian relief. On December 27, 1991, the outgoing secretary-general, Javier Pérez de Cuéllar, initiated the first attempt by the UN to broker a political deal that might bring a cessation of hostilities, allowing the secure access of the starving population to humanitarian supplies.

At first this seemed to gain some traction, and an agreement on the implementation of a cease-fire was brokered between President Mahdi and General Aidid in Mogadishu on March 3, 1992. As part of this deal and subsequent agreements, in April the Security Council created the UN Operation in Somalia (UNOSOM). This was a peacekeeping mission of fifty unarmed observers to monitor the cease-fire in Mogadishu, including further troops who would accompany humanitarian convoys delivering relief around the country.

On August 25, 1992, we heard from the Red Cross that eleven of its workers had been killed in the southern Somali port of Kismayo. This was a particularly bad case among scores of other attacks on relief workers and supplies in the days and weeks before. Nine days earlier, on August 16, I arrived in my office at DPKO in New York to discover that gunmen and looters had blocked food trucks in Mogadishu. UN World Food Programme workers attempting to move food aid from the capital's port to the communities beyond were once again being thwarted with force. That was not all: at the same time, a band of gunmen had just broken into the harbor at Kismayo and stolen 250 tons of food.

Relief workers in the Somali countryside were providing us with increasingly harrowing reports of the conditions of the population, and the consequences of this denial of food aid: at Baidoa, 150 miles from Mogadishu, children were dying daily at the actual feeding centers, even though those centers had been established over a month before. As the relief workers explained to us, the road from Mogadishu to Baidoa was now strewn with bodies.

It was horrifyingly clear, as these all too regular events went by, that political reconciliation was not taking hold, peace was not settling, and looting by armed gangs was continuing to disrupt and stop humanitarian supplies. The reality of the situation on the ground repeatedly demonstrated that the capabilities of the UN mission were inadequate. By the end of August 1992, the Security Council approved a series of moderate measures to expand UNOSOM's observation and escort operations, as recommended by Boutros-Ghali.

But regardless of efforts to deliver aid, as long as the fighting continued in Somalia's fluid civil war, so would the deterioration of the humanitarian situation in much of the country—and this then worsened steeply from November 1992. As the effort to deliver food and the volume of aid expanded, so did the level of effort to disrupt it. Whole factions, not just loose gangs, were now openly blocking the delivery of food. Huge amounts of supplies were being delivered to the country, but only a tiny portion of this was reaching the starving.

At DPKO, our prime concern was getting food to the people. This meant more troops dedicated to ensuring the safe delivery of supplies.

The situation was outrageous for all to see: food warehouses at Somalia's ports were now full, while an estimated 3,000 Somalis were dying every day, with perhaps 300,000 already dead. It was a situation, as I said at the time, that diminished every one of us a little more each day.

A more urgent and purposeful course of action was clearly necessary. We believed that capabilities and a mandate to use force were going to have to be provided if we were to get the bulk of the food beyond the ports and airfields and into the hands of the starving. On November 29, 1992, Boutros-Ghali responded to a request from the Council for options on how the uninterrupted delivery of humanitarian supplies might be achieved. He recommended mandating the use of force, under Chapter VII of the UN Charter, as the only feasible option.

In response, on December 3, 1992, the Security Council unanimously adopted resolution 794, mandating the use of "all necessary means to establish as soon as possible a secure environment for humanitarian relief operations in Somalia," including, under Chapter VII of the Charter, the deployment of a new, unified military force. This was issued with the understanding that the United States would take the lead in delivering this new military capability. The next day, on December 4, the U.S. outgoing president, George H. W. Bush, authorized Operation Restore Hope, declaring his recognition that "only the United States has the global reach to place a large security force on the ground in such a distant place quickly and efficiently and, thus, save thousands of innocents from death." On December 9, the spearhead of an American force of 28,000 of some of the world's most professional soldiers landed in Somalia, to be supported by 17,000 additional troops from twenty other countries.

The Security Council and the troop contributors saw this as a decisive measure that would rapidly stabilize the situation in the country. So sure were they of this, the Council emphasized the operation should be of only a short duration "to prepare the way for a return to peacekeeping and postconflict peacebuilding."

Despite this intervention, a situation resembling "postconflict peacebuilding" remained far beyond the horizon. Once humanitarian supplies had been securely delivered to the main relief areas of Somalia by the U.S.-led task force, its effort came to an end. Responsibility for the situation transferred to a new UN operation in March 1993, in the form of UNOSOM II; the same month I replaced Marrack Goulding as head of DPKO and received the rank of under-secretary-general.

The U.S.-led task force was highly successful in securing population centers in much of Somalia and ensuring the delivery of humanitarian supplies to 40 percent of the country—but the fighting still continued afterward. For this reason, Boutros-Ghali recommended to the Security Council that UNOSOM II be provided with a Chapter VII mandate to use force as in Operation Restore Hope, and to disarm the factions in Somalia in order to restore law and order in the country. The result was Security Council resolution 814, adopted on March 26, 1993, which U.S. ambassador to the UN Madeleine Albright declared "an unprecedented enterprise aimed at nothing less than the restoration of an entire country as a proud, functioning, and viable member of the community of nations."

The problem, however, was that with the removal of much of the U.S. troop presence, the ambitions of UNOSOM II were expanding enormously just as it was being stripped of capabilities. It was now a smaller, far less well-equipped force with a much more fragmented command structure. Before March 1993, there had been around forty thousand international troops deployed, mostly from the United States. But although still supported by some U.S. troops, UNOSOM II was now made up of troops from Turkey, Malaysia, Pakistan, and elsewhere in a force that never went above twenty thousand. If UNOSOM II was going to succeed, it would need rapid progress in the political reconciliation of the parties and the establishment of a peace deal. Otherwise, UNOSOM II would not have the power to force the issue.

But a deal was not forthcoming, and the civil war continued, particularly with the fighting in southern Mogadishu, which UNOSOM II could do little to stop with its limited resources. What is more, UNOSOM II's effort to disarm the Somali factions dragged the force directly into the conflict. In a situation of ongoing war such as this, any faction that was targeted for disarmament then found itself disadvantaged in relation to its enemies. No Somali warlord was simply going to let this happen. On June 5, 1993, following a series of incidents involving attacks on UN-OSOM II forces, twenty-five Pakistani peacekeeping troops were killed and over fifty others wounded. General Aidid was blamed, and the response of the Security Council—and particularly the United States—was to focus attention on arresting Aidid, whom they now perceived as the greatest threat to the mission.

This distracted the mission from important strategic questions. In my view, we needed a stronger force as a whole, not a focus of limited resources on one man in Mogadishu. Sahnoun had also argued that the alternative to the approach of dealing with—and so empowering—warlords was to focus instead on local leaders outside Mogadishu. This would, in his view, help build Somali structures and reconciliation through leaders with real legitimacy in their communities, not just the men with the most guns in Mogadishu. But the obsession with Aidid left little space for considering such alternatives.

Much of UNOSOM II was run by Boutros-Ghali in his secretive style. Through his personal negotiations with troop contributors, Boutros-Ghali kept most people at the UN, including the leadership of DPKO, out of much of the decision making.

Most significant of the developments that Boutros-Ghali kept to himself was the deployment of U.S. Special Forces to hunt for Aidid: the forces arrived in Somalia in late August 1993 in a unit made up of U.S. Rangers, Delta Force, and Navy SEALs under a chain of command entirely separate from the UN mission. But the first we in DPKO knew of this was on October 3, 1993, when news broke that there had been a disastrous attempt to capture the Somali warlord. Boutros-Ghali's hard-nosed attitude to dealing with Somalia had come together with the new-found U.S. obsession with catching Aidid. Two helicopters had been shot down, eighteen U.S. soldiers killed, and scores of others wounded, trapped in different parts of the city, only to be retrieved from the jaws of a mob of armed Somalis by UN peacekeeping troops who, like us, had been un-aware of the operation. In horrifying images screened around the world, dead U.S. soldiers were stripped naked and dragged through the streets of Mogadishu.

For a humanitarian mission this was devastating. The American public was shocked. It did not matter that U.S. and other UN troops had been engaged in significant episodes of combat for several months in Mogadishu as part of UNOSOM II's mandate—it had still been under-stood as "peacekeeping" and the American people had not been prepared for casualties. The politicians who opposed the intervention were now full throated in their call for an end to the United States' involvement.

The U.S. swiftly announced its departure from Somalia. This gutted UNOSOM II as it took the best-trained, best-equipped features with it. The rest of the troop contributors, now even more exposed, followed suit, and the UN mission in Somalia collapsed in the weeks and months that followed. Thus ended the greatest experiment ever attempted to use peace enforcement in a mission motivated purely by humanitarian goals. Going in under the cover of peacekeeping only to meet the fire of combat meant political momentum had swung decisively and rapidly toward withdrawal—and with it all the help that had proudly been offered to the Somali people.

The world abandoned Somalia, allowing it to create for the world whole new forms of civil chaos and human suffering. Somalia would from then on be ignored by Western countries—until years later, when interna-tional terrorists emerged there in force, and when scores of well-organized pirates took to the high seas to threaten one of the lifelines of international commerce. But in 1993, the concept of the "enlightened self-interest" of international humanitarianism had barely been grasped in the international community.

The failure of the raid on October 3 brought the dysfunctional nature of the peacekeeping system into plain view. The response to this, however, did not trigger a careful reassessment of the tool of peacekeeping by member states, but snap reactions: President Bill Clinton announced that U.S. troops would never again be put in harm's way in a UN peacekeeping mission. The debacle in Somalia meant the aversion to taking any risks now ran even harder through the instincts of the troop-contributing nations. But peacekeeping operations continued to be deployed to complex and rapidly shifting civil war zones elsewhere.

This only deepened the dysfunction in peacekeeping. A peacekeeping mission in Haiti, mandated in September, soon collapsed after a U.S. warship, bearing U.S. and Canadian troops, was turned back from the country on October 11 in the face of the presence of only lightly armed criminal gangs on the shore. The resentful attitude toward peacekeeping immediately fed into the negotiations for the creation and implementation of other peacekeeping operations after October 3, 1993, leading to angry resistance in the Security Council to any mandate or deployment that might include the use of force. Fatefully, the first operation to be created in this climate was the mission to Rwanda.

Rwanda: In the Shadow of Somalia

Code Cable, 11 January 1994.

To: Maurice Baril, DPKO, UN, New York.

From: Romeo Dallaire, Force Commander, UNAMIR, Kigali, Rwanda.

Subject: Request for protection of informant.

Force Commander put in contact with informant by very very important government politician. Informant is a top level trainer in the cadre of interahamwe-armed militia of MRND [the ruling Hutu political party]. He informed us he was in charge of last Saturday's demonstrations . . . [There] they hoped to provoke the RPF battalion [the unit of the rebel army stationed in Kigali as part of the peace agreement] to engage (being fired upon) the demonstrators and provoke a civil war. Deputies were to be assassinated upon entry or exit from Parliament. Belgian troops [the core component of the peacekeeping force] were to be provoked and if Belgian soldiers resorted to force a number of them were to be killed and thus guarantee Belgian withdrawal from Rwanda . . . Since the UNAMIR mandate he [the informant] has been ordered to register all Tutsi in Kigali. He suspects it is for their extermination. Example he gave was that in 20 minutes his personnel could kill up to 1,000 Tutsis. Informant states he disagrees with anti-Tutsi extermination . . . Informant is prepared to provide location of major weapons cache with at least 135 weapons . . . He was ready to go to the arms-cache tonight . . . It is our intention to take action within the next 36 hours . . . Recce of armed cache and detailed planning of raid to go on late tomorrow. Possibility of a trap not fully excluded . . . Peux Ce Que Veux. Allons-Y.

By January 1994, DPKO was locked in an ongoing effort to manage eighty thousand troops engaged in seventeen peacekeeping operations worldwide, from over sixty troop-contributing countries, and all with a staff at the New York head office that had expanded little alongside. In the midst of this dizzying situation, and in the shadow of Somalia, we received this urgent and deeply disturbing message from the force commander of our peacekeeping mission in Rwanda.

Three months later, an estimated 800,000 people were killed in Rwanda in one hundred days. Our reply to General Dallaire's cable was in stark contrast to the tone of his closing words in French: "Allons-Y," or, "Let's Go." Instead, we warned Dallaire against the offensive action envisaged in his plan to raid the arms cache, reminding him that it would not be allowed by the Security Council or his existing mandate, and instructed him only to convey the information as a warning to other more influential parties on the ground, including the three countries with the most influence in Rwanda. He was to go, we told him, to the diplomatic missions of France, the United States, and Belgium in Rwanda, and also to approach the president of Rwanda himself. We believed it to be the best—indeed, the only—option that we could take.

In light of what came after, how did we come to that conclusion? The answer, in many ways, cuts to the heart of everything that was going wrong in UN peacekeeping at that time.

Rwanda had long suffered from an ethnic power struggle between the minority Tutsi population (who, before independence, had occupied a privileged position in the colonial administration of the country) and the majority Hutu population. The former Tutsi dominance of the colonial era was overturned during a violent power struggle that accompanied decolonization from Belgian rule. Following independence in 1962, there were many who would remain ever fearful of a return of Tutsi hegemony over the Hutus. On October 1, 1990, the predominantly Tutsi Rwandese Patriotic Front (RPF) launched an assault from neighboring Uganda against the Hutu-dominated government of Rwanda. To the Hutu government, the RPF invasion represented the threat of a return to Tutsi domination in Rwanda.

The RPF proved itself a formidable rebel force and gained an increasingly strong foothold in northern Rwanda, several times threatening the capital, Kigali, in the months and years that followed. The Hutu-dominated Rwandan government of President Juvenal Habyarimana had an ally in France however, and on several occasions French paratroopers were deployed, along with troops from Zaire and Belgium, to secure key sites in Kigali to free more Rwandan government troops for the increasingly faltering campaign to halt the RPF. On February 8, 1993, the RPF launched one of its biggest offensives and came within fifteen miles of Kigali. The French intervened, sending six hundred additional paratroopers to shore up the defenses of the government in Kigali. This helped stall the RPF advance, and under diplomatic pressure from France, Belgium, and the United States, the RPF entered into concerted negotiations designed to find a peaceful settlement to the conflict.

The result was a peace deal, known as the Arusha Accords, signed in August 1993, which established the conditions for a power-sharing, democratic government representing both sides and a unified army composed of government and RPF forces. Part of the agreement was the provision that a neutral international force should be deployed in Rwanda to assist in upholding the deal on the ground. This final detail of the agreement was largely a result of French lobbying. The French, interested in facilitating a deal that ensured the survival of its ally, the Habyarimana regime, albeit in a power-sharing deal with the RPF, pushed from the outset of the Arusha negotiations for a UN force to be deployed to Rwanda to support the peace deal.

Other than from the French, there was at first little appetite among permanent members of the Security Council for mandating a new peacekeeping force in so distant and, to many, so obscure a country—especially when they were so preoccupied with other complicated, sizeable, and deeply troubled missions in Somalia and Bosnia. But the French made a deal to support peacekeeping missions in Haiti and Georgia, which the United States and Russia wanted, in return for backing on a Rwandan mission. The result was resolution 872, passed by the Council on October 5, 1993, creating the UN Assistance Mission in Rwanda (UNAMIR).

Of utmost importance to understanding resolution 872 was the context of hostility to any robustly equipped peacekeeping mission that prevailed in the Council at that time, particularly and acutely emanating from the United States. The vote on the creation of UNAMIR occurred just a few days after the Mogadishu debacle—the United States, supported by other states, was now insistent in its rejection of peacekeeping operations that might put troops on a course leading to the use of force and the complications and casualties that could come with them. Furthermore, within domestic U.S. politics there was now an agenda for reducing the cost of all peacekeeping missions, which many members of the United States Congress now argued to be excessive, absorbing too many U.S. tax dollars.

As a result, at first the United States argued for only a tiny force of one hundred observers for UNAMIR, preferring a far cheaper option to the eight thousand, optimal number of troops recommended by a UN reconnaissance mission sent in August. That mission had argued that a force of five thousand was the minimum feasible to support the Arusha Accords, but in the end only twenty-five hundred troops were mandated.

The outcome of the Mogadishu raid had caused a flurry of anger at the UN in the United States. The Clinton administration now blamed the UN for the debacle, including falsely claiming that the UN Secretariat had been in command of U.S. troops and thus was responsible for the calamity of October 3, 1993. Given that we had not even known about the planned raid to capture Aidid or even that U.S. Special Forces were in the country, stomaching this accusation was tough for all of us in DPKO.

As a result, at the time of the establishment of UNAMIR and the weeks after, there was a sense that the future of UN peacekeeping was hanging in the balance. This was not least because the United States Congress, in approving the U.S. budget for 1994, had also thrown out a proposed peacekeeping contingency fund designed to enable the United States to provide emergency financing for the rapid start-up of peacekeeping operations. It seemed that the United States was looking to cut itself loose entirely from peacekeeping. Given that the U.S. government also owed some $900 million in unpaid contributions to the regular UN budget and its peacekeeping expenses—the payment of which Congress refused to approve despite the legal obligation as a UN member state—it felt as if UN peacekeeping, and all the benefits it brought to international peace and security, might be on the verge of rapid decline. Some feared it might wither entirely.

In our analysis at the time, UNAMIR seemed to exhibit none of the risks that had caused the disaster in Somalia and the continuing problems in Bosnia. A three-year civil war had ceased and a full peace deal had been agreed to. Unlike in recent controversial operations, the force would not be deploying to an environment where there was no peace to keep. The peacekeeping operation was part of the Arusha Accords and so would exist with the full consent of the parties to the conflict. Furthermore, the operation was deployed as a Chapter VI mission, without any powers or agenda for peace enforcement. Finally, the operation was launched under the explicit provision that its existence and continuation was entirely dependent upon the ongoing commitment of the RPF and the Habyarimana-led government to the Arusha Accords. Any collapse in the agreement would mean the termination of the operation—and this was seen as a sensible caveat that would protect the mission from any messy entanglements in a civil war, as was then causing the problems in Somalia and Bosnia.

We were aware of a history of ethnic violence in Rwanda, and the fact that there had been major ethnic killings in neighboring Burundi, too, but we did not translate this into any serious fear for a collapse in Rwanda. Unlike in Burundi, the parties had accepted a UN role in sustaining a peace agreement. From a traditional peacekeeping operations perspective, Rwanda seemed much safer ground for involvement than other missions of that time.

We were not alone in our optimism. The international development community had been engaged for years in Rwanda, and right up to March 1994, reports were still being written by leading development organizations that praised Rwanda as an unusual success story. But the international community had a thin appreciation of Rwanda's society and history and the forces at play there. As one CIA officer later admitted, when he was assigned to Rwanda in 1990, his first task was to locate the country on a map. At DPKO, we certainly had no genuine, deep expertise on the country. Handed to us by the Security Council were over a dozen operations that we now had to manage worldwide with a tiny DPKO staff. A limited knowledge of the countries in which our operations were taking place had simply become a necessary way of life at DPKO.

Even for the tightly limited tasks of UNAMIR, mandated to conduct traditional peacekeeping and oversee only a cease-fire, the deployment got off to a bad start. By late December 1993, the capabilities of the force were totally inadequate. A report from UNAMIR on December 30 outlined its severe deficiencies. No country had been willing to supply a self-contained, 800-man infantry battalion, which had been considered essential for securing the Kigali area. Instead, they had to use two smaller infantry battalions, one from Belgium, consisting of 398 men, and one from Bangladesh, which was supposed to consist of 370 men of which only 266 had arrived. The lack of any armored personnel carriers or helicopters also meant, the report stressed, the "absence of this deterrent capability and the lack of a mobile reserve force not only for Kigali, but also for the demilitarized zone, which was forecast as a critical requirement in the Secretary-General's report." Among an extensive list of other problems with the force, the report stated that engineers and logisticians were being reassigned as infantry due to the severe shortfall in the number of troops.

UNAMIR was meant to receive twenty-two armored personnel carriers and eight helicopters to enable some flexibility in its response capability. But no country was willing to provide any helicopters, and only eight armored personnel carriers could eventually be sourced for the force, which were cannibalized from the UN mission in Mozambique. The vehicles finally arrived but they were dilapidated, and only five were serviceable; some of these often broke down and had to be towed by the remaining armored personnel carriers. Such humiliating exhibitions of the force's lack of capacity often occurred in Kigali and in full view of Rwandan government forces. Years later, Paul Kagame, president of Rwanda and leader of the RPF, would tell me that it was clear to him at the time that Dallaire did not have the necessary means to carry out his mission, and that he did not even trust Daillaire's ability to protect him when he made official visits to the UN field headquarters.

It was in this context—less than two weeks after the damning December UNAMIR report on the military incapacity of the operation—that we received the January 11, 1994, cable from Dallaire informing us of the tense situation on the ground and his plan to raid an arms cache. My deputy, Iqbal Riza, received it and sent the response to the SRSG in Rwanda, Jacques-Roger Booh-Booh, as was the proper chain of communication, telling him to curtail any plan to raid. It stated that we could not agree to his planned raid, stressing the overriding consideration being "the need to avoid entering into a course of action that might lead to the use of force and unanticipated repercussions."

Our greatest fear at that moment, given the precarious position of UN peacekeeping at the time, was for another military disaster to befall a peacekeeping operation leading to significant casualties. In Dallaire's cabled request to raid, we saw the ingredients of a disaster akin to the failed raid on Aidid in Mogadishu three months earlier—but with a force that was a thousand times weaker in military capabilities and entirely isolated from any possibility of reinforcement. In Dallaire's plan there lay the potential for a scenario that, for the peacekeeping force, could have proved even worse than the events in Somalia. In a remote country surrounded by two armies made up of tens of thousands of potentially hostile and well-armed soldiers, with no contingency for the deployment of additional, robust fighting troops or any standby force, I believed such a raid would set them up for a confrontation they would not be able to deal with. It could have led to not just a few dozen peacekeepers exposed, as had happened in Somalia, but hundreds, perhaps even the entire force of 2,165.

What is more, in the post-Somalia international climate, there was no appetite in the international community for taking even the slightest risks with the lives of peacekeepers, certainly not in the United States. A small-scale encounter with only a few casualties would have set off a withdrawal by the Security Council and the collapse of yet another peacekeeping mission, perhaps triggering the collapse of the entire peace process.

With the information we had then, it was impossible to countenance the raid. Later, in April, when ten Belgian troops were captured, as predicted by Dallaire's informant, Dallaire at that time was in a car on the way to meet leading members of the government's armed forces. He passed a compound where he saw two of the Belgian peacekeeping troops being held and beaten. This was the first he knew of their capture, and he realized then, he would explain later, that he could do nothing to save them other than engage in negotiations. "At that moment I was already saying: 'I just can't get those guys out of there. I just don't have the forces,'" he would recount. He considered a rescue option irresponsible due to the risk to his other troops, and it was this same overriding consideration that dictated our response to his January 11 request.

Dallaire's cable also warned of a potential trap. Even if it had not, we would seriously have considered this possibility. There were always parties with an interest in manipulating peacekeeping forces. The supply of false information was a common feature of missions to conflict zones. There was a delicate balance in the Arusha peace process, and this intelligence had come out of the blue from an isolated source. There was the real risk that it could have been planted by elements from either side precisely to trigger the offensive action envisaged by Dallaire and so set a course of events that would restart the war.

Furthermore, if we had agreed with the plan to raid, it would have had to have gone to the secretary-general and the Security Council to be authorized. All cable traffic from force commanders was automatically copied to over a dozen people, both among senior staff in DPKO and the secretary-general's office. Given its contents, the cable certainly caused a stir in DPKO and in the office of the secretary-general, but there was no dissent to our response. The reason for this was clear to all: there was no appetite whatsoever in the Security Council to even consider the use of force in a peacekeeping mission—as it had been made clear to us repeatedly in the weeks and months earlier.

The atmosphere in the Security Council was grim, and its attitude regarding any initiatives from the Secretariat, whom the United States was publicly blaming for recent failures in Somalia, was skeptical at best. Any recommendations contrary to the attitudes of the Security Council were met with a mix of derision and anger at that time. In one instance, for example, Maurice Baril, the senior military advisor at DPKO, in a rare opportunity for anyone other than Gharekhan to meet the Security Council, joined me to brief the Council with a military analysis of the plan to set up "safe areas" in Bosnia, which he explained were subject to severe deficiencies under current conditions. Maurice said he felt as if he was being "skinned alive" by U.S. ambassador Albright and UK ambassador David Hannay for implying that he might know better than the Council's members about the conditions necessary for a successful peacekeeping operation. The attitude was very much one of "who do you think you are to come here and lecture us?" and they made sure they punished Maurice verbally for it.

Within these constraints, we sent our response to Dallaire's request. But we still took his warning seriously. In our cable we instructed him to implement an alternative, diplomatic course of action that seemed to have the best chance of preempting any plan to carry out a massacre in Kigali. To add further pressure on President Habyarimana, we also said to Dallaire:

> on the assumption that you are convinced that the information provided by the informant is absolutely reliable . . . you should advise the President that, if any violence occurs in Kigali, you would have to immediately bring to the attention of the Security Council

the information you have received on the activities of the militia, undertake investigations to determine who is responsible and make appropriate recommendations to the Security Council.

Our tactic here was to try to create the impression that the president was on notice from powerful forces in the world—from the most militarily active foreign nations on the ground in Rwanda to the UN itself—that could bring serious repercussions upon him if he was complicit in any violence.

On the day after we sent our cable, on January 12, 1994, the UN special representative Jacques-Roger Booh-Booh and General Dallaire met with the ambassadors of those three countries as instructed by us, in response to which the ambassadors said they would inform their capitals and coordinate strategy. There was the later claim that members of the Security Council were unaware of the warning conveyed by Dallaire's informant. Given that permanent Council members, particularly the United States and France, had far more advanced and established intelligence-gathering capabilities in Rwanda than UNAMIR, this could not have been true.

On April 6, 1994, a plane carrying President Habyarimana of Rwanda and President Cyprien Ntaryamira of Burundi was shot down while carrying its passengers from negotiations in Tanzania, just as it was nearing its destination at Kigali Airport. All passengers were killed. Immediately following this, violence initiated by government Hutu forces erupted in Kigali. The day after the assassinations, ten Belgian paratroopers who were part of UNAMIR and assigned to protect the prime minister of Rwanda were captured by government troops. Radioing for instructions from their commander, Colonel Luc Marchal, they were told to lay down their weapons and not engage in combat. The prime minister was then murdered, and soon after the ten Belgian paratroopers were killed and their bodies mutilated.

Our fears from January were now being confirmed—troop contributors looked likely to withdraw, with the mission set to collapse, and there were now massacres occurring in Kigali. But over the coming days, reports came in of something Dallaire had not warned us about. The violence and massacres were clearly spreading beyond the capital. Civilians were being killed in the open by government troops, militia groups, and bands of civilians under the direction of local commanders and state officials, mostly with agricultural tools, and at a rate and intensity none of us had ever heard of before.

A senior Rwandan official later said of the plan to kill the Belgian peacekeepers that "we watch CNN too, you know." He was referring to the lesson that they had garnered from Somalia the year before: that the death of just a few foreign peacekeepers would be enough to end the appetite for intervention and allow them to get on with their murderous plans. They were right. Five days after the grisly killing of its soldiers, the Belgian government announced that it would withdraw its troops—the core fighting capability of UNAMIR—from Rwanda immediately.

The first instructions to come from the Security Council on April 8 were for UNAMIR to do everything it could to facilitate an agreement that would reestablish a cease-fire. On the ground, meanwhile, the UNAMIR force was in no way equipped to intervene in any meaningful way without seriously jeopardizing the lives of all its troops. On April 15, Dallaire said to a *New York Times* journalist: "We have been sitting now eight or nine days in our trenches. The question is how long do you sit there or attempt to get it settled? Ours is not a peace enforcement mission . . . If we don't see any light at the end of the tunnel, if we see another three weeks of being cooped up watching them pound each other then we have to seriously assess the risk of keeping these soldiers here." Dallaire took full responsibility for protecting his troops and did his duty for them. But when the time came to draw down and leave Rwanda, as he was expected to do, he himself decided to stay. He remained for a further three months, and very much in harm's way, with a tiny contingent of Ghanaian and Tunisian peacekeepers to save what Rwandan civilians they could.

In New York—with feelings of shock and disbelief that only escalated each day—we read the reports and news releases as they came in. By April 21, it was clear that the violence was being conducted in a systematic and intensifying fashion across the country. On that day, the Security Council then voted to draw down the UNAMIR force to just 270 troops. There was no interest in getting involved. As Bob Dole, the Republican leader in the United States Senate, said a few days before the Council's decision: "I don't think we have any national interest here. I hope we don't get involved . . . The Americans [U.S. citizens in Rwanda] are out. As far as I'm concerned, in Rwanda that ought to be the end of it."

The choice offered to the Security Council on that day by Secretary-General Boutros-Ghali included options for the complete transformation of the force and a major military intervention. This was summarily rejected. The Security Council took no responsibility for the situation in Rwanda and the growing number of lives lost, and its key members flatly denied the notion that a genocide was taking place. However, a CIA briefing report, dated April 23, 1994, two days after the Security Council decision to withdraw, demonstrates that at least by this date the conflict was considered and referred to as a "genocide" by officials in the U.S. administration.

The Security Council turned its back, but the news reports did not stop in their growing testimony to atrocities that were beyond imagination. On April 29, the Office of the United Nations High Commissioner for Refugees (UNHCR) published statistics indicating that over 250,000 Rwandans had crossed into neighboring Tanzania alone, which made this the largest mass exodus of refugees ever witnessed by the UN agency. At that same point, the UN estimated that over 200,000 people had been killed inside Rwanda. By early May, we at the UN were officially describing the killings in Rwanda as genocide, having dispatched Iqbal Riza to

Rwanda to make his assessment of the situation. These different points of pressure finally compelled the Security Council to restart deliberations on Rwanda on May 6. The secretary-general, supported by us at DPKO, submitted options to the Council for a response, including a range of interventions involving different levels of force. Eventually, on May 17, the Council issued resolution 918, mandating the reestablishment of the UNAMIR mission (with the new name, UNAMIR II) with a force of 5,500.

However, not one of the Council's members was willing to provide troops. At DPKO, we spent endless days frantically lobbying more than a hundred governments around the world for troops. I called dozens myself, and the responses were all the same. We did not receive a single serious offer. It was one of the most shocking and deeply formative experiences of my entire career, laying bare the disjuncture between the public statements of alarm and concern for the suffering of other people on the one hand, and, on the other, the unwillingness to commit any of the necessary resources to take action. The world knew the scale of the killing in Rwanda, and yet we could not get anyone, from governments across the world, to do anything serious to help.

What brought the genocide to an end—but not before it saw a staggering 800,000 Tutsis and moderate Hutus killed in just 100 days—was the victory of the RPF over the government. The RPF military drove the government's genocidal forces from Rwanda in a military campaign that came to its completion in July, and a new government under the RPF was established. It was only after this, in August, that troops were finally sent to form UNAMIR II, by which time the genocide and the civil war were firmly over.

The lesson of the RPF victory was that ending the genocide and protecting civilians on a large scale would have required military capacity and the political will to act to stop the killing. But in 1994, there was simply no culture or precedent in the international system of UN intervention in an internal conflict to use military force decisively to protect civilians. Combined with the impact of events in Mogadishu, the result was total inaction. It would take another war, and the deaths of thousands more civilians—this time in Europe—for the world to learn to take sides.

BOSNIA: FACING UP TO FAILURE

"A fantastic gap between the resolutions of the Security Council, the will to execute these resolutions, and the means available to commanders in the field." That was Belgian general Francis Briquemont's acerbic observation and summation of the UN mission in Bosnia at the end of his command of the peacekeeping force there. This gap would be filled, once again, with dead civilians, and on a scale not seen in Europe since World War II.

The UN was, and will probably always remain, an easy target when it comes to analyzing failed peacekeeping operations. The limits on our resources, the extreme reluctance of troop contributors to take risks with their troops, and, above all, the profound divisions over policy and strategic direction that often existed among members of the Security Council were often conveniently forgotten when apportioning responsibility for what was routinely referred to in those years as the "crisis in UN peacekeeping." Nowhere was this more so than in Rwanda and Bosnia, where between 1992 and 1995 the UN was asked to keep the peace in the midst of an ongoing and brutal war.

I had taken up my post as deputy to Marrack Goulding, undersecretary-general in charge of peacekeeping, in early March 1992, just as the situation in Bosnia-Herzegovina was about to take a dramatic and violent turn for the worse. With the disintegration of Yugoslavia alongside the end of the Cold War, and after an intense but relatively brief war in Croatia, the Security Council in February 1992 authorized the deployment of UN peacekeepers, the United Nations Protection Force (UNPROFOR), to oversee the separation of warring parties along the confrontation line between the Krajina Serbs and Croatian forces. Deployed firmly on the basis of traditional peacekeeping principles—host state consent, impartiality, and minimum use of force—UN blue helmets were to establish three so-called Protected Areas, ensure their demilitarization, and control access to them. They were also tasked to verify the withdrawal of the Serb Yugoslav National Army (known as the JNA) and irregular forces from Croatia, many of whom, as it turned out, would soon be providing logistic support to and fighting alongside Bosnian Serb militias in neighboring Bosnia.

Two months earlier, following the recognition of Slovenia and Croatia by the European Community on January 15, 1992, Bosnia held a referendum on independence. It was boycotted by the Bosnian Serbs but, unsurprisingly, overwhelmingly supported by the majority of Bosnian Muslims and Croats in the republic. On April 6, Bosnia's independence was duly recognized by a majority of European Community members, and what had hitherto been sporadic fighting exploded into full-scale war that crossed the new internationally recognized borders.

It proved a one-sided affair. Over the next three months, a savage onslaught by Serb militias and paramilitary forces, aided and abetted by the rump Yugoslav army, resulted in the displacement of some 1 million people from their homes. The attack on the town of Bijelinja by forces commanded by Željko "Arkan" Ražnatović—a notorious career criminal turned paramilitary leader and later indicted for crimes against humanity—set the pattern for a campaign of murder, rape, looting, and destruction aimed at ethnically cleansing a swath of territory in the north and the east of the country. Conducted with the utmost brutality, Bosnian Serb forces sought the wholesale expulsion of the non-Serb, largely Muslim population from towns and cities where, in many cases, non-Serbs had constituted the majority population before the war. The offensive was as swift as it was brutal, and, in fact, most of the territory captured by the Bosnian Serbs during the war in Bosnia was secured within the first sixty days.

Alarmed by these developments, pressure began to build from member states, as well as some of the key Council members, for the international community to "do something" and for the UN to expand its activities into Bosnia. While Boutros-Ghali was reluctant to take on yet another large-scale peacekeeping commitment in the Balkans, President François Mitterrand of France urged him to consider it in light of the catastrophe that was unfolding on the ground. He responded by sending Marrack Goulding on a fact-finding mission to Bosnia in May 1992 in order to assess the possibility of deploying a peacekeeping mission to the republic. Goulding reported back on the ongoing war, noting how Bosnian Serbs supported by JNA were deliberately seeking to create "ethnically pure" regions by terrorizing, killing, and expelling non-Serb populations from hitherto mixed areas. However, he also concluded that "in its present phase this conflict is not susceptible to UN peacekeeping treatment." Boutros-Ghali accepted the conclusion, as did the Council on May 15.

By this time, much of UNPROFOR's headquarters in Sarajevo had been evacuated due to the fighting, and although some forty military observers had been sent to the Mostar region in late April, there was only a very limited UN presence throughout the republic in the period when Bosnia Serb forces consolidated their hold on much of eastern and northern Bosnia. The accompanying scenes of barbarity that saw thousands, mostly Bosnian Muslims, killed or expelled from their homes, were not, in general, witnessed by UNPROFOR officials.

The full scale of the horrors taking place in Bosnian Serb–controlled territory, however, could not long be hidden from the international community, particularly in light of the evidence of the rapidly growing population of refugees. To Europeans, who had recently lived through the end of the Cold War and had come to expect that transitions from communist rule to democracy could be both orderly and peaceful, the reports that emerged from Bosnia in the summer of 1992 were deeply disturbing. The images of emaciated prisoners, frightened, traumatized, and huddled behind barbed wire, evoked memories of the darkest days of European history. There was also an ongoing, systematic rape campaign that clearly became common practice in the conflict. Particularly abhorrent were the "rape camps" where Bosnian women were held at the disposal of Serbian soldiers and paramilitaries.

The demand for further action only grew in intensity—even though the conditions that, back in May, had been found to rule out a traditional peacekeeping mission had not changed. In June, UNPROFOR troops assumed control of Sarajevo Airport from Bosnian Serbs, thus establishing a vital lifeline for humanitarian supplies into the country, which was kept open by the UN throughout the period of the war. The first significant expansion of the UN's role in Bosnia, however, came in September, when the Security Council, in response to the deteriorating situation in Sarajevo and elsewhere, authorized an increase in UNPROFOR's strength in order to protect UNHCR convoys delivering humanitarian aid.

Although deployed into what was plainly an ongoing war, member states insisted that the enlarged force should operate in accordance with the "established principles and practices of UN peacekeeping." The emphasis was significant and telling: "doing something" did not at this stage, nor, indeed, at any time until after the fall of Srebrenica in the summer of 1995, involve war fighting. On this much, at least there was agreement among the permanent five member states as well as the major troop contributors to the mission.

The Secretariat viewed this as an inescapable reality. Again and again I learned, in my regular meetings with troop-contributing countries as head of DPKO, accompanied by my trusted and insightful special assistant Shashi Tharoor, that no one was willing to reconfigure the mission to engage in war fighting. To do so, I was told, would expose their troops to "unnecessary" risks. Yet as the war dragged on, the international media and key member states, notably the United States and Germany, publicly and rightly questioned the viability of the nonconfrontational peacekeeping basis on which UN involvement was based. Rather than risk soldiers, they pressured us to take more forceful action through the use of air power.

Every new resolution, however, also reaffirmed previous resolutions, which rejected active war fighting. Although some forty thousand UN peacekeepers were eventually deployed, Bosnia remained essentially a peacekeeping mission: lightly equipped, widely dispersed with limited mobility and no strategic reserve, vulnerable logistics, and reliant on the consent of parties to carry out its tasks.

Some said, as a result, that the UN was effectively abandoning the Bosnians. Yet the way in which the public sympathized with the victims of the conflict sometimes overshadowed their understanding of what obstructed the UN from doing what ought to be done—and from what the UN *was*, in fact, doing.

UN peacekeepers in the former Yugoslavia were deployed originally in support of three major purposes. Chief among them was the effort to alleviate the human suffering caused by the war. This meant keeping Sarajevo Airport open and the airlift going; supporting the efforts of UNHCR to deliver food and medicine as well as protecting their storage centers and other UN facilities; providing protection for other humanitarian agencies and, when requested to do so by the International Committee of the Red Cross (ICRC), providing protection for convoys of released detainees. It was a large and complex operation for which many peacekeepers and aid workers paid with their lives. By the end of 1995, the airlift operation had delivered nearly 160,000 metric tons of food in nearly 13,000 sorties, while UNPROFOR-supported convoys had delivered more than 850,000 metric tons of aid by road.

The second broad purpose for which the UN was deployed was to contain the conflict and mitigate its consequences as far as possible, making sure it did not spread within or beyond the territory of the former Yugoslavia. This involved imposing various constraints on the warring parties, through such arrangements as the no-fly zone over Bosnia adopted in October 1992, weapons-exclusion zones, and the preventive deployment of UN troops, the first mission of its kind, to the Former Yugoslav Republic of Macedonia in December 1992.

The third objective was to facilitate the efforts by the warring parties—both locally and at the strategic level—to reach a peaceful settlement to the conflict. To this end, the UN negotiated local cease-fires and provided support for an overall political settlement. The latter included support for activities of the International Conference on the former Yugoslavia and those of the contact group established in April 1994.

While these were all important goals, they did not constitute a clear political objective for the UN mission. The peacekeepers had not deployed to end the war in Bosnia, nor was it an army sent out to fight on one side.

By 1993, the Bosniak town of Srebrenica—a refugee-filled enclave containing some sixty thousand trapped Muslims—was besieged, bombarded daily by Bosnian Serb forces threatening extreme ethnic cleansing. Consequently, on April 16, 1993, the Security Council demanded that "all parties treat Srebrenica and its surroundings as a safe area which should be free from armed attacks and any other hostile action." A few weeks later, the Council conferred the same status on five other threatened towns: Zepa, Gorazde, Bihac, Tuzla, and the capital city, Sarajevo.

The decision to accord the status of "safe area" to Srebrenica provided no more than a temporary respite from violence. The fighting around the enclave and shelling of the town ratcheted up once more, and it soon became clear that the Council would have to return to consider their professed commitment "to ensure full respect for the safe areas."

In mid-May, the self-styled Bosnian Serb Assembly in Pale rejected a peace plan proposed by UN special envoy Cyrus Vance and European Community representative Lord Owen, after which both the nonaligned caucus—led by Venezuela, which was then on the Council—and the United States called for more "forceful" action to be taken, including a lifting of the arms embargo on Bosnia combined with NATO air strikes against Bosnian Serb targets. The UK and France, both with large contingents of troops on the ground and deeply opposed to U.S. ideas of air power, sought another option. The result was resolution 836, adopted on June 4, 1993, again extending the mandate of UNPROFOR in the safe areas, affirming its responsibility for their protection and allowing for the potential use of air power in or around the safe areas.

At this moment I was acutely aware of the complexities of our new plan in Bosnia and how difficult it would be to raise more troops. The force was already stretched dangerously thin on the ground, and I was alarmed at the ambiguous and imprecise wording of the resolution. Although members did not appreciate being reminded of the gap between mandate and resources, I was determined to raise my concerns regarding the troop numbers that would be required to implement the safe-areas plan.

In this case, none of the cosponsors—the United Kingdom, France, Russia, Spain, and the United States—offered to increase their contingents, nor were they willing even to redeploy existing contingents in theater to the newly established safe areas. This was concerning enough, but I was particularly eager to clarify three aspects of the resolution: the precise meaning attached to the word "deter," the provisions they envisaged for demilitarizing the safe areas, and the conditions under which air strikes would be justified and under whose authority they would be initiated. I asked the force commander in Bosnia at this time, Lieutenant-General Lars Eric Wahlgren, to draw up a staff study of the implications of the safe-area concept, asking in effect what it would take to make the concept at all credible and if it could be done with their existing force.

At a meeting with the cosponsor countries, I asked my military advisor, General Maurice Baril, to give an oral presentation on UNPROFOR's preliminary military staff study. It called for thirty-two thousand *additional* troops "to credibly implement the safe areas concept." I did not expect that we would be able to raise that number, but I was determined to get the message across about the consequences of taking on new commitments. The cosponsors, especially Britain and France but also the United States, reacted with anger to the presentation, accusing DPKO of incompetence and failure to do its job properly. Their preference and what they wanted DPKO to spend their time on was the "light minimum" option, which had been drawn up earlier by France and which envisaged the deployment of only five thousand troops.

David Hannay, the UK permanent representative, was especially unhappy with our performance and did not mince words. As for the actual language of the resolution, he made it clear that the phrase "to deter attacks against the safe areas" had been chosen deliberately rather than "to defend" and, likewise, that "to promote withdrawal of military and paramilitary forces" had been chosen rather than to "ensure or enforce." The cosponsors, he stressed, wanted UNPROFOR's "deterrent capacity" to derive from its *presence* in the safe areas—not from its actual military strength. As for demilitarizing the safe areas, UNPROFOR should "seek assurances" and, if possible, negotiate "voluntary agreements" with the Bosnian government. Reporting back on the meeting to General Wahlgren, I wrote that none of the six representatives present "seemed to envisage a force capable of effectively defending these areas" and, crucially, that none of them were willing to contribute any additional troops to UNPROFOR.

Justifying their stance, the cosponsors stressed that the creation of the safe areas was only a "temporary measure" adopted in anticipation of an overall political settlement. We knew however that "temporary" measures had a habit of becoming permanent and of acquiring a life and logic of their own. Moreover, even if only temporary, commitments of this kind inevitably created expectations, and, crucially from our point of view, they required resources. Even the light-minimum option proved impossible to meet, and we would be forced to muddle through with the limited resources we had.

There were several fundamental features driving the political dynamics at this time, limiting our room for maneuver. The first and most important of these were the deep divisions that existed throughout much of the war between key members of the Security Council—notably between the UK and France on the one hand and the United States on the other—about the nature of the Balkan conflict and, crucially for us in DPKO, the appropriate way forward on the ground. Unlike other operations at that time, including successful ones in Cambodia, El Salvador, and Mozambique, agreement among Council members and troop-contributing countries frequently extended only to the need for action, not to the definition of what kind of action to take. In Bosnia the persistent source of disagreement concerned the use of air power in support of UN peacekeepers.

There was a standoff between countries with peacekeeping forces on the ground, mainly the Europeans, and the Americans, who were not on the ground. The Europeans felt that any attempt to use air power would place their troops at risk—they might then face a military backlash they had not been deployed to sustain. The Americans, meanwhile, felt that the only way to resolve the issue and stop the Serbs was to use air power. The French and others demanded that this could happen only if the ground troops were reinforced with troops prepared to fight.

Second, member states were reluctant to provide additional troops, nor were they prepared to redeploy existing troops within theater in order to meet new commitments. The governments of troop-contributing nations tended to deal directly with the commanders on the ground, further undermining unity of command.

Third, there simply was no appetite among troop contributors for abandoning peacekeeping in favor of a combat mission, however much the wording of individual resolutions appeared to suggest greater toughness and resolve. This created the "fantastic gap" that General Brique-mont spoke of.

Finally, it seemed to me and many of us in DPKO that the complexity of the situation was sometimes missed, other times willfully ignored, by certain member states. No one within DPKO ever questioned the over-whelming primary responsibility of the Bosnian Serbs and its allies in Belgrade for the tragic course of events in Bosnia, their duplicity, and the untold horrors and suffering caused daily by their campaign of ethnic cleansing. But there were other aspects to the war that UNPROFOR on the ground could not ignore. The ferocious war that raged between Bos-niak forces and those of the Croatian Defence Council supported by Za-greb in 1993 and 1994, for example, barely registered in the U.S. public discussion about the war, even though some of the worst individual atroc-ities save for Srebrenica—in Stupni Do and the Medak pocket in Septem-ber 1993—were committed during that struggle.

By the spring of 1995, it was becoming increasingly clear that "mud-dling through" another year in Bosnia was simply no longer an option. In mid-March, General Rupert Smith, in his first directive as force commander in Bosnia, noted that UN efforts to advance the exist-ing cease-fire were failing while warlike preparations by the parties were intensifying. The vulnerability of the peacekeeping force in Bosnia, thinly spread out as an effectively indefensible force, was further underscored by the capture of some four hundred UN personnel in late May following NATO air strikes against a few targets around Sarajevo on May 25 and 26. The personnel were held hostage in retaliation for those strikes, and although their capture was humiliating enough, the air strikes then stopped in acquiescence to this Serb tactic. The response of troop-contributing countries to that crisis—retrenchment and a reaffirmation of the peacekeeping character of the mission—only sharpened the dilemmas confronting us, as we made very clear in the secretary-general's report to the Council on May 30. After more than three years, it concluded, UNPROFOR was still "deployed in a war situation where there is no peace to keep." As a result, we now found ourselves obstructed, targeted, denied resupply, and restricted in our movements. At the time, we had great difficulty seeing a way out of the situation. But the real prison, of course, was the one that caged Bosnia's civilians with no escape from the deadly conflict.

After a series of demonstrations of the Security Council's lack of commitment to take serious action to protect the safe area, on July 11, 1995, Bosnian Serb forces under the command of General Ratko Mladic overran Srebrenica. The reports began only a few days after the fall of Srebrenica that thousands of young men and boys were unaccounted for, and the stories grew each day with thousands of women desperately trying to discover the whereabouts of their husbands and sons. As the days passed, the worst suspicions were increasingly confirmed. We later learned that, within days of Srebrenica's capture, thousands of Bosniak men and boys were summarily executed by Serb forces, many of them mercilessly hunted down as they desperately sought to reach government-controlled territory. The precise figure of those massacred has yet to be established, though at least eight thousand Bosnian Muslims are known to have been murdered in the immediate aftermath.

The safe area of Zepa would fall shortly after, and one might have thought that this would have finally compelled the Security Council to more fervent action. I vividly recall, however, at the international conference of defense ministers in London in the aftermath of the fall of Srebrenica and Zepa on July 21, that deep differences persisted among member states about the way forward. While the meeting did threaten air strikes if the Serbs attacked the remaining enclave of Gorazde, I remained deeply skeptical whether this was a serious commitment.

By this stage, however, a raft of key developments had come together. First, UN troops were finally concentrating their positions, with remote units pulled into tighter and better defended positions, negating the threat of hostage taking that had been used to such effect by the Bosnian Serb forces in May. Second, in early June the European countries created a Rapid Reaction Force (RRF) consisting of British, French, and Dutch elements, which, although initially set up to cover a possible withdrawal of UNPROFOR, also provided the mission with a genuine, self-contained and combat-capable force of some seven thousand troops. In particular, the RRF provided heavy artillery, which General Rupert Smith, UNPROFOR's highly capable commander, who had been in post since February 1995, then deployed on Mount Igman.

Under General Smith, UNPROFOR was transformed, enabling it finally to apply credible military force. The key to this transformation was the third development, which was a change in the rules governing the use of NATO air power in support of UNPROFOR. This had been a long-standing tension between the United States and the Europeans, who had troops on the ground. The London meeting on July 21 had threatened the Serbs with sustained air strikes if they attacked Gorazde. It was clear to all that this commitment, especially in the cold light of Srebrenica, required changes to the existing dual-key system—whereby the secretary-general of NATO and the secretary-general of the UN both had to approve any air attacks—and which was now recognized as being unwieldy and far too slow. It had to be replaced by a more flexible arrangement.

The course of events was also shaped by another critical development. This was Operation Storm, the Croatian military offensive in the Krajina region in early August aimed at reasserting Croat control over the whole of its territory, following their earlier offensive in western Slavonia in May 1995. The operation owed much of its speed and success to tacit support from the United States and other key member states. Thousands of Serbs were driven from their homes by Croatian army units in a campaign whose brutality matched many of the atrocities committed across the border in Bosnia. Despite these atrocities, the Croat offensive did weaken the military position of the Bosnian Serbs.

While nearly one hundred thousand lives had been claimed in Bosnia by this stage, the spark that lit the fuse for a decisive military intervention was a single mortar attack on Sarajevo on August 28, 1995. It hit one of the city's main markets where people were queuing for bread, and thirty-nine people were killed. The outrage in the press around the world was instantaneous, and after years of brutal atrocities in Bosnia—and the changes on the ground that had taken place in the previous months—it seemed that, finally, enough was enough.

On the first night alone, over one hundred aircraft from the United States, the UK, France, Spain, and the Netherlands took part and destroyed twenty-four targets to the south and east of Sarajevo, including strikes near the Bosnian Serb headquarters in Pale. These were not pinprick, symbolic attacks, as had occurred on previous occasions when attempts to deter assaults on the safe areas were made. Fast jets were now attacking arms depots, command and control centers, artillery positions, and surface-to-air missile batteries. Most important, the UNPROFOR troops were now shored up in secure positions, and the bombing could go on without fear of reprisals and hostage taking against them. Over eleven days, more than thirty-five hundred sorties were flown by NATO warplanes and nearly four hundred targets were attacked. Artillery and mortar batteries of the RRF added their power to the air strikes, with the units on Mount Igman able to neutralize the Serb guns firing on those using the Mount Igman road running into Sarajevo, or those bombarding Sarajevo itself. This was Operation Deliberate Force, and it broke the hold of the Bosnian Serbs, who were already being pushed back by the Croat forces.

By this time, the Bosnian Serbs were also under pressure from Milošević in Belgrade to cut their losses. The Security Council by now had decided to take sides in the conflict, choosing war in firm rejection of peacekeeping. Doing so dangerously weakened the Bosnian Serb forces

and compelled them to the negotiating table. Having gone from control-
ling around 70 percent of the country to only half in just a few weeks, on
September 17, the Serbs agreed to withdraw most of their artillery from
the hills surrounding Sarajevo. By November, all parties were locked in
concerted peace negotiations in Dayton, Ohio.

The resulting deal, or Dayton Accords, brilliantly negotiated by the
U.S. ambassador Richard Holbrooke, finally ended the war in Bosnia
and the brutal cruelty to civilians that accompanied it. It was an uneasy
peace, with deep and recent wounds inflicted across Bosnian society
and between communities that would have to now be carried forward,
and there were many contradictions and tensions in the agreement,
particularly surrounding the governance and policing of respective territories by different communities—but it is a peace that has held for nearly
twenty years.

THE COMPLICITY WITH EVIL

"Could we have a moment alone please?" I asked the crowd of politicians,
aides, and reporters who surrounded us. In far greater numbers than our
entourage were the hundreds and hundreds of skulls and other bones—
some clearly broken by force—stacked on simple green tarpaulin-covered
tables. Underneath the timber and corrugated iron shelter in which these
remains were displayed at a site thirty miles southeast of Kigali, Nane
and I took a quiet few minutes as the crowd backed away. We stood there
while we let this symbol of suffering—and what had happened in Rwanda
four years earlier—speak for itself.

The day before, on May 7, 1998, early in my first tenure as secretary-
general, I had addressed the Rwandan parliament. I believed it important that, as head of the UN, I should pay this official visit to the nation
that had suffered the most while under the UN's gaze. I publicly called

it "a mission of healing," and it proved a difficult visit politically. In my address, I fully acknowledged the failure of the UN and the international community in Rwanda: "We must and we do acknowledge that the world failed Rwanda at that time of evil. The international community and the United Nations could not muster the political will to confront it. The world must deeply repent this failure." And I went on to say: "Rwanda's tragedy was the world's tragedy."

There was a reception scheduled for after the speech, but as we were walking toward the venue, it became clear that the president and his cabinet had boycotted the event in a show of anger—one that they were already taking steps to publicize across Rwanda. The president's spokesman soon announced that the reason for the boycott was the "arrogance" displayed that was "insulting to the Rwandan people." In the speech I had used the line that Rwanda's horror "came from within," and this was now a lightning rod for criticism. I had used this phrase as part of what should have been an uncontroversial point: that, while the international community and the UN had failed to act when it could have done so much more, the source of Rwanda's suffering came from demons within the country itself. This was a testament to the scale of the challenges their country now faced, particularly for national reconciliation. It was the biggest single issue facing the country and required acknowledgment. I also felt it would be counterproductive, for the UN and Rwanda, to in any way endorse the idea that the UN and the international community, while sorely culpable, was somehow the prime perpetrator.

As I stressed at the time in briefings with the press, the problem had been in the international community's collective refusal to act, through the UN in particular. But the mistaken idea that the UN peacekeeping force itself could have stopped the genocide—therefore implying that a full and ready instrument for ending the genocide was already there and waiting in the country and had just stood by—was now circulating, as if it were an accepted fact. The UN force in Rwanda could not alone have stopped the genocide. It was a peacekeeping force, sent in a deliberately weak and vulnerable form to engender the trust of both sides, which emerged as even weaker in reality due to the challenges of finding troops and equipment. UNAMIR could have been reinforced to save more lives, for certain. But a very different force would have been needed to stop an entire national campaign of genocide. Such a force would have needed full war-fighting capabilities similar to those of the Rwandan Patriotic Front, whose army had to conquer the entire country before it ended the genocide.

It was not long after this visit to Rwanda in 1998 that I began a concerted process of reform of UN peacekeeping. The first step was to acknowledge the recent history of failure, fully and honestly. The UN's association with the worst atrocities of recent civil wars was a terrible stain on the organization. But this was a painful reminder that we could use: a shock to us all that we could turn into a productive and powerful instigator of reform. In this endeavor I commissioned two reports, one investigating the UN's failure leading up to the massacres at Srebrenica in Bosnia, and the second investigating the sources of the UN's failure in the lead-up and response to the Rwandan genocide. Both of these reports were produced and delivered to me in November and December 1999. Both reports were critical of many parties, particularly of member states and their political leaders, but also of the UN Secretariat and, specifically, of my own former office in DPKO.

In follow-up I informed the Security Council of my intention to use the stern findings of both reports to begin a major process of learning and reform in UN peacekeeping. Contrary to the urgent advice of some, I ordered both reports to be released in full without amendment to the public. I knew no real process of reform and healing could begin without absolute candor, honesty, and openness.

What followed was the Brahimi Report, named after the remarkably capable and experienced diplomat Lakhdar Brahimi, whom I selected to lead a high-level panel of experts to investigate what was required to reform peacekeeping in the post–Cold War world. On completion, I had the report released to the Security Council, the General Assembly, and the public on August 21, 2000.

The report recognized the particular challenges posed by UN peace operations in territories torn by civil war as the most important qualitative change. Consent of the belligerent parties, impartiality, and the use of force only in self-defense still had to remain the bedrock of peacekeeping, as it had before. Otherwise, peacekeepers would rarely be accepted by any belligerent parties. But the greater fluidity of civil wars rendered peacekeepers more exposed and vulnerable to changes in the balance of force and aggression between parties, as well as more prone to manipulation as belligerents jostled for advantage. This meant peacekeepers needed more credible means of self-defense.

The report also stressed the need for the integration of peacekeeping and peacebuilding activities. Sustaining a peace process after civil war required a whole range of activities beyond traditional peacekeeping, including long-term development efforts. To ensure the possibility of an exit for peacekeepers, the activities of their operations had to include efforts more usually understood as state building if they were to ensure any long-term success and the self-sustainability of the peace they left behind.

The report also heavily stressed the need for improvements in the relationship among the Secretariat, the Security Council, and troop-contributing governments—to communicate and coordinate more cohesively during fast-moving crises. Yet the tripartite structure, no matter how dysfunctional, could not be replaced. Therefore, troop contributors needed to be brought into the Security Council to consult directly with its members and the Secretariat at every stage of mandate formulation and other key decisions. Furthermore, the Secretariat needed to exert a stronger advisory voice during this process, to be firm in conveying its expertise in the face of the Security Council, telling it what it *needed* to hear, not what it *wanted* to hear.

The Brahimi Report covered these problems and many others regarding the doctrine, strategy, and decision making of peacekeeping. But the biggest issue it had to reckon with was the epicenter of the peacekeeping storm: the complicity with evil. As the Brahimi Report states: "UN peacekeepers—troops or police—who witness violence against civilians should be presumed to be authorized to stop it." Never again should they stand aside and not help the people who thought they were there to save them. But the report also pointed out that peacekeepers could, naturally, only do this "within their means."

This left a major problem: the consistent weakness of peacekeeping forces who could be expected to do little to intervene substantially in a civil war and stop atrocities wholesale. As the Brahimi Report suggested, the greater responsibility was for member states, particularly on the Security Council, not to use the deployment of peacekeeping forces as a fig leaf designed to conceal their unwillingness to intervene with the true commitment necessary, as a means of appeasing demands for forceful humanitarian intervention.

Peacekeepers cannot decisively change the balance of force in any conflict. In this sense, peacekeeping can be only a secondary instrument of peace, not a primary one. In certain circumstances, it must be stressed, UN peacekeeping can accomplish significant achievements, as it did throughout the Cold War and in several other operations in the early 1990s, including in Central America, Mozambique, Namibia, and the huge operation in Cambodia. But in other circumstances it can be deeply inadequate. This is because peacekeeping cannot take the lead in driving outcomes in war zones. Those instruments are the commitments of the armed factions to peace or war, and the commitment of the international community to affecting the balance of forces on the ground. Only a decision to deploy a self-contained fighting force—capable of defeating other military formations—can match the ambition of altering a civil war. This was what happened in Bosnia, when the decision was eventually made to reform the force and to take sides.

During my time in the senior management of the UN, we could chalk up as one of our collective achievements the adaptation of the instrument of peacekeeping from a relatively simple tool—designed for limited conflict between countries during the Cold War era—into one that could valuably be applied to aiding the resolution of complex civil wars, the dominant form of conflict in the modern world. Testament to this was the fact that UN peacekeeping did not wither away after the disasters of the mid-1990s, as some thought it might, but instead would return again in force alongside our reform efforts, with operations repeatedly sent to territories torn by civil war. It is in these conflicts where by far the most war-related deaths occur in the world, and where, therefore, some of the greatest contributions to peace are to be made. Indeed, almost all UN peacekeeping operations since 1992 have been deployed to conflicts that cannot be readily categorized as between countries, and there are now, at the time of writing, almost one hundred thousand uniformed personnel serving on sixteen such operations.

But the crucial fact was that the biggest problem encountered by UN peacekeeping operations in the early 1990s could not be solved by UN peacekeeping. We could do what we could to help salvage and preserve the reputation of peacekeepers in the field, guided by the Brahimi Report and adapting our management of operations. But such reform could not end the true problem of the early 1990s: the international community's complicity with evil—of standing by in full knowledge of horrors on the ground that it had the power to stop. Notwithstanding the inherent limitations on what force alone can achieve, there were clearly times when the international community could, and should, decisively intervene.

From the Department of Peacekeeping Operations to the office of the secretary-general, I took with me, above all, the lessons of Bosnia and Rwanda. Evil in civil war zones occurs due to the will of the conflict protagonists, which must be rounded upon, confronted, and stopped—and through force if necessary. But while I was serving as secretary-general, there were many in the international community, in diplomatic missions, and in capital cities around the world, who clung to a vision of the UN Charter that, in their view, said that the use of such force was unacceptable.

This left me with what would become my greatest challenge as secretary-general: creating a new understanding of the legitimacy, and necessity, of intervention in the face of gross violations of human rights.

SOVEREIGNTY AND HUMAN RIGHTS

Kosovo, East Timor, Darfur, and the

Responsibility to Protect

FIVE MINUTES TO MIDNIGHT IN EAST TIMOR

We are in your hands now," Xanana Gusmão told me. It was September, 5, 1999, and I had called the East Timorese independence leader in the Indonesian capital of Jakarta. He was being held under house arrest by a government whose militias had unleashed an orgy of violence in his homeland following the UN-sponsored referendum six days earlier. Our worst fears were coming true. Xanana warned me in a concerned but calm and determined voice that "a new genocide" was threatening his people. I told him I would do everything I could to end the onslaught, and concluded the call by urging him to take every precaution to ensure his personal security in the coming days. If his people were being murdered in the streets of Dili, the capital of East Timor, he was in no less danger in Jakarta.

In the preceding weeks and days, I had been warning publicly and privately of the threat of violence in the aftermath of a referendum that would give the people of East Timor their long-sought opportunity to determine their own destiny. In negotiating the process leading to the vote, I had established a close and confidential relationship with the Indonesian president Bacharuddin Jusuf "B. J." Habibie. In many ways an accidental president who had succeeded his country's long-term leader Suharto a year earlier, Habibie had convinced me of his desire to see the conflict in East Timor resolved peacefully.

His ability to do so, however, was clearly a different matter. He was neither in control of his own armed forces operating in the region in collusion with local militias, nor was he being told the truth about the killing and burning that they had unleashed. I had called him five days earlier to say that we were pleased that the polling had taken place under largely peaceful conditions, with the vast majority of voting-age East Timorese casting their ballots. Habibie told me that his government had acted "without dirty minds" and that they would "accept and honor any decision by the people." He said directly that if the decision was for separation, he was ready to withdraw the Indonesian police and military. The result was similarly unambiguous—some 80 percent had rejected the option of autonomy within Indonesia and voted for full independence.

On the ground in East Timor, however, a horrifying reality then began playing out one that would test the will and ability of the United Nations and the international community to manage a separatist process within the borders of a major country. By the time I spoke with Xanana, I had concluded that an international force was needed to bring security to the territory. I also knew that it could be inserted only at the invitation of the Indonesian government. This became my overriding focus in the days ahead, and my peacekeeping experience had taught me that an effective lead nation for the intervention force was critical. On the day Xanana warned me of the scale of the violence threatening his people, I called the prime minister of Australia, John Howard. As the looting and killing was metastasizing throughout the territory, I asked him if his country would lead a multinational intervention force with the authority to end the violence.

To his—and his nation's—great credit, he immediately agreed, but not before saying that we were "at five minutes to midnight" in getting an agreement out of Habibie. In a call with President Clinton later that day, it became clear to me that the U.S. president's major concerns were securing a Security Council authorization for a mission against a key U.S. ally, and, at the same time, addressing congressional hostility to U.S. participation in such an operation. The urgency of the situation on the ground did not seem to have been impressed on the president. This did not prevent my friend Richard Holbrooke, U.S. ambassador to the United Nations, from asking me if this was "Srebrenica all over again," while adding that there was what he called a "Bosnia-style" division within the U.S. administration on what to do.

What was clear was that no one—and certainly not the United States—was prepared in this case to contemplate war with Indonesia to protect a minority under siege within its borders. Only an intensive diplomatic campaign could succeed in convincing Jakarta that its own future relationship with the international community depended on allowing the long-developing issue of East Timor to be resolved peacefully, and that required an outside presence on the ground. The question haunting us all was whether it all would be too late for the people of East Timor.

SOVEREIGNTY AND INTERVENTION

The crisis over East Timor was, like every other challenge we confronted, not happening in a vacuum. There were other conflicts, such as those in

Kosovo, Congo, and Sierra Leone, that challenged our conceptions of sovereignty and intervention. I took office as secretary-general in early 1997 with a deep personal conviction that we had to put the individual at the heart of everything we did at the United Nations. An organization of member states had to become focused, once again, on the rights and protections of the "We the Peoples" in whose name the Charter was written. I also knew that, in addition to shifting the burden of the UN's focus and engagement, I needed to make a broader case for intervention and challenge the conventional views on national sovereignty as immutable and inviolable no matter what outrages were committed within the borders of states.

In strengthening our focus on the sanctity and universality of human rights—in word and deed—we sought to make them a core element of all our work, from development to health to peace and security. When civilians are attacked or killed because of their ethnicity, the world looks to the United Nations to speak up for them. When women and girls are denied their right to equality, the world looks to the United Nations to take a stand. In a world where globalization has limited the ability of states to control their economies, regulate their financial policies, and isolate themselves from environmental damage or human migration, states cannot and must not have the right to enslave, persecute, or torture their own citizens.

Human rights to life and basic security were being threatened, in an increasingly visible fashion, by conflicts that were internal to states, and this meant that we needed to reframe the relations between citizens and governments. We needed to convince the broader global community that sovereignty had to be understood as contingent and conditional on states' taking responsibility for the security of their own people's human rights— and for this to be taken as seriously as the states' expectations of noninterference in their internal affairs. I had come to this conclusion through the trials of UN peacekeeping—from Somalia to Rwanda and Bosnia.

And in the words often spoken by my most trusted aide and advisor, Chef de Cabinet Iqbal Riza, we needed now to insist on a moral dimension to our engagement with the conflicts of the world—whether they took place between or within states.

I had recognized this looming conundrum for the international community for some time. At a press conference in New York in 1993, when I was still under-secretary-general for Peacekeeping Operations, amid the growing tensions in dealing with the militias of Mogadishu, I was asked if our operations entailed a new definition of the UN's role. I answered by noting that what we were trying to do was to rid southern Mogadishu of weapons by proceeding rapidly with a disarmament program with the cooperation of the Somali people—but there were also elements who did not hesitate to use violence against this effort. I asked if the best way really was to appease criminal elements and to give in to them? "The UN," I continued, "is caught in a very difficult situation where we are accused in Bosnia of not doing enough, of having too weak a mandate, of standing by when these criminal elements attack women, shell cities, and kill civilians. For the first time, here in Somalia, we have a mandate to try to check some of these criminal elements. And I think these are questions that the international community, the politicians, and the world at large will have to deal with. We have to go beyond the traditional UN concepts of intervention. If we do intervene in the face of massive human rights abuses, in the face of cruel humanitarian situations, and we do have a mandate to settle the situation, are we going to become engaged or do we not? Do we stand by and let these things go on?"

Later that year I asked this question again, in starker terms, putting it to a room full of reporters sitting with me in a hot Mogadishu briefing room, some of whom were again questioning the use of force in the Somalia operation going on outside. I was, once more, begging the answer that decisive action was needed: "What do you do when people are starving, dying, not because there is drought but because people, a group of men, are stopping them [from] getting the food?" I asked. "What do you do? Sit? Negotiate? Or what?" No one answered at that moment, but the thinking was beginning to change.

In 1995 I was appointed Special Envoy to the Former Yugoslavia and NATO. At a ceremony that year in Zagreb marking the handover of military authority in Bosnia from the UN to NATO following the Dayton Agreement, I again urged the assembled officials to reflect on the high price paid by the people caught in the conflict, this time in Bosnia: "In looking back, we should recall how we responded to the escalating horrors of the past four years, and ask ourselves the questions, What did I do? Could I have done more? Could I have made a difference? Did I let my prejudice or indifference or my fear overwhelm my reasoning? How will I react the next time?" I did not spare the UN from the condemnation this implied for our own policy of neutrality between the parties during the Bosnian war—which for too long made us too-passive witnesses to the Serbian campaign of ethnic cleansing. I knew that this wouldn't be the last time that our principles and practices in relation to state sovereignty would be tested in a world riven by civil wars.

The fact was the environment had changed—we saw it in Bosnia and later in Congo and other conflicts where neutrality and "not taking sides" in the deployment of peacekeepers would not work; indeed, where sticking to neutrality could result, however inadvertently, in abetting the aggressor and punishing the victim. In some cases we had to take action to stop aggression, to protect the innocent, and that meant going far beyond traditional forms of UN intervention.

Kosovo: The Return of the Balkan Wars

In the year prior to the East Timor referendum and its ensuing violence, the world had gone through a major crisis over Kosovo. There, in a similar set of circumstances, an ethnic minority had been punished with gross violations of human rights for its desire for self-determination. What set Kosovo apart for all of us—the United Nations, Europe, NATO, and the United States—was that it was an all-too-familiar crisis with an all-too-familiar predator setting fire to yet another corner of the Balkans.

In the case of Kosovo, we were dealing with a region that had been at war for several years and had been deformed by the behavior of one state and one leader, above all, who was still on the prowl. This was Slobodan Milošević, and his eyes were now fixed on Kosovo. In the wake of Bosnia, we had good reason to suspect that if the international community did not act, the ethnic Albanian population of Kosovo would receive treatment similar to the Bosnians. The link with Bosnia was very much on our minds as the crisis in Kosovo escalated. There was a powerful sense that we could not sit back and watch the Serbs do the same to the Kosovar Albanians.

There was no trust in Milošević on the part of anyone in the international community—not even from the Russians, his ally—and little sense that he would be persuaded of the merits of peaceful compromise over Kosovo. Even as I warned other governments of Milošević's habit of miscalculation, I had also seen him act as a master manipulator. Milošević told me more than once that he considered Kosovo the cradle of their civilization and would never let it leave Serbia. The year 1389 was when Ottoman Turks defeated Serbs at the battle of Kosovo Polie, leading to Ottoman dominance of their lands for nearly five centuries. Milošević had ruthlessly and effectively exploited this mythical importance of Kosovo to the Serbs, and in 1989, in what later became seen as the trigger of the Bosnia war, he had gone to Kosovo to stoke the ethnic tensions there, declaring to his Serbian audience, "Nobody has the right to beat you."

Some three years after the end of the Bosnian war, in early 1998, tensions on the ground began to escalate in Kosovo between Serbian forces and ethnic Albanian militias seeking independence. Milošević's response to the Kosovo Liberation Army's resistance campaign was as brutal as it was familiar. Rather than seek to resolve the dispute peacefully—or focus his wrath on the armed men of the militias—he directed his forces to embark on a wholesale campaign of ethnic cleansing, with hundreds of thousands of civilians the target of the operations.

The campaign appeared to have one aim above all: to expel or kill as many ethnic Albanians in Kosovo as possible. The result was a calamity for the people of Kosovo and a humanitarian disaster throughout the region. This time, the leaders of Britain, France, and Germany decided that Europe's own future depended upon responding forcefully to Milošević's campaign. Principally through NATO, they began issuing warnings that this time a Balkan war on civilians would not be allowed to stand. For the United Nations, the crisis presented a different, if equally important, challenge. Without a ground presence in Kosovo, we were unable to provide assistance to civilians. That meant the interventions we could make would have to be political and diplomatic—in my statements and in our work with the Security Council—to try to unite the international community around halting the abuses of human rights and preventing a wider war.

Beginning in early 1998, we managed to place Kosovo on the agenda of the Security Council, allowing us to present the Council with periodic reports on the developments on the ground. By summer, some two hundred thousand Kosovars had been made refugees, 10 percent of the province's population. At this point I started speaking out with greater frequency about the need to avoid another Bosnia. As the crisis escalated in the summer and autumn of 1998, I decided that this time we would place the United Nations squarely on the side of the victims of aggression in the Balkans and offer no legitimacy to the well-worn propaganda coming out of Belgrade. This became a careful balancing act, as the pressures to act from Europe and the United States were met with implacable opposition by Russia, which still saw Serbia as a key ally and did not want to see a repeat of the punishment Milošević received at the end of the Bosnian war.

I decided to speak out for two reasons: First, because I believed the best way of halting the terror and violence and preventing a wider war—even one fought for humanitarian reasons—was to make clear to Milošević that he would not be able to use the United Nations, or at least its secretary-general, in a drawn-out diplomatic dance while his forces went on a rampage in Kosovo. A united international front, I believed, would lead him to capitulate on his most egregious war aims sooner. Second, and of equal importance, was the opportunity that the crisis in Kosovo provided: to draw a new line in international affairs, to set a new standard in how we held states responsible for the treatment and protection of the people within their own borders. We had to make clear that the rights of sovereign states to noninterference in their internal affairs could not override the rights of individuals to freedom from gross and systematic abuses of their human rights.

The shift in policy, controversial as it was among many member states wedded to the sacrosanct principle of sovereignty, was not without its challenges within the United Nations Secretariat itself. The Kosovo crisis led to a fierce debate among my advisors that cast into stark relief the lessons of our past decade in peacekeeping. On one side were the views of the career diplomats and Secretariat officials: they maintained that the duly recognized government in Belgrade had the right and the duty to maintain order within its territory, and that it was not for the UN—and certainly not its secretary-general—to call attention to violations of human rights in Kosovo and urge a forceful response by outside powers. On the other side were those advisors who argued that for us to maintain a blind neutrality in the face of the recidivist behavior of a well-known predatory regime intent upon ethnically cleansing yet another group in the Balkans would destroy our standing—especially with all those who looked to the United Nations to protect would-be victims of atrocities.

My own instinct was to maintain our credibility and authority with the main parties of the Security Council, including Russia, who were seeking to put an end to the violence, while making clear that this time, our own response would be different—the UN, I believed, needed to stand for the rights of the individual as strongly as it did for the rights of states. Post-Bosnia and post-Rwanda, I knew that the UN in the eyes of many was being judged on its ability to deal with gross violations of human rights and crimes against humanity.

I signaled this early on, during a visit to a NATO conference in June 1998. NATO leaders were meeting on the question of Bosnia as a test case for collective security in the next century. Traditionally, a UN secretary-general would appear at a meeting of a military alliance to urge the peaceful resolution of disputes, above all other values. On this occasion, I urged the intensification of diplomacy backed by the credible threat of force and sought to impress on them a sense of urgency. Calling on our experience of Bosnia, I urged them to ensure that the future of collective security would be both effective and legitimate. One without the other—as we had learned, and would learn again later in Iraq—would not do.

"Credible force," I noted to the NATO leaders, "without legitimacy may have immediate results but will not enjoy long-term international support. Legitimate force without credibility may enjoy universal support but prove unable to implement basic provisions of its mandate." I insisted that all the talk of lessons learned about the credibility, legitimacy, and morality of intervention would be hollow without applying those lessons practically and emphatically where horror threatens. Kosovo, I said, was now that threat. This time, we could "not be surprised by the means employed or by the ends pursued," I warned, and I explicitly applauded the determination of NATO governments to prevent a further escalation of the fighting. I concluded my remarks with as direct a call for the use of force as I ever made during my time as secretary-general: "All our professions of regret; all our expressions of determination to never again permit another Bosnia; all our hopes for a peaceful future for the Balkans will be cruelly mocked if we allow Kosovo to become another killing field."

Later that month, at a conference in Britain, hosted by the Ditchley Foundation, I set out the case for humanitarian intervention more broadly by examining its history. In that speech, I defined it as part of other interventions, including, say, a case of a surgeon who intervenes to save a life, or a teacher who intervenes to prevent the malicious bullying of a child in school. My point was that intervention was a cause for everyone, and one not limited by any means to the use of military force.

Even during the Cold War, I went on in my speech, when the UN's own enforcement capacity was largely paralyzed by divisions in the Security Council, there were cases of extreme violations of human rights within a country that led to military intervention by one of its neighbors. In 1971, an Indian intervention ended the civil war in East Pakistan, allowing Bangladesh to achieve independence. In 1978, Vietnam intervened in Cambodia, putting an end to the genocidal rule of the Khmer Rouge. In 1979, Tanzania intervened to overthrow Idi Amin's erratic and brutal dictatorship in Uganda.

In all three of those cases the intervening states cited refugee flows across their borders to legitimize their action under international law. But what justified their actions in the eyes of the world was the internal character of the regimes they acted against. History has largely ratified that verdict. Few would now deny that, in those cases, forceful intervention was a lesser evil than allowing massacres and extreme oppression of that kind to continue.

When people are in danger, I insisted, everyone has a duty to speak out. No one has a right to pass by on the other side.

I n Kosovo, meanwhile, as we were debating the necessity of intervention at UN headquarters, the violence continued to escalate into
the autumn of 1998 with tens of thousands of Kosovar Albanians being
forced from their homes. Seeking to end the crisis, Richard Holbrooke—
then the U.S. special envoy for the Balkans—negotiated the insertion of
two thousand unarmed Organization for Security and Cooperation in
Europe (OSCE) verifiers to monitor a fragile cease-fire agreement. And
on September 23, the Security Council adopted resolution 1199, which
demanded the withdrawal of Yugoslav forces from Kosovo. NATO followed this up with its own threat of action if Milošević refused to comply. It was a surprise to no one when Milošević continued his campaign
unabated.

In my own reports to the Security Council, I pointed with increased
urgency to the escalating violence and placed responsibility squarely on
the Yugoslav authorities for the killings gaining in pace. On October 4, I
described what was happening as a "campaign of terror and violence."
Reflecting the widening chasm between Belgrade and the international
community, I received a letter later that day from the Yugoslav foreign
minister, whose first sentence stated that "Peace prevails in Kosovo"
and that "full freedom of movement had been ensured." When I called
Milošević a few days later to urge acceptance of the UN's demands, he
repeated this claim and said that over the past two weeks, there had been
"no conflict in Kosovo." He added for good measure that "the problems
are only with the Albanians."

That same week, I spoke with British foreign secretary Robin Cook,
who drew his own parallels to the worst acts of ethnic violence in the
Bosnian war. We agreed, on the basis of our common experience with
Milošević, that he would likely respond only to force. I reminded Cook
that Milošević was an expert in creating a "mirage" of cooperation when

the reality was one of applying brute force as long as he was able to get away with it.

As most of us feared and expected, the Kosovo Verification Mission increasingly became a powerless witness to an escalating Serbian campaign, which culminated in mid-January with the massacre of some forty-five men, women, and children at the village of Racak. In the following two months, as the violence and fighting intensified, new attempts to negotiate a settlement continued with talks in Rambouillet, France. There the Kosovars were persuaded to sign an agreement on substantial autonomy within the Federal Republic of Yugoslavia. The Serbs, however, refused to sign, bent on maintaining their pattern of aggression and miscalculation until the very end.

Throughout the crisis, I had maintained a very close relationship with Javier Solana, the cerebral and shrewd Spanish NATO secretary-general who combined a deep aversion to war with his own determination, as a proud European, not to allow Milošević to make a mockery of the continent's commitment to peace and human rights once again. In a call on March 17, we spoke of how no one seemed to be getting through to Milošević—not his Russian allies nor Holbrooke, with whom he had negotiated an end to the war in Bosnia.

It was clear that the moment of truth had arrived when the OSCE observers were ordered to leave Kosovo. On the evening of March 23, Solana called me again to say that Holbrooke would be returning from Belgrade to the NATO headquarters in Brussels with "very bad news." He told me that he would be transferring the authority to launch a military operation to the Supreme Allied Commander Europe imminently, meaning that military action by NATO would soon begin. With Russian opposition to any resolution mandating the use of force, this meant NATO would be breaking with the will of the Security Council. But something had to be done, and we discussed our shared view of how out of touch with reality Milošević seemed—and that once again this was leading to war in the Balkans.

The next morning, on March 24, I received a call from Madeleine Albright, who wanted to emphasize that NATO had had no choice but to act. Albright spoke in that tone that I had come to expect from her by then: though a friend and ally, she had never quite understood that although the United States had supported my candidacy for secretary-general, I had to maintain an independent dedication to the principles of the Charter and be seen to be responsive to the wishes of all member states of the United Nations.

I told her that I'd be issuing a statement in response to the NATO military action speaking of the failure of the Serbs to comply with the demands of the international community, while emphasizing that it would have been "preferable" if the action had been authorized by the Council. When I said that I would be indicating that the Council should always be involved with the decision by states to use force, she replied bluntly: "We don't agree." I thought her State Department lawyers may have thought differently on this matter, but recalled her response to a similar legal point made by Robin Cook, the UK foreign secretary: "Get yourself some new lawyers" had been her retort. In ending our call, she acknowledged, nonetheless, that "you are Secretary-General of the United Nations, and I am the Secretary of State of the United States—that's life. But if we had put this to a Security Council vote, the Russians would have vetoed it, and people would have continued to die." I left my response unspoken, but I agreed.

Later that day, NATO began a campaign of air strikes to drive the Serbian forces from Kosovo and bring an end to their campaign of killings and mass expulsion of the civilian population of the province. I saw this as a tragedy—as is every resort to war. Those who believe otherwise have seen nothing of its consequences. But I also knew that a greater evil would have been to allow the unfettered rampage of Serbian forces in Kosovo.

What made the situation more complicated for me was the fact that I was secretary-general of the United Nations at a time when NATO had taken this action without seeking Security Council authorization. The Charter of the United Nations is clear: except in cases of self-defense, the use of force must be authorized by the Council in order to be in conformity with international law. What was equally clear to me, however, was that Milošević had left the international community with no other option, and that none of the international community's claims to never allowing another Bosnia would be credible if he was permitted to continue his campaign of cleansing against yet another Balkan people.

Throughout the Kosovo crisis, with no United Nations peacekeeping or diplomatic presence on the ground, I had focused my efforts on ensuring that the challenge before the international community was understood as clearly as possible. If we were to avoid a conflict, Milošević would have to understand that this time the United Nations would recognize his wars as the wanton acts of aggression that they were—and that he had no option but to agree to the demands of the international community. Now that NATO had acted to enforce those demands, the debate among my advisors returned to the surface.

The Department of Political Affairs drew up a statement for me that focused on the Security Council's primary responsibility for the maintenance of peace and security, emphasizing my regret at the use of force without the Council's authorization. Aides in my office reacted strongly to this draft. They argued that it would be a betrayal of all that I had said in the preceding months about the need to hold Milošević accountable—and about placing the United Nations on the side of civilians under siege from their own government—if I were now to merely lament the enforcement action. In conformity with my instructions, they amended the draft and began the statement instead by assigning responsibility for the recourse to military force to the Yugoslav authorities:

> Throughout the last year, I have appealed on many occasions to the Yugoslav authorities and the Kosovar Albanians to seek peace over war, compromise over conflict. I deeply regret that, despite all the efforts made by the international community, the Yugoslav authorities have persisted in their rejection of a political settlement, which would have halted the bloodshed in Kosovo and secured an equitable peace for the population there. It is indeed tragic that diplomacy has failed, but there are times when the use of force may be legitimate in the pursuit of peace.

The statement then concluded with a call for the Security Council to be involved in any decision to resort to the use of force. As secretary-general, I had to affirm this principal—fundamental as it was to nothing less than international order—even at a time when, in anomalous circumstances, it was being set aside out of moral necessity. As Kieran Prendergast, my senior political advisor and head of the Department of Political Affairs, argued: "If you won't stand up for the Charter, who will?"

The day after the bombing began, the *New York Times* headline read: "The Secretary-General offers implicit endorsement of raids"—much to the relief of the NATO countries, and to the consternation of the Russians. But while there was no choice in my mind of the need to resort to force, I had in my response to the bombing also emphasized to NATO countries the value, and legal requirement, of a Security Council authorization that made this situation a stark exception. It was an uneasy—and in many ways unsatisfactory—compromise, but it reflected the reality of an international system whose balance of priorities required a broader shift if the United Nations was to be an organization that truly served those whose human rights were under threat.

In this debate the dilemmas facing the United Nations in the cause of intervention were laid bare. I had to chart a course that combined a clear defense of the primacy of the Security Council in matters of peace and security, with an equally clear recognition that the UN was never intended as a pacifist organization and that there were times when force was not only necessary but legitimate. Rwanda and Bosnia had taught us this essential fact.

Two weeks later, at the opening of the annual United Nations Human Rights Commission meeting in Geneva, I began to set out the parameters of what I called an "evolving international norm" against the violent repression of minorities that must take precedence over concerns of state sovereignty. "Even though we are an organization of member states," I concluded, "the rights and ideals the United Nations exists to protect are those of peoples."

On the ground in Kosovo, however, the military intervention was having nothing like the impact that NATO commanders had hoped or expected. When it began, Solana told me that it would be a matter of three or four days of bombing and then it would be over. Milošević, however, had his own ideas. In his own diabolical manner, he had clearly prepared for this moment, and intensified his campaign of repression and expulsion. By March 24, 1999, UNHCR estimated that more than 250,000 Albanians had been forced from their homes within Kosovo and another 200,000 had sought refuge in neighboring countries. Over the next three months, nearly a million Kosovars joined this throng of refugees.

In early April, faced with the escalating humanitarian disaster, I decided that the United Nations needed to enter the diplomatic game more actively. NATO and the United States had taken upon themselves the responsibility of enforcing the wider demands of the international community, and the United States in particular made little secret of its desire to keep the UN—and me—out of the day-to-day management of the conflict.

On April 9, I issued a call to the Yugoslav authorities to halt all offensive operations and withdraw from Kosovo, in return for which NATO should suspend its bombing campaign. From increasingly nervous European leaders such as Jacques Chirac and Gerhard Schröder, I received positive responses, but from Albright and Clinton, some hesitation about my intervention. I then spent the next six weeks in intense consultations with all the active parties, in order to reinvigorate the diplomatic track and bring the Russians back into the fold in order to apply the necessary pressure on Milošević.

From the outset, Secretary Albright was opposed to my active role, and even more so to my decision to appoint two UN mediators: Eduard Kukan of Slovakia and Carl Bildt of Sweden. Her resistance led to one of those drawn-out diplomatic merry-go-rounds that ended where we began, with valuable time lost in the process and with the humanitarian situation deteriorating by the hour. In the middle of a set of intense, almost hourly negotiations with Albright, former Russian prime minister Viktor Chernomyrdin, Chirac, and other European leaders, I received a call from Henry Kissinger. He was concerned about the impact on the United States' standing of the bombing of Serbia, and he was incredulous as to the administration's opposition to my intention to appoint Bildt, rating him by far the strongest of the candidates under consideration. He then offered to make his own appeal to the White House, which I accepted. Ending our call, he quoted Bismarck's adage: "Woe to the statesman whose arguments for entering a war are not as convincing at its end as they were at the beginning" and added that "although I am a Republican, we have to save the administration's face." Otherwise, "it would undermine the U.S. position around the world."

Albright then shifted the game by asking me to appoint the Finnish leader Martti Ahtisaari as a UN envoy to work with the Russian envoy Chernomyrdin. While I was not opposed to a role for my friend Ahtisaari,

I was concerned about the confusion that this would create on the envoy front. On the other hand, the Russians had indicated that Ahtisaari's participation might win Yugoslav agreement to a deal. I then received a call from Strobe Talbott, the U.S. deputy secretary of state, who said that Washington had changed its mind on Bildt, something I suspect had a great deal to do with Kissinger's intervention.

On May 9, Javier Solana called me to say that the situation had turned into a "nightmare." A NATO air strike had hit the Chinese embassy in Belgrade, enraging Beijing and deepening doubts in Europe and around the world about the value of the bombing campaign. Albright called to ask me to speak to the Chinese and tell them that it "would have been insane for the U.S. to bomb the Chinese embassy deliberately." Bildt soon confirmed the U.S. fears about his outspokenness by asking publicly what would have happened if the Chinese had bombed a U.S. embassy. However legitimate his question, this was not a way for us to play a constructive role in ending the war. Our efforts could not be part of a diversion from the real causes of the war—a diversion that would only serve Milošević's purposes and delay his capitulation. Five days later, I told Bildt: "Neither you nor Kukan will go to Belgrade. And I will not ask for a halt to the bombing."

With the military campaign nearing the end of its second month, I used the opportunity of a speech on the centennial of the 1899 Peace Conference in The Hague on May 18 to take the argument for intervention one step further. I called the world's attention to the dilemmas of statecraft provoked by the NATO action taken without Security Council authorization. I warned that unless the Security Council was restored to its preeminent position as the sole source of legitimacy on the use of force, we would be on "a dangerous path to anarchy." But equally important, I stressed that unless the Security Council could unite around the aim of confronting massive human rights violations and crimes against humanity on the scale of Kosovo, it would betray the very ideals that inspired the founding of the United Nations.

From The Hague I traveled to Macedonia and Albania to see for my-self the humanitarian consequences of the ongoing war, and to visit the refugee camps that now were holding some two hundred thousand refu-gees. With the roar of jets and thuds of bombing raids in the background, I made my way to Kosovo. As we approached the border posts, I saw what looked like an endless line of refugees coming down the road—men and women of all ages, children carrying their few belongings. Nane and I spoke with a ten-year-old boy who was crying helplessly and sat with a one-hundred-year-old woman who kept questioning, "Why is this hap-pening to us, why is this happening to us?" She then looked at me and asked me if this was the way her life would end. Milošević had, once again, acted with utter contempt for the lives and dignity of a civilian population in the former Yugoslavia, and with the bombing unable to move him to compromise, at that moment it seemed difficult to offer the woman any genuine hope. The inherent limits to what force alone can achieve were reflected in both the turmoil around us and in the wrench-ing desperation in the woman's eyes.

But hope again resurfaced. A few days later, on May 22, the War Crimes Tribunal for the former Yugoslavia indicted Slobodan Milošević for crimes against humanity. Then, finally, after a seventy-eight-day bombing campaign, on June 3, Milošević met with Chernomyr-din and Ahtisaari and—to their great surprise—abruptly agreed to the demands of the international community. A week later, the Security Council voted 14-0, with only one abstention, to authorize the presence of an international military force, led by NATO, and a civilian mission, led by the UN, in order to provide an interim administration for the territory. The Serbian campaign was halted, Milošević now had the prospect of being held to account by a court of law, and the people of Kosovo were secured safe passage to their homes and given the opportunity to rebuild a society with international support.

In the conclusion to the report that I had previously commissioned on the fall of Srebrenica, I urged the international community to heed the cardinal lesson of Srebrenica; namely, that "a deliberate and systematic attempt to terrorize, expel or murder an entire people must be met decisively with all necessary means, and with the political will to carry the policy through to its logical conclusion." In the Kosovo conflict, the international community resolved to apply that lesson—however belatedly and imperfectly. The NATO intervention had presented a profound challenge to those in the international community that remained dedicated to the principle of military action under international law but increasingly refused to accept the right of governments to abuse the human rights of their citizens under the cover of sovereign immunity. At the very least the international community had proved it was now willing to stop this in the Balkans, where, in Bosnia, the UN, the United States, and Europe had previously been unwilling to halt a savage war of ethnic hatred in the early 1990s. A high price had been paid by the people of Kosovo for the world's dithering, but the rapidity and determination of the response, at least, had changed.

TO SAVE A NATION: EAST TIMOR

Dili, the tiny, destitute, and isolated capital of East Timor, could not be further removed from the great cities of Europe where the fate of the people of Kosovo was being determined in the spring and summer of 1999. Whereas the Balkan wars of the early 1990s had provided the international community with an intimate familiarity with ethnic differences exploited with ruthless efficiency, it was almost entirely ignorant of the suffering of the East Timorese, who were caught in an orphaned conflict at the edges of one of Asia's largest and most powerful countries, Indonesia.

A former Portuguese colony, East Timor had been annexed by Indonesia in 1976 in a bloody and vicious campaign. The United Nations never recognized Indonesian sovereignty over East Timor, and through the years of repression and exploitation, which are estimated to have cost between 100,000 and 250,000 East Timorese lives, Portugal was among the few nations that sought to keep the world's attention on East Timor's right to self-determination.

Talks between Indonesia and Portugal were initiated by my predecessor, Secretary-General Perez de Cuellar, in 1983, but these had made little if any headway. When I took office in 1997, I identified East Timor as one of the long-running diplomatic negotiations to which I wanted to give new impetus. I appointed Jamsheed Marker of Pakistan as my personal representative and we accelerated the pace of talks and pushed for some bold moves with greater involvement of the East Timorese themselves. After the end of the Cold War, the 1991 Santa Cruz massacre, and the awarding of the Nobel Peace Prize in 1996 to Bishop Carlos Ximenes Belo and Jose Ramos-Horta, the warning signs for Indonesia were all there that the world would not simply accept the legitimacy of its rule in East Timor without some form of consent by the population.

With the end of the Suharto regime in Indonesia, and the coming to power of President B. J. Habibie in 1998, a new possibility arose. Habibie made clear that he was willing to allow some kind of vote or referendum on the future status of the territory—whether it would become an autonomous entity within Indonesia or become wholly independent. For the UN, there was an opportunity to play a valuable role, as no major power had a strategic interest in the dispute—unlike, say, in the case of the Middle East peace process where our influence was always limited by the U.S. dominance of the issue. In response, we at the UN structured a negotiating process that included the Portuguese and the Indonesians to pave the way for what we termed a "popular consultation" on the future of East Timor, to be held at some point in 1999.

In their foreign minister Ali Alatas, the Indonesians had a tough and able negotiator. Jaime Gama represented Portugal's historic interest with equal skill. I appointed Jamsheed Marker to lead our side of the diplomacy. From time to time, I intervened personally in the negotiations in the slow lead-up to the referendum and brought Alatas into my private office to urge him to stay on the path of compromise and not be distracted from the ultimate goal of a secure and peaceful outcome that would serve to improve Indonesia's international standing. I told him repeatedly that we were there as honest brokers, had no vested interests, and that we would put the referendum question fairly. We were able to reach the point where there was sufficient trust in the process for both sides to believe they might be able to win the referendum.

While Jamsheed Marker led the talks with superb skill and patience, I formed an unusual bond with President Habibie. Over time, he came to trust me and understood that I was not looking to weaken Indonesia. He realized that I wanted a peaceful outcome reflecting the wishes of the people of East Timor but that I was also looking for a way for Indonesia to come out of this in a stronger position with the international community. Day by day—and often hour by hour—I managed to hold his commitment, despite immense pressures from within his own military and security apparatus to take a much harder line. By the end of August 1999, I was speaking daily with Habibie. On more than one occasion I was able to tell him—later with increasing resonance—that what he was hearing from his own aides and advisors simply did not reflect the reality on the ground in East Timor.

Once the go-ahead for the referendum was finally agreed, we were given only a few short months to organize it. On the critical question of security, the Indonesians were adamant: they would maintain responsibility for security on an exclusive basis, with no other troops of any kind allowed on Indonesian soil. I pressed Habibie to accept an armed force to protect civilians and UN activities during the process, but this was vetoed by the Indonesian military, which insisted on its own prerogatives—a fateful decision with severe consequences for them and for the people of East Timor.

The reason we were so concerned was that Timorese militias backed by the Indonesian military had now made clear that they would intimidate and threaten the local population. Throughout this process, and as I reminded my own staff and others, there was a basic reality shaping the context of the diplomacy: the Indonesian military could do what it wanted in the region as no foreign power would contemplate militarily challenging Indonesia's right to maintain control in whatever way it wished within what it considered to be its borders. That it was also the largest Muslim-populated country in the world and a close ally of the United States, with ever-closer relations with China, did not make the diplomacy any easier. We were given no choice by the Indonesian government but to accept their pledge to maintain security.

However, the agreements of May 5 gave me the authority not to proceed with the ballot if the necessary security conditions for a peaceful vote were not present. I wrote a letter to Habibie outlining the elements of what would constitute such a peaceful environment, including bringing the militia under strict control as an urgent first step and confining Indonesian troops to designated areas ahead of the vote. The Indonesians would not accept the letter. I therefore decided to put the same elements in a memorandum to both sides as a way of putting everyone on notice as to what my expectations on security conditions were. In the end, these conditions were not met. But given the historic opportunity represented by Habibie's agreement to grant the people of East Timor the chance to determine their future status, and in light of the Tiomorese leaders' appeals not to delay the vote, we decided to proceed with the referendum.

I spoke with Habibie on the morning of August 24, six days before the vote, to thank him for his efforts, especially, I stressed, for ensuring "a peaceful environment" for the vote. This was, for me, the best way of alerting him to my concern about the increasing violence. On August 26,

I issued a public statement condemning the incidents of violence that had been reported, and on the eve of the vote I issued another statement encouraging a free vote and warning the government about any threat of intimidation or violence against the East Timorese people.

Amid an atmosphere of distrust, menace, violence, and intimidation, on August 30, 1999, the people of East Timor voted overwhelmingly in favor of independence, with nearly 80 percent seeking separation from Indonesia. The actual day of the referendum passed in a largely peaceful and orderly fashion. Shocked and infuriated by the outcome, however, the Indonesian-backed militias went on a rampage of killing and burning after the announcement of the result on September 4, laying waste to vast areas of the already impoverished territory. At UN headquarters and among UN staff in East Timor, we felt a terrible burden of responsibility. We had managed to secure for the people of East Timor a referendum on their future; the voting itself had taken place in peaceful circumstances, and no one could claim that we had an alternative to Indonesia's insistence on maintaining security on its own. We had given the people of East Timor every reason to believe that we had organized this referendum so that they could choose their own future in peace and safety—but now it had become a pretext for a campaign of slaughter by Indonesian forces. To me, personally, the moment evoked the darkest days from our peacekeeping years when restrictive mandates and incomplete resources had put our troops in conflict zones unable to help civilians who had every reason to believe that we were there to protect *them*, and not just ourselves.

This time, unlike in the case of Kosovo, it was not a matter of just using the bully pulpit of the United Nations to change the understanding of sovereignty and intervention. Given our own central role in negotiating and organizing the referendum, and our presence on the ground, I knew my own intervention could alter the trajectory of the tragedy now under way. I began an around-the-clock schedule of meetings and phone calls on the crisis, which included daily conversations with the leaders of

Indonesia, Australia, the United States, the United Kingdom, Portugal, Malaysia, and Thailand, among many others.

When the violence started, we had no troops or police on the ground except for the military liaison officers and UN police advisors. We needed to get help in quickly, and for over two weeks I worked the phones nonstop on two tracks. From New York, I dedicated the nighttime hours to working on Habibie, who was on Indonesian time, to make him understand the critical importance of restoring security in East Timor. Each night I pressed him on the need to enable an end to the violence—by Indonesian troops if possible, or by others if they were to fail. During the daytime hours, I lobbied the Security Council and potential troop-contributing countries to assemble what had to be a credible intervention force. It would have to have sufficient capabilities for the intervention and have a significant Asian component if it were not to be seen as a Western invasion of Indonesia.

As in other crises, from Kosovo to the Middle East, I soon became a central node of diplomatic communication between the various parties to the conflict, and, it seemed, the only one they all felt comfortable speaking with in trust and confidence. What this meant in many instances was that I often ended up with a better—and a more up-to-date—understanding of the state of play and the positions of all parties to the crisis. Each party shared its interests, knowledge, and even some of its intelligence with me. While this would often represent biased or slanted information, designed to persuade me of the merits of each case, this was still helpful because it enabled me to broker agreements with more insight and impact than otherwise. East Timor was no exception to this practice.

The possibility of Australia's leading any potential intervention was fraught with tensions given its own status within Asia. Australia had a robust, competent military with an ability to lead the operation effectively and convincingly. But they were not considered truly Asian by their neighbors, and I needed other regional powers to commit, such as Thailand, Malaysia, and Singapore. They, in turn, would not even consider being involved—or want it to be known publicly that they were even speaking to me about it—without an explicit invitation from the government of Indonesia. All roads now led back to Habibie, a decent, responsible, but utterly besieged leader. If I could convince him, I knew I could assemble the other pieces of the puzzle.

In Dili, every day was bringing new reports of massacres, assassinations, and arson attacks by Timorese thugs and militias clearly enjoying some level of backing by the Indonesian military contingents posted in the territory. Even as I received increasingly alarming reports from our own people and other foreign representatives, Habibie was being told an entirely different story by his military and security forces. During one call, he insisted that no hostile operations had been directed at the Timorese. What looting was taking place, he said, was simply the actions of Indonesians torching their own homes in anger over the outcome of the referendum. My reports, he insisted, were false.

I had to break this counterproductive cycle of dialogue, and began to warn Habibie that he would be held personally responsible if the killings continued and he was unable to protect the people. I emphasized in hour-long calls that an intervention force would not be an imposition, or an invasion; instead, he should accept the outside help because his troops clearly were unable to restore order on their own, even if they wanted to.

On a personal level, I sympathized with Habibie. I sensed he wanted to do the right thing, but he was under tremendous pressure from powerful hard-liners within the military. Even though I suspected he was never alone when on the phone with me, I had to inform him that his soldiers were not telling him the truth. But I also knew I had to be careful not to push him too hard. There was always a risk of the dialogue breaking down and with it the chance of a breakthrough. When this possibility loomed, I knew it was better to resume the next day, however agonizing the lack of progress. A temptation in such circumstances, when atrocities are being committed on the ground, is to express one's moral outrage during dialogue with those responsible. But this delivers only an immediate personal satisfaction, one that must be resisted when one's goals lie in the outcome for victims on the ground.

Following the chilling call from Xanana on September 5, warning of a genocide against his people, I called Habibie to tell him that the international community was increasingly alarmed by the deteriorating security situation. He again claimed that everything was under control and complained that it was all a matter of rumors, exaggerations, and emotions. I assured him it was not. Instead, I pushed explicitly for what I called a security component to be sent into East Timor. His counteroffer, no doubt suggested by those around him, was the imposition of martial law, something he proceeded to do two days later. As Xanana said to me in a call later that day, the last thing East Timor needed was more Indonesian troops with greater license to act at will.

I then received John Howard's agreement that Australia would lead the force. When Howard asked me if its main purpose would be to protect the UN mission, I was unequivocal in my reply: it would have to go in with the overriding mission of protecting the East Timorese civilian population. Force protection alone, as we had learned from Bosnia, was not the answer.

R umors of a coup in Jakarta against Habibie then began circulating, and the campaign of violence turned directly, and terrifyingly, on the United Nations. Just after 3:00 a.m. in New York on September 8, I received an urgent call from my under-secretary-general for political affairs, Kieran Prendergast. He reported that our head of the UN mission in East Timor, Ian Martin, had called from Dili saying that militias were now besieging the UN compound. Martin wanted to evacuate the UN staff to ensure the safety of the hundreds of UN civilians in the compound.

For my chef de cabinet, Iqbal Riza, and me, there was no question of the seriousness of the challenge we now faced. Our concerns focused immediately on the fate of the fifteen hundred Timorese civilians who had sought shelter in our compound in Dili, as well as the hundreds of UN staff now threatened by the militias who were shooting at the compound and waving grenades at the front gate. Riza and I had gone through the experience of the Rwandan genocide together in the Department of Peacekeeping Operations, and its lessons were never far from our minds. Over Rwanda, a key breakdown had taken place in the three-way relationship between the field, the office of the secretary-general, and DPKO. At a meeting later that morning following Martin's call, we agreed that we simply could not depart the compound and leave the civilians behind—not this time.

After a tense twenty-four hours, we agreed to evacuate the bulk of the UN staff, but in a moment of great and lasting pride for us, more than eighty members of the UN staff volunteered to stay behind along with Martin and a skeleton team, to serve as a shield for the East Timorese sheltering within the compound. Our East Timorese national staff, who were a particular target of the militias and their military backers, had by then been evacuated to Darwin, Australia.

I called Habibie to make sure he was clear about the danger the UN staff were in. I told him that I was being forced to evacuate our personnel. Habibie sounded shocked—he even seemed disoriented. He then spoke for some thirty minutes, without stopping, often repeating himself, and made it impossible for me to interject. As he spoke, he still maintained that the Indonesian forces were the only answer and that the arrival of Australian soldiers to assist with the evacuation would be dangerous. Then he paused, and I spoke to him in as direct a manner as I had ever done before: his information was simply false. A rampage, aided and abetted by the Indonesian military, was ongoing. And now it was targeting the United Nations. I could no longer risk the lives of our personnel. He responded that the arrival of Australian troops could mean war. I ended the call by telling Habibie that he had forty-eight hours to improve the situation—otherwise the international community would have to be invited in to restore peace and security.

Later that morning, I called President Clinton to tell him that I had issued this deadline. Clinton then provided useful support, ordering that Indonesia be pressured by letting them know that future U.S. military cooperation and loans from the World Bank and the International Monetary Fund would be put at risk if Jakarta allowed the violence to escalate. For my part, I also gave a public interview warning that military and civilian leaders could be held individually responsible for violations of human rights.

Over the next forty-eight hours, a delegation of Security Council envoys, led by Namibian ambassador Martin Andjaba and including UK ambassador to the United Nations Jeremy Greenstock, arrived in East Timor along with the top Indonesian military official, General Wiranto. It was clear that Wiranto was embarrassed by the lawlessness that was taking place under his officers' command. From Jakarta, Greenstock called me: "This place is surreal," he said. "The president is not in charge. The people who are in charge are telling a lot of lies. There is absolutely no doubt that the violence is orchestrated." Greenstock's analysis was further confirmed later that day by a single but symbolic killing: the murder of Xanana's eighty-two-year-old father by pro-Jakarta militiamen.

In one of the most difficult telephone conversations I had to make as secretary-general, I immediately called Xanana to offer my condolences. His response to my words of sympathy was that his father was one of far too many civilians who had died in East Timor. He quickly returned to the wider cause and conflict: "I know you are doing everything for us, but I can't help feeling that the situation is getting worse. I don't know how many more days martial law will prevail. I want to ask you to define a time for martial law. It is very difficult to accept martial law in East Timor." I replied that I had given Habibie forty-eight hours, after which he would have to accept an international force. As we ended the call, he spoke about his father: "He was a small part of East Timor's people. Thank you so very much for your solidarity."

Our solidarity, of course, was not enough. To convert the pressure on Indonesia into a shift in policy, I decided it was time now for me to turn from private dialogue to public diplomacy. At a press conference in New York, I laid out the same arguments to the attendant reporters, to take on board and relay to their audiences around the world what I had put to Habibie. "Before the eyes of the world," I said, the East Timorese were being subjected to an orgy of looting, burning, and killing for participating in a UN-organized ballot. The time had clearly come, I emphasized, for Indonesia to seek help from the international community, to fulfill its responsibilities for ensuring the security of the people of East Timor. I warned Jakarta that unless it allowed international troops into the territory, it could not escape responsibility for what could amount to crimes against humanity.

When a journalist asked me why the international community was still seeking the consent of Indonesia for going in, I used the occasion to remind the press—and our own team in the UN—of the realities of this intervention: "The question of just going in is very simple. To go in, you must have a force, and governments must be prepared to go in. We all talk of the United Nations and the international community. But the international community is made up of governments—governments with the capacity and will to act. They have made it clear that it will be too dangerous for them to go in." I went on to stress, "They will not do it without the consent of Indonesia. That is why Indonesia must be pressured to change its mind."

The turning point, at long last, came two days later, early in the morning on September 12, when I received a call from Habibie. Exhausted, concerned, but also resolved, he began by recalling the agreement we had made a few days earlier that he would call on our help if he concluded that martial law would not succeed in restoring peace to East Timor. "As a personal friend of mine and the friend of Indonesia that you are," he began, "I am now calling you to ask for your advice and assistance in efforts to restore peace and security in East Timor." This was the signal I needed to authorize the UN force. He agreed to send his foreign minister that night to New York to negotiate with me the deployment of the force. I thanked him for his important and courageous decision—which it was, given his position—and I assured him, once again, that the force would not be an imposition, but rather there to cooperate with Indonesia. He ended the call with a startling confession of his failure to restore order and his government's acceptance of our terms: "There are no concessions or conditions from my side: I have full confidence in you and in the United Nations."

On September 15, the Council unanimously passed a resolution authorizing the multinational force, to be known as INTERFET. And five days later, the first Australian troops landed on the beaches of East Timor in a force that, crucially, included Malaysian and Thai troops. After the swift restoration of order by the international force, the United Nations Transitional Administration in East Timor (UNTAET) was established in October 1999 with a mandate to rebuild the devastated country and prepare it for independence. I visited East Timor six months later, in February 2000. As I drove into town with my special representative Sergio Vieira de Mello, I saw the remains of burned-out buildings and the wanton destruction wrought by the Indonesian forces and their militias. My team and I then traveled by helicopter to the town of Liquica, where the postreferendum killing had been the most extensive. Nane and I went to the village church where hundreds had been massacred, and laid a wreath. As we were standing there, one Timorese after another came up to us in silent embrace. Later that afternoon, even as a crowd of some five thousand people gathered to hear their independence leader, Xanana Gusmão, and me speak of a peaceful future in freedom, I could not help thinking back on the terrible price paid by the Timorese for their freedom.

When the UN Transitional Administration was established in East Timor following the postreferendum violence, almost every structure—homes, shops, government buildings, churches—had been looted, gutted, or torched. In this wreckage we were tasked with building a whole new government where there had been none before. For this difficult undertaking I turned again to my trusted senior humanitarian official Sergio Vieira de Mello, to lead the UN's mission in the war-torn country. On arrival, Sergio spoke to the press about the approach we would apply in governing East Timor and preparing it for independence. Reflecting the debates around the culture and practice of peacekeeping and intervention that had been consuming the UN, Sergio's words indicated that we were determined to avoid the traps and trials of the past: "This time we chose not to opt for the usual and classical peacekeeping approach: taking abuse, taking bullets, taking casualties, and not responding with enough force, not shooting to kill," Sergio said. "The UN had done that before and we weren't going to repeat it here."

When I returned two years later, in May 2002, to celebrate East Timor's independence by lowering the UN flag and raising the Timorese one, I recalled in my words to the crowd the excitement and optimism that we had felt at my own country's independence day forty-five years earlier. At the midnight independence ceremony at the main stadium in Dili, Xanana then spoke in powerful terms on the prospects ahead: "We gained our independence to improve our lives. I remind everyone, especially the leaders: discipline to affirm our power, tolerance to affirm democracy, reconciliation to affirm unity." For the United Nations, this day marked a genuine and important achievement, a testimony to our ability to alter the course of nations under siege—when we could summon the will of the international community behind the principles of human rights and self-determination—and then guide them to self-rule.

We had honored our word to the people of East Timor; stood with them in their hour of greatest peril through a diplomatic campaign that secured the agreement of Indonesia and the support of the international community; stopped the killing, looting, and burning; and brought the country back from the brink of collapse and onto a path of self-determination. The cost to the people of East Timor had been staggeringly high. But in a world with too few examples of the vindication of the just demands of a people for security and self-determination, we had won a rare victory.

THE RESPONSIBILITY TO PROTECT: INTERVENTION AS DUTY OF CARE

The turnaround in Jakarta was the dramatic, but ultimately hopeful, backdrop to the United Nations General Assembly of September 1999. Over the previous eighteen months, the world had confronted two separate crises—Kosovo and East Timor—that had triggered a global debate on intervention and sovereignty, the rights of peoples and the responsibilities of states. I had combined my own intense diplomatic engagement on both crises—with the UN playing a central role in the case of East Timor—with a determination to reframe the question of intervention, and restore the United Nations to a central place in setting the boundaries for what states could do within their own borders. Throughout this period, I had sought to acknowledge the complexity and conflicting demands of this issue of intervention—both as matters of principle but also given the context of a diverse global community with deeply held views on both sides.

Ultimately, the success of our efforts on the question of intervention should not be measured in wars launched or sanctions imposed but in lives saved. Truthfully, therefore, if we can succeed in changing the behavior of potential conflict protagonists before intervention becomes necessary then we will save far more lives. Prevention is complex and can take many forms. One form is sustained and dedicated diplomacy in response to an evident fault line of potential conflict. It was this philosophy of preventive intervention that I later applied to a more submerged—but still very real—crisis over the Bakassi Peninsula, a territory claimed by both Nigeria and Cameroon. This was a long-standing cause of hostility between these two countries, and a ruling on the status of the territory by the International Court of Justice (ICJ), expected in 2002, could inflame communities on both sides, including the inhabitants of Bakassi, thus threatening significant internal violence of some form as well as interstate hostility. I had seen too many times how complicated such conflicts could become once they began, and long before the ICJ ruling was given, I took steps to ensure a set of diplomatic structures and avenues for dialogue between the parties so that this contentious issue could be managed peacefully. And over the years of diplomacy that followed and the breakthroughs in Nigerian-Cameroonian dialogue that we brokered, we succeeded in maintaining peace and stability—an important success in this alternative form of intervention.

But there is a harder side to prevention in the global system that is more contentious: the deterrent effect created by an international system that includes the threat of a military response to gross violations of human rights. As secretary-general, I believed strongly that the credibility of the UN in the minds of the citizens of poor and rich states would depend on where we stood on this issue of humanitarian intervention: the question of whether we were dedicated not to the power of states but to saving lives and defending the human rights of individuals. If states bent on criminal behavior knew that frontiers were not the absolute defense— if they knew that the Security Council would take action to halt crimes against humanity—then they would not embark on such a course of action in expectation of sovereign impunity. As I warned in the September 1999 speech to the GA, "If the collective conscience of humanity cannot find in the United Nations its greatest tribune, there is a grave danger that it will look elsewhere for peace and for justice."

Having posed a series of questions, I did not wish to leave anyone in any doubt about where I stood: "This developing international norm in favor of intervention to protect civilians from wholesale slaughter will no doubt continue to pose profound challenges to the international community," I observed. "Any such evolution in our understanding of state sovereignty and individual sovereignty will, in some quarters, be met with distrust, skepticism, even hostility. But it is an evolution that we should welcome. Why? Because, despite its limitations and imperfections, it is testimony to a humanity that cares more, not less, about the suffering in its midst, and a humanity that will do more, and not less, to end it."

The last year of the twentieth century—the bloodiest century in the history of humanity—was ending, it seemed with these developments in international relations, on a hopeful note. The new century would, of course, have its own wars and conflicts. That we knew. It would confront the oldest enemies of peace and coexistence, and encounter new challenges from emerging powers and unimagined conspiracies of hatred. And even where governments continued to repress ethnic groups and minority populations, we knew that the ideal of intervention would be balanced by the reality of power, capability, and political will.

In September 2000, the government of Canada, in the figure of Lloyd Axworthy, took up the baton that I had presented in my intervention speech to the UN General Assembly in 1999. It assembled a distinguished group of scholars and diplomats led by the dynamic former foreign minister of Australia Gareth Evans, and Mohamed Sahnoun, the distinguished Algerian UN diplomat, to draft a report on the implementation of the new norm that I had charted. Its most lasting contribution, however, would be in the title of its report and reframing of the issue from a right of intervention on the part of the international community to a "responsibility to protect" that had to be accepted by governments as well as the international community.

At the same time as the Canadian commission was carrying out its deliberations on a doctrine for the international community, a culture of humanitarian intervention seemed to be growing also in the actions of many of the global powers. This was evident in the determination of some of the more impressive international leaders during my time as secretary-general to respond to this call. After a deeply troubled period for the UN peacekeeping mission in Sierra Leone in 1999 and early 2000, in which the entire mission looked set to collapse due to the intransigent and brutal intentions of the factions to the conflict there, I was able to call upon the staunch support of the UK prime minister Tony Blair. Rather than watch Sierra Leone fall into another bout of atrocious civil war of the kind that had devastated the country throughout the 1990s, what followed in May 2000 was a decisive military intervention by a British military task force that routed the rebel factions and returned the balance to Sierra Leone's political system. The UN operation was saved, as was Sierra Leone, in large part through the courageous leadership of Tony Blair, and this ushered in a from-then-on stable peace process that endures to this day.

I also found a strong and determined partner in France's Jacques Chirac, in particular over the intractable crisis in the Democratic Republic of the Congo (DRC). In 2003, and with the withdrawal of thousands of Ugandan troops from the peacekeeping mission who had been based in the eastern Congo province of Ituri, a collapse in the security situation threatened to engulf the entire civilian population of the area. A firm military intervention, of the kind that went beyond the impartial peacekeeping that had been implemented hitherto in the province, was urgently necessary to buy time for the peacebuilding process in the area. The problems of eastern Congo were deep and protracted, and remain so, but Chirac responded to my call for a force to protect the people of Ituri from at least this imminent danger. He swiftly dispatched a well-armed French unit to lead this brief but essential intervention by a wider European force to strengthen the UN presence in the DRC.

While the debates on humanitarian intervention were often divisive—challenging as they did a right to noninterference that justly was considered sacred by developing countries in particular—the question of a "responsibility to protect" was, by definition, more inclusive, cooperative, and nonconfrontational. It was a brilliant innovation, which helped take the argument further. The launch of my report *In Larger Freedom* in 2005 generated a formal member state endorsement of the Responsibility to Protect. Six years after I had launched the debate on sovereignty and intervention, the members of the United Nations formally adopted a principle of individual and collective dignity.

This was less of a radical break with United Nations practice than its opponents would suggest. Of course, a legitimate concern was the fear of selective application of the principle by some members of the Security Council, guided by other, less noble, motives. Still, the old orthodoxy of distinguishing between internal conflicts and "threat to international peace and security," in the language of the Charter, was never, in fact, absolute. The Charter, after all, was issued in the name of the "We the peoples," not the "We the governments" of the United Nations. Its aim is not only to preserve international peace—vitally important though that is—but also to "reaffirm faith in fundamental human rights, in the dignity and worth of the human person." The Charter was never meant as a license for governments to deny human rights or human dignity. Sovereignty always implied not just power, but responsibility.

The Universal Declaration of Human Rights was not meant as a purely rhetorical statement. The General Assembly that adopted it also decided, in the same month, that it had the right to express its concern about the apartheid system in South Africa. There the principle of international concern for human rights took precedence over the claim of noninterference in international affairs. And the day before it adopted the Universal Declaration, the General Assembly had adopted the Convention on the Prevention and Punishment of the Crime of Genocide, which puts all states under an obligation to "prevent and punish" the most heinous of crimes.

The Responsibility to Protect is a deceptively benign-sounding concept. In fact, as we've seen, it represents a deep and disturbing challenge to those leaders who wish to treat their people with impunity. As Kosovo and East Timor taught us, the realities of power, the utility of force, and the summoning of political will can on occasion come together in a near-perfect combination for reality to match rhetoric in the commitment to shield civilians from gross abuses of human rights.

But if anyone doubted the limits of the new understanding of sovereignty and intervention, or the scale of the ever-present challenge of political will, events in the remote Sudanese province of Darfur would show just how far one government could go in persecuting a people, and how little the world would do about it.

DARFUR: THE FAILURE TO PROTECT

Just as the doctrine of the Responsibility to Protect was beginning to make progress in the corridors of international diplomacy and the minds of statesmen, the practice of protecting civilians was collapsing into one of its greatest and most agonizingly protracted failures in history: Darfur.

In December 2003, I issued my first statement of alarm at the situation in Darfur. But with a Security Council that had no desire to place the complicated and heavy demands of Darfur on its agenda, I could do little more than make verbal appeals and try and negotiate throughout this protracted period—but with few carrots and sticks in my hands.

Where Rwanda was staggering in its intensity, leaving eight hundred thousand dead in just one hundred days, Darfur was equally so in its protraction. Many chart the beginning of the conflict from February 26, 2003—only days before the United States and the UK conducted their invasion of Iraq without Security Council authorization—when a largely unknown rebel group conducted a raid on a small airfield in a corner of Darfur, an act that few, including the UN in New York, took any notice of at the time.

While the Sudanese government's response began in only the weeks and months after, Darfur's population, in truth, had been in the grip of insecurity and violence for years. Hard-pressed communities had long faced sporadic attacks on their villages, livelihoods, and bodies. The absence of any rule of law or government sources of protection partly underpinned the rebellion that triggered the conflict. But what came in the months after February 26, 2003, was a torturously long, unfolding war that would bring violations of human rights on a colossal scale.

Even before the raid in March 2003, the government of Sudan was already embroiled in several other violent conflicts within its borders, tying up most of its military resources. First, it was faced with a conflict in the east, near the border with Eritrea. More important, there was the issue of the south, where the government was still dealing with the remains of a twenty-year civil war with that region's secessionist movement—a conflict in the final throes of an arduous and, until then, long-faltering peace process. On top of these wars, Khartoum now faced another, and highly potent, insurrection drawn from the non-Arab communities of Darfur. Under these circumstances, with stretched military resources, the government of Sudan, from mid-2003, began developing its counterinsurgency strategy for Darfur: a war by proxy and atrocity.

To tackle the threat of the Darfur rebellion, the government unleashed a lawless coalition of proxy actors. It was a form of warfare waged through local militias, armed bands, and other tribal groups. It was fluid and shifting, but it came together to create a terrifying and devastating force against the people of Darfur in a process that became increasingly apparent to the international community by late 2003. It was at this time that my senior UN staff began to issue public warnings to the international community that something terrible was unfolding in Darfur.

The core component of this marauding army of gangs and tribal fighters was the camel- and horse-mounted Janjaweed, armed herders from the Arab Baggara tribes. They were supplied with weapons by the Sudanese army and were allowed free rein to carry out raids on the non-Arab villages of Darfur. The previous pattern of sporadic raiding in the region was now replaced with an unrestrained and systematic assault on the lives and livelihoods of the non-Arab communities across the province. The brutal strategic logic underpinning this method was simple: if the population was driven from its places of refuge, then the rebels would be, too.

With the Janjaweed supplied by Sudanese military intelligence, and closely supported by government military assets in the form of helicopters and fixed-wing aircraft loaded with rockets, bombs, and heavy machine guns, there was little Darfur's people could do to protect themselves from this hybrid modern-medieval rampage of pillaging and mass rape. There could be no refined targeting with a force such as the Janjaweed. The government of Sudan had willfully unleashed and supported a process that would grow without restraint into an assault against an entire population. The choice for civilians, when faced with Janjaweed attacks, was to be raped, mutilated, and killed, or flee and take to the barely preferable desert landscape.

E arly in the crisis, on March 29, 2004, in the midst of a series of telephone calls to other heads of state and actors engaged in the conflicts in Sudan, with knowledge of these terrible developments in Darfur heavy on my mind, I made a personal telephone call to the president of Sudan, Omar al-Bashir. I was in Bürgenstock, Switzerland, involved in hard negotiations on the Cyprus peace process, which we were trying to herd into an endgame. Juggling multiple crises was our bread-and-butter by now, and I had been trying to reach Bashir for some time, so I broke from the proceedings when this opportunity finally arose.

"I'm calling about the situation in Darfur, which I consider to be grave," I said, pausing to allow the interpreter to convey my words. "The situation is very bad, indeed," I continued. "I have received sustained and credible reports that Janjaweed fighters are continuing to rape, murder, and drive people off their lands. There are an estimated seven hundred thousand internally displaced persons, as well as large numbers of refugees in Chad. The people need protection from the Janjaweed. This is a situation that is urgent and, I must stress, unacceptable."

I saw no point in cloaking the purpose or tenor of my call, but I was acutely aware that my statements to Bashir were a slim recourse compared with the threats of force—whether implicit or explicit—that would surely be needed to have any hope of obtaining Khartoum's full compliance with our demands. But with the Security Council taking little interest in its responsibilities for the plight of Darfur's civilians, and without any member state with the resolve necessary to issue serious and credible threats of an intervention in Darfur, this was the only route I could take.

Even so, in the face of my frank words, I was still amazed by the response from Bashir. Greased with easy diplomacy, he even thanked me for my concern. He waved away my worries with the claim that the situation was entirely overblown in the media. "The situation in Darfur is quiet," he said. As far as he was concerned, the only problems in the province were those caused by the rebels, not the government-backed Janjaweed.

He then evaded a question I put to him on his view of the feasibility of a cease-fire. He was not going to offer me, or anybody, a promise to soften his government's counterinsurgency campaign. Without any Security Council resolve I knew, as he knew, that there was nothing I could do to push his government off a course it was determined to take.

But I was able to try to pressure Bashir, at least, on the issue of access for humanitarian supplies and humanitarian workers. In our conversation, he repeatedly claimed that, given the "quiet" situation in Darfur, there was no obstacle to humanitarian supplies across the province.

"So, if my people have difficulties with humanitarian access or deliveries, they can come to you?" I inquired. Given his stance, I sensed that even a slight personal desire to maintain his credibility, if only on an amicable level with me, meant that he would have to agree to this suggestion. This would be a promise that I could then hold him to later. "OK," Bashir affirmed, in an uncharacteristically curt response.

Using his words to box him into this slight corner seemed to give us a small result. The one thing that did improve in the coming weeks was the increase in the accessibility of humanitarian supplies to certain parts of Darfur. This was barely a positive outcome, given the magnitude of the situation. But I thought it might at least do something to help some people in Darfur who otherwise would have suffered or died without this assistance.

That phone call, and other conversations that followed regarding Darfur, happened in a dangerous vacuum—one of political pressure and political will among powerful states regarding Darfur, particularly on the Security Council. Over the coming months and years, as the conflict wore on, estimates suggested that upwards of a half million people would die as a result of the Sudanese government's strategy in Darfur, alongside millions more who were forcibly displaced and their livelihoods destroyed. The government of Sudan was not willing or able to protect its population from mass violations of human rights—and it would prove this time and again over the weeks that became months that became years of crisis.

The solution was clear, if difficult. Outside actors had a responsibility to protect civilians in Darfur, to step in and stop the assault—with or without the permission of the government of Sudan.

By late 2003, different voices were calling for action, including our own at the UN. The international community had to do something. After Rwanda, the world had said "Never again." But the Security Council refused to provide the leadership and resolve necessary to tackle the crisis in Darfur head-on. This reluctance appeared at the earlier stages to be motivated by well-meaning concern for the success of the Sudanese North-South peace process, which we all hoped was nearing an end in late 2003 and early 2004. The North-South civil war in Sudan had lasted over twenty years and had taken millions of lives, hitherto proving impervious to any peaceful resolution. Ending this conflict was a huge prize for peace, which the parties to the negotiations—led by a troika of the United States, the UK, and Norway—were rightfully determined to see through. When the reports of violence against Darfur's civilians began to accumulate in December 2003 and January 2004, it was explicitly recognized among all diplomatic parties to the negotiations that to hammer hard on the Darfur issue now could derail the entire North-South peace process— and with it the benefit to millions of Sudanese.

In December 2003 and early January 2004, given the stakes in the conflict in the South, and with peace there within our grasp, I agreed with this analysis. I instructed my staff that if we were not to lose the North-South peace process, we would have to, for now, only subtly pursue the emerging Darfur issue, discussing it on the margins of other meetings, rather than allowing it to appear center stage in negotiations with the government. It was terrible to have to make such a choice. We could either pursue a condemnatory route, which could potentially then destroy the delicate peace processes in the south, in turn doing little for the west; or, continue on course to complete the peace process in the south while doing what we could to persuade the government to curtail and end the crisis in Darfur. At best, we hoped we might conclude the major steps of the North-South process quickly enough to then apply full and decisive diplomatic attention to Darfur.

Within two months, developments in Darfur rendered this approach irrelevant. The mass of evidence of gross violations of human rights in Darfur that emerged made it clear that to continue the North-South peace process without serious inclusion of the Darfur issue was unviable. Events in Darfur were entirely inconsistent for any supposed partner for peace. I began to issue warnings to the various negotiators and mediators to the conflict, including foreign ministers and heads of state and government, that the Darfur issue could not be considered separately from the south. But the lack of resolve to do anything now demonstrated a different logic in the Security Council to one dictated by a concern for the North-South peace process.

As always, there were divisions on the Council. Pakistan, in particular, which held the presidency of the Council in early 2004, rejected requests to put Darfur on the Council agenda. In Darfur, Pakistan saw an issue that could lead to a campaign for intervention, and Pakistan stood in principle against what it saw as meddling in the affairs of sovereign states, particularly a fellow developing, and Muslim, country. China was another obstacle. With a skeptical attitude to humanitarian intervention not dissimilar to Pakistan's, China had also wedded itself to the Khartoum regime with contracts for the supply of Sudanese oil to fuel China's growing economy. China looked set throughout to obstruct any attempt to bring the more forceful options of the UN Charter to bear against Khartoum.

But, in theory, there was scope for negotiation and the alteration of the Chinese and Pakistani positions, as well as those of other skeptical Council members. More concerted pressure and innovations in diplomatic dealings could have been tried. An obstinate Syria, for example, had been persuaded a few months previously to cast its vote on the Security Council in favor of a tough resolution on Iraq. In the run-up to the vote, many thought Syria's representative would vote against the resolution. But in the end, after a sustained period of pressure from multiple parties, it voted for it. Furthermore, in Kosovo, NATO had proudly gone outside the mandate of the UN Charter, in response to the threat of a Russian veto at the Council, to conduct a forceful humanitarian intervention to protect the Kosovar Albanians. If there was another case for such a side step of international institutions in the face of enormous suffering, then Darfur was surely it.

But no real attempt to help the people of Darfur materialized. The province was the size of France; it was in an Arab-ruled country, with a government quick to point out that if Western forces intervened, they would be the third Muslim country in a row to be invaded after Afghanistan and Iraq, and one rich in oil and gas at that. As Bashir reportedly put it privately on occasion: "If they want jihad, let them come." The situation on the ground was enormously complex, too—not one like Rwanda, where there was a centrally organized and deliberate attempt to wipe out a clearly identified ethnic group. Instead, the divisions were unclear, fractured, and shifting, and who controlled which faction and when was blurred to a similar measure. In some ways, in terms of the level of disorganization and confusion, the war in Darfur was a situation better resembling Somalia or Congo than Rwanda. All this enhanced the preference for inaction among the members of the Security Council.

In the midst of the dithering, we made an official visit to Sudan, arriving on July 1, 2004. It was to include a visit to some of the refugee camps in Darfur and neighboring Chad. The state of the Darfuris was a terrible thing to witness—something which the Sudanese government made more difficult for us to achieve by physically moving a refugee camp, practically overnight, so that it would not be there for us to examine upon our arrival. This was a government with something terrible to hide. From the refugees we were able to meet came endless stories that only gave face to the other countless stories we had already heard—stories of horrific suffering across the province at the hands of viciously unrelenting, marauding forces.

On July 2, we held meetings with President Bashir and other senior members of his government. As I had found when meeting leaders responsible for the most terrible of atrocities, it was remarkable how genteel he was. One always imagines that those responsible for great evil should exude it from their very pores. But as with Saddam Hussein—whom I met with on a special visit to Iraq in 1998 in order to attempt to broker a deal that would stop a war—this was a man who seemed cool, polite, and friendly. It seems paradoxical, but this is often the way with those responsible for massive bloodshed.

Bashir had been in power since 1989, a degree of longevity in power that takes cunning and ruthlessness. As we sat down to our discussion in the presidential palace in Khartoum, Bashir opened by thanking me for the visit and expressing his eagerness to hear my views. I responded in kind, thanking him for his hospitality and then quickly moved on to Darfur.

"The international community wants comprehensive peace in Sudan," I said. "I have discussed this issue with the U.S. secretary of state Colin Powell and ministers of other members of the Security Council many times, who all want Sudan to take rapid and effective action." Bashir did not seem too impressed or concerned by this and repeatedly knocked back my extensive comments on the plight of Darfuri civilians and the ongoing violence against them, including my reference to particular incidents in Darfur during the previous two days. Bashir seemed keen to emphasize in response that the conflict had been started by the rebels—a typical argument of governments responsible for atrocities—and that this had created the security vacuum that they were now trying to rectify.

"The world firmly believes that the government of Sudan has control of the Janjaweed, including providing them with aerial support," I said.

"Specific action to protect vulnerable people needs to be taken immediately." Bashir waved off this demand with a comment indicative of his scornful attitude toward the mass of people in Darfur, and a callous lack of concern for any individual suffering:

"We have bombed the Janjaweed attacking villages. If the villages were more honest, they would admit that our planes also bomb the Janjaweed."

I have been asked by some journalists, privately, why I did not fire a threat of military intervention at Bashir during this meeting. In answer: This would have been the worst thing to do. If I had stood up and threatened him with the prospect of looming military intervention, knowing full well the Council was far from approving any kind of action, it would have undermined the credibility of the Council further. The inevitable lack of follow-through would then have made the Sudanese even bolder. Furthermore, the key to action on the part of the Council was unity between its members. A secretary-general making threats on the Council's behalf, on an issue that was deeply divisive for its members, would only have enhanced those divisions. The fallout would only have been to make the Sudanese even more certain that there was no international military action over the horizon.

It was clear from my discussions with Bashir and other Sudanese leaders that they were confident that there was no threat from the Security Council or any of its members. With the size of the province of Darfur, the complications of its geography, and the nature of the conflict, and the fact that the insurgency and sectarian war in Iraq was scaling up and consuming the endeavors of the U.S. and UK troops there, they were sure no one in the international community was coming for them. Their calculation proved entirely correct.

We left Sudan with what we could: a negotiated joint communiqué between the UN and the Sudanese government. In this document they pledged to disarm the Janjaweed, to pursue rapidly a comprehensive and peaceful settlement for the province, and to bring to justice all those accused of human rights violations "without delay." Unsurprisingly, these proved to be entirely empty promises.

The question on many people's minds at this time was: Is Darfur a genocide? The reason for this emerging obsession in the debates was the mistaken assumption that this question was effectively synonymous with "Should the world take action against Sudan?" Yes to one of these questions, it was believed, meant yes to both. But this was a mistake. NGOs and human rights groups had led a huge global campaign for international action on Darfur. Previous great events of suffering that all agreed should have compelled international military intervention—the Holocaust in Europe and the massacre of Tutsis in Rwanda—had clearly been genocide. The mistake was to believe that for intervention in Darfur to be considered legitimate, it had to be labeled "genocide," just like those previous disasters. The campaign became, in part, to push governments to recognize Darfur as a genocide.

In response to this pressure, the United States Congress voted on July 9 to declare the conflict in Darfur a genocide. Many thought that surely something would now happen. But they were wrong. The problem was that Darfur, by any careful legal examination, was not clearly a genocide, and this declaration, endorsed by Congress, meant that the debate on the definition of the conflict in Darfur—as opposed to what should be done to help the millions suffering—now took center stage at the Security Council. On September 7, 2004, for example, Jack Straw, the British foreign secretary, repeatedly questioned me on what he saw as the important issue of whether the conflict was genocide—as this had become key to the international debate. "What answer would you give today if you were asked if this is genocide?"

I replied in a similar manner to how I had treated this question for many months: "The fact is, whatever we call it, there are clearly gross and systematic violations of human rights and of international humanitarian law happening in Darfur, and the situation is the largest humanitarian catastrophe in the world." I believed this was all that really mattered. But he asked me to be clear on my view as to whether it was genocide. "I have stayed away from calling it genocide, because teams of experts have gone there, and they cannot conclude if a legal definition of genocide applies, or even, strictly speaking, ethnic cleansing, given the complexity of the situation on the ground." Straw then continued to discuss this question of what to call the conflict, despite my attempt to cast this concern, which was vexing all leaders engaged on the issue at that time, as irrelevant. But this had clearly become an important question in domestic political debates, whether in Britain or elsewhere.

"Is it conceivable that it could fall to you to advise the Security Council on whether it is a genocide?" he asked.

"That is possible," I said. "But let me stress that we are here debating whether this is a genocide, when we all can agree that this is a terrible situation and it has to be dealt with."

This message, which I had been pushing in speeches and interviews and conversations with other politicians for months, failed to resonate. Instead, the obsession with the correct label for Darfur continued. Two days after my meeting with Straw, on September 9, 2004, Colin Powell referred to the conflict in Darfur as "genocide." Rather than ending the debate on the label and moving on to the question of action, this move only stoked it. (Powell also made it clear that U.S. policy on Darfur would not change, despite the new rhetoric.) The result that then came out of the Security Council was the formation of a commission of inquiry to investigate whether the conflict in Darfur was a genocide. This investigation, led by the respected Italian judge Antonio Cassese, concluded that the campaign of the government of Sudan could not technically be deemed a systematic attempt at genocide, although there were clearly major crimes against humanity and war crimes taking place for which individuals should be held responsible. But this was not conveyed until the commission reported back to the Council, by which time it was January 2005.

There is always a danger with labels in international affairs. Protagonists become obsessed with definitions instead of focusing on what matters, namely the suffering of individuals. The label "genocide" was irrelevant to the fact that hundreds of thousands were suffering in Darfur. But as a result of the obsession with the word "genocide," as if only genocide could signify an evil worthy of our collective horror and concern, the debate about what *action* should be taken was delayed further.

For the suffering of the civilians it did not matter what the situation was called, or what motive had led to their desperate situation. They were still dying, and in vast numbers, as a result of a government's decisions and the actions of its armed proxies. This was a crime—whatever its form. What Darfur demonstrated, and hopefully should never have to be demonstrated to world leaders ever again, is that the "genocide" label does not hold a monopoly over the most heinous of crimes against humanity, and should not be the sole trigger for action. The sheer numbers that were made to suffer and die in Darfur is proof enough of that.

I n the end, it took almost four years of continued mass rape, mutilation, slaughter, and the deaths of hundreds of thousands to exposure, disease, and malnutrition, as well as the forcible displacement of millions more, before the Security Council issued anything resembling a serious response and dispatched international troops to Darfur. But even with this change, which came in late 2007 and several months after my tenure as chief of the UN had ended, the force that was sent was only a "robust peacekeeping" mission. It was not a true humanitarian intervention upholding the Responsibility to Protect. A forceful intervention was needed to have any real impact on the ground, to bring about the sustained protection of Darfur's civilians.

Instead, a peacekeeping force of nineteen thousand was approved in August 2007, to be deployed by the end of the year. The mission would provide the usual secondary role that such a peacekeeping force can only offer. They would support largely voluntary disarmament, monitor events, and protect humanitarian efforts, and they would be able to defend themselves. They would be helping, of course, but they would not be capable of having any drastic impact on the dynamics around them.

Furthermore, the 2007 mission was also permitted to enter Darfur only with the full permission of the Sudanese government. The force was still mandated to protect any civilians it could. But in its resources, mandate, and intent, it would not answer the fundamental challenge of protecting the people of Darfur from gross violations of human rights.

The Responsibility to Protect is not just about planes, tanks, and helicopters, of fast-moving military interventions sent to vanquish the forces of mass murder. While history has shown that atrocious violations of human rights, or the obvious threat of such, can sometimes make it devastatingly clear when force is needed, the Responsibility to Protect is also made up of a much broader range of activities, of a whole spectrum of interventions, to safeguard the lives and rights of individuals around the world. In some cases, this may require the urgent use of military force, as in Kosovo—but this alone can never be sufficient. Ultimately, the long-term protection of civilians depends upon the peaceful structures and institutions under which they live, their stability and robustness in the face of the subversive efforts of those who would do evil to others. The Responsibility to Protect, properly defined, is above all about ensuring lasting institutions—mostly within states—for the peaceful safeguarding of human lives and human rights.

In the future, I see the Responsibility to Protect as becoming a norm that gives nations and peoples a yardstick—a standard by which they can hold their government to account. An example is the Universal Declaration of Human Rights, which today we take for granted and refer to as a bedrock document of the international community. If the declaration had existed before the Second World War, would it have made a difference? Would it have helped people prevent the outrages committed in their name? How could governments, individuals, and civil society have used it to stop some of the excesses? Today everybody knows about a universally acknowledged set of human rights, and it is used to demand their protection. The Responsibility to Protect builds on this and puts responsibility also in the hands of those global powers with the capacity to intervene for the better.

We have challenged the argument that the lives and rights of individuals are an internal affair of state that is of no concern to outsiders. We have also told the dictators that sovereignty is no longer a shield behind which gross violations of human rights can be committed. You are responsible and you are accountable.

A PEOPLES'
UNITED NATIONS

Reforming Global Governance and

Restoring the Rule of Law

W hat is the United Nations for? That is the question that I
found myself asking more and more as I looked at the range
of issues facing us, and how we addressed them. My years in
peacekeeping had brought me face-to-face with the deepest tragedies suffered by men and women caught in conflict. Too often they had looked to
the United Nations for safety and found an organization unable to secure
it. As I sought to rethink our responsibility to our mission, I realized that
we needed to make clear whom we were fighting for.

An organization of member states jealously guarding their privileges, the United Nations had drifted toward becoming an institution
focused, above all, on self-preservation. In so doing, we had in many respects lost our way—forgetting the first words of the Charter: "We the
Peoples." We needed to refocus our lens on the individual man, woman,
and child in need of security, health, and opportunity. We needed to bring
the United Nations back to the peoples in whose name it was founded.

B efore dawn one morning in October 2001, I received a phone call from Fred Eckhard. Fred had been my spokesman since I had taken office as secretary-general, and such calls were not unusual—though they typically heralded bad news. On this occasion, however, Fred had been telephoned by someone from a Norwegian radio station who spoke little English but kept repeating my name. "I think you got the Nobel Peace Prize," Fred concluded, in his usual calm manner.

At first I dismissed the idea. I told Fred that surely the Nobel Committee itself would contact the recipient. Then I received another call, this time from my in-laws, Nane's parents, Gunnar and Nina Lagergren, in Stockholm, congratulating us. Later the Nobel Committee itself did, indeed, telephone, apologizing for the unusual manner of releasing their decision.

The prize—which I shared together with the United Nations—was an important act of recognition for our efforts to reenergize the institution and restore its place in global politics. The committee emphasized its own belief in the centrality of the UN in advancing global peace and security, and applauded our new initiatives in the areas of human rights and the fight against HIV/AIDS. Recognizing that the UN is an organization of member states, the committee underlined its support for our efforts to redefine sovereignty as a responsibility as much as a right—and commended me for "making clear that sovereignty cannot be a shield behind which member states conceal their violations."

For the United Nations staff, it was a vital acknowledgment of the sacrifices made in some of the most desperate and dangerous parts of the world; for member states, it was a reminder of the values for which the UN stood. This was particularly important as we were all still reeling from the September 11 attacks. Only a month earlier, staff and diplomats alike had been evacuated from UN headquarters.

When I accepted the prize that following December, I began my acceptance speech by observing that we had entered the third millennium "through a gate of fire." The twentieth century had been the bloodiest in human history, yet, out of the ashes of World War II, inspired leaders had created an organization with the aim of securing peace and development for all peoples. The September 11 attacks warned that the twenty-first century could be bloodier still, and that our work on behalf of the poorest and most vulnerable communities would be faced with new threats and challenges. In the UN's fundamental choice, however, between justice and neutrality, actor and bystander, I had placed the United Nations squarely on the side of intervention and in support of the people in whose name the Charter was written.

The Nobel Prize was as unexpected as my election to the role of secretary-general four earlier. I had spent my career within the UN Secretariat, and in my last role, as under-secretary-general for peacekeeping, achieved as senior a position as seemed possible for an international civil servant. Never before had a career UN staff member been elected to lead the organization.

But when I returned from a mission to Bosnia as special representative of the secretary-general in April 1996, the tension between the United States and Secretary-General Boutros Boutros-Ghali was palpable. Secretary of State Albright and Boutros-Ghali were increasingly at loggerheads. Rumors started to circulate that the United States might not support him for a second term. He had been appointed at the start of 1992 for a five-year term, and each previous secretary-general had served two full terms, except for Trygve Lie, who resigned and Dag Hammarskjöld, who died in a plane crash in present-day Zambia.

Boutros-Ghali brought to the role of SG a fierce intelligence and a global perspective, an academic mind-set and a visceral distaste for the post–Cold War dominance of the United States. However, his souring relationship with the Americans was as much a function of his own lead-

ership style as it was a perennial U.S. intolerance for any UN leader acting independently. Though he had escaped criticism for the UN's failure
in Rwanda, in 1994 and 1995 he seemed to obstruct the increasingly robust U.S. position on the Balkan war.

Added to this was Boutros-Ghali's autocratic and secretive style,
which had long caused difficulties within the UN, alienating large numbers of staff and diplomats. This left him in a highly vulnerable position
when the Americans turned on him. In mid-1996 Albright arranged a
meeting with me and said that they were considering my candidacy for
secretary-general. I had worked well with her and over time developed a
genuine friendship based on our common interest in a more relevant and
responsive United Nations. A critical advantage was my knowledge of the
workings of the United Nations system—from its far-flung missions to its
New York staff to the diplomats who crowded its corridors.

By the time the United States used its veto in a special meeting of
the Security Council on November 11, 1996 to prevent Boutros-Ghali
from winning a second term, I was prepared to step into the role of
secretary-general, with all the challenges and difficulties that I knew it
would entail.

The UN Charter is a stirring document, setting out a vision for world
order based on right, not might. On the role of secretary-general,
however, it is far less clear and comprehensive. It defines the secretary-
general as the chief administrative officer of the organization, but that
doesn't capture all that the job entails. There is, naturally, a great deal of
administration, overseeing an annual budget of around $10 billion and
a staff of forty-four thousand. On top of that, the bureaucracy of the
UN has grown organically, and not always logically. Alongside the intensive work of marshalling the divisive and deeply contentious Security
Council—the supreme decision-making body in international law, peace,

and security—and providing overall leadership for the UN's diverse work around the world, a big part of the job is simply making sure all the agencies and associated organizations that make up and work with the UN are working together properly.

From my years as head of peacekeeping, I had learned important lessons about the limits of the UN's capabilities, the value of building constituencies of support, and of forging consensus in a universal organization tasked with meeting global challenges. I knew—from extensive and often trying experience—that a secretary-general's effectiveness comes from his ability to convince others of the justice and urgency of his cause. Convincing others that my success was in their own interest—and that I was neither a threat nor an obstacle to their own agenda—was a key condition of progress. Without the support of member states—and the other actors in global affairs, from businesses to NGOs and citizens' groups— there was little I could achieve. With it, I knew we had the power to change the dynamic of progress in every arena of global affairs, from poverty to health to human rights and conflict.

As for the great geopolitical questions of the day, it is essential for a secretary-general to choose where he can make a difference. One advantage of the position is that you can serve as the honest broker, the interlocutor acceptable to most parties. It is usually quite clear that the only interest the secretary-general has is in achieving peace and advancing development. However, it can also be a problem when member states use the secretary-general as an alibi for inaction. Within the organization, my title was routinely abbreviated as "SG." I sometimes joked that this stood for "scapegoat."

Of course, no decision in an organization of states escapes some degree of politicization. If I asked for money for human rights, developing states would complain that I had forsaken their interests; if I pressed for resources for development, the developed states would protest that I was letting their agenda slide. Here it was helpful that I had worked in the UN for a long time before moving to the thirty-eighth floor of the UN's main building in New York—where the secretary-general's office is—and understood better than most of my predecessors how the system worked.

Contrary to what many suspect, the UN has few resources of its own. For a peace operation, I had to go to the troop-contributing countries and ask for peacekeepers. For development assistance and humanitarian relief, I had to go to the donor governments. Given the stakes involved, I realized that this was something that I had to become good at. So I learned how to ask, what buttons to push and, importantly, how to listen and judge my response. And also *whom* to ask, because sometimes it is a bureaucrat rather than the minister or even the head of state who can get resources moving. This is the soft power of a secretary-general— the ability to convince others that your success is in their own best interests.

The Nobel Peace Prize of 2001 was an important vote of confidence in the institution, and for me as its secretary-general, at a critical moment in our institution's history. Less than a year later, the inexorable march to war in Iraq was dividing the member states and calling into question the relevance of the organization. The architecture of global governance was tested almost to the breaking point. And whatever the particular agenda of the U.S. administration—or the specific roots of the Iraq War—it was clear to all that we needed a new vision of security and of the place of the UN in achieving it. Out of crisis I saw an opportunity— and the urgent necessity—for reform.

Addressing the key global threats of our age—which included terrorism but also poverty, organized crime, disease, and climate change— required cooperation between states and other actors. I believed then and believe now that the United Nations offers the best forum in which the necessary compromises can be struck and concerted action carried out. The problem was that the organization was about to be challenged in ways that went to the core of its mission—and credibility. What should the UN's role be in the use of force by the most powerful? What place should it have in the global exercise of power?

Within the UN building and among the member states there was a great deal of anger and even more disillusionment surrounding the Iraq invasion. As secretary-general, I wanted to help people focus on issues that would unite them and direct that anger toward something positive rather than toward raw division. The year 2003 could well have become a year of retreat—with the Iraq War and the beginning of the Oil-for-Food investigations we certainly felt under siege. But I decided that what the UN needed was not to retreat into obscurity but to confront these challenges—of the structure of the organization, of the willingness of member states to support it, of the very principle of an international order governed by law—head-on.

"Excellencies," I said in my address to the General Assembly in September 2003, "we have come to a fork in the road." I described the moment as comparable to the founding of the United Nations, when a group of farsighted leaders had drawn up rules to govern international behavior and founded a network of institutions, with the UN at its center, in which the peoples of the world could work together for the common good. Two generations on, we had to decide whether it was possible to continue on the basis agreed then, or if radical changes were needed.

The core problem at the top of the UN's power structure is the composition of the Security Council. Today we have five permanent members with veto powers—the United States, Britain, Russia, France, and China—based essentially on the geopolitical reality that existed at the end of World War II. The other ten nonpermanent members are elected by the General Assembly for two-year terms, on the basis of geographical representation. This situation is intolerable to some; unjustifiable to most. Japan and Germany pay the second- and third-largest contributions to the UN but do not have a fixed seat at its most important table. India has over a sixth of the world's population but no seat. There is no permanent member from Africa or Latin America.

For the Security Council to enjoy legitimacy in the twenty-first century, it needs to be not only effective but also representative. Often in the past it was neither. Whatever the challenges of collective action, it is evident that economic and political power has shifted in the world. Why emerging and regional powers will accept structures in which they have a second-class status is a question no one has answered credibly. The problem will not be that such countries will actively oppose the Security Council. It's that they will ignore it.

We are starting to see this playing out in the jockeying for positions around new tables—the G8, G20, and all the other Gs. But I have to remind friends who celebrated joining the G20 that they were deeply unhappy when they were outside the G8, and that there are still 172 countries outside the G20.

So, as part of my reform agenda following my September 2003 speech, I proposed two models to be considered. Both models involved increasing the number of seats from fifteen to twenty-four. The first model included adding six permanent seats to the Council—without vetoes—and three additional rotating seats. The second model would have added just one rotating seat but eight new semipermanent seats, which could be held for four years at a time on a renewable basis. I then laid these options down as the basis for negotiations on what shape a reformed Security Council should take.

It was clear that those aspiring to permanent seats favored the first model—indeed, India was unhappy not to be getting a veto as well—but which countries should get the seats? Japan, Germany, India, and Brazil pressed ahead on this basis, assuming their candidacy, while member states in the Africa group could not decide among the competing claims of Nigeria, South Africa, and Egypt. The continent's traditional rivalries came to the fore, with Egypt arguing that there had to be a seat for the countries north of the Sahara, and South Africa maintaining that it would be able to represent all countries from its position. To this, Nigeria responded that its size, population, and resource base justified a seat for Abuja. On the Latin American side, the divisions between the big countries were equally apparent, with Argentine president Carlos Menem charging furthermore that a fight over representation on the Council would serve only to resurrect bitter rivalries that at long last had been put behind them.

The divisions that ensued were welcomed by some states that saw new permanent seats as a mistake—and, of course, a threat to their positions of privilege. Indeed, the policy of a good number of countries appeared to be to support Council expansion in theory but to oppose any specific proposal in practice. There were some who opposed particular states: Pakistan essentially said India would get a permanent seat over its dead body; China was deeply ambivalent about Japan; and so on.

This jostling was shortsighted. If the Council is to remain relevant, then some expansion is needed. In light of past efforts, the semi-permanent model is the most promising, with the creation of a half dozen extra seats that could be held on a long-term basis by regional powers, perhaps renewed every eight to ten years. Divisions such as those that plagued the Africa group might be resolved through regional mechanisms like the African Union—in the same way that the European Union coordinates some of the foreign policies of its members.

Critics of my decision to press for Security Council reform in 2003 argued that it was a distraction from other problems plaguing the UN, or that it would create division at a time when unity was required. But to propose reform of the UN without addressing the problems on the Council would have been seen as dodging a fundamental issue for many member states, making it harder to get countries to focus seriously on the other reform questions.

Other people said I tried to do too much, and perhaps that was true. The UN (not unlike the Vatican) doesn't always treat reformers kindly.

But this ignores the real achievements of the 2003 reform drive that we were able to extract in the months and years that followed.

The problems confronting the UN at that time were not only structural. In many ways, a more fundamental problem was the different manner in which member states perceived the world and its dangers. This issue became particularly acute after September 11, 2001. From that point a great many Americans and others were primarily concerned about the threat of terrorism. This was understandable, and the UN provided a vehicle for addressing some of those threats through support to the United States in Afghanistan, curbing terrorist financing, and other measures. But for those, for example, in Africa or South Asia that found themselves with not enough to eat, the perception of threat was quite different. And if you are in a region where there is serious conflict or a possible explosion of ethnic conflict, you have different fears again.

So what I tried to make clear was that we needed a comprehensive understanding of these threats. To say the world is interdependent had become the worst kind of cliché—true in the literal sense, but unable to generate the kinds of multilateral engagement befitting a world where no threat was limited to one country or region. Member states engaged selectively, and sporadically, on the major issues: some cooperating on threats like terrorism and, to a lesser extent, disease, but dividing when it came to confronting the proliferation of weapons of mass destruction.

Major reforms in an international institution of such size usually coincide with a crisis. It took World War I to establish the League of Nations, and World War II to create the UN. The Charter had only been amended in the 1960s following decolonization and the near doubling of the UN membership. When crisis came during my tenure over the invasion of Iraq, it was unclear whether it was of a kind that would bring the world together or tear it apart.

From late 2003 we set about devising an extensive package of reforms. These included reform of the governing bodies of the UN, particularly the Security Council, but also the creation of new bodies and norms governing the activities of the organization. In my address to that year's General Assembly, I announced the creation of a High-Level Panel on Threats, Challenges and Change to propose new ideas for advancing collective security in the twenty-first century. We suggested the creation of a Human Rights Council, to replace the long-maligned Commission on Human Rights, in order to energize the issues surrounding human rights violations at the heart of the UN. We set forward proposals for the creation of a Peacebuilding Commission, one that would serve to bring together the multifaceted requirements of intervention in civil war zones, across the spectrum of military, development, and humanitarian activities that also reflected the long tail of involvement required for effective intervention in such territories. And we included the new doctrine of the Responsibility to Protect as part of this reform package, alongside issues of WMD in international security and—most controversially—preemptive war, as core questions regarding the future of the UN's governance, outlook, and sense of mission.

One of the great ironies of that period was the manner in which the United States—which had done more than any other country to establish the UN—found itself in the position of being the main obstacle to reforming it. Another irony was how that opposition actually made some reforms possible.

The creation of the Human Rights Council was one example. As we approached a vote on the reforms, the chief opponents were the United States, Cuba, and Pakistan—a curious coalition. At the time, I was traveling in South Africa, and I called the president of the General Assembly, Jan Eliasson, to find out how things were going. "It's very tough," he told me. "I'm not sure we will get an agreement." The problem, he said, were these three countries. By that point the U.S. ambassador John Bolton—so deeply opposed personally to the entire existence and purpose of the UN—had isolated himself so much that he was out on his own. But I suspected he was still hoping to hide behind Cuba and Pakistan, so that they would be blamed for the failure of the creation of the Human Rights Council.

In response, I decided to call the president of Cuba. Fidel Castro was sleeping, but I got Foreign Minister Felipe Pérez Roque on the line and I explained that Cuba could not play this role. The member states, especially the developing countries, needed an improved human rights institution. Cuba held itself up as the voice of developing countries, but now it was on a path that would lead to its being blamed for killing human rights at the UN. Cuba should be backing, not obstructing, this move, I said.

Later, Pérez Roque called back and said that he and Fidel Castro had discussed it and decided to instruct their ambassador in New York to remove their objection to the Human Rights Council. I then told Jan, who was delighted.

This left only Pakistan. It was late, but I managed to get the ambassador, Munir Akram, on his cell phone. "I understand you have very strict instructions not to let this go through," I told him. "I see you are in a difficult position, so I want to help you. I will call President Musharraf and ask him to give you flexibility to remove this objection. You should also know that among the developing world, you are alone. You're the only one blocking it. The Cubans have lifted their objection."

"What?" he said. "The Cubans?"

"Yes," I replied. "Talk to the Cuban ambassador and he will confirm it. I've been on the line with Havana and it's done. I'm prepared to help you the same way. I will call Musharraf."

"No," he said. "Give me fifteen minutes."

This was typical of some ambassadors who routinely claimed to have "very strong instructions" but could then change those instructions if needed. Akram lifted his objection.

And that left the United States on its own. Bolton had nobody to hide behind, and we didn't hear from him again on this issue.

In September 2005, the member states finally voted on the reform package. There were anxious days in the lead-up to the vote. Indeed, I had my speechwriters prepare some remarks that I could use if the whole process fell apart and there was no agreement on anything. In the end, however, the vote was unanimous in support of reform.

Although we tried harder than ever before in the UN's history, reform of the Security Council remained elusive due to the intense divisions over what form it should take. There was, however, progress on some other important priorities—the Human Rights Council, the Peacebuilding Commission, the Responsibility to Protect. One thing that was missing as a result of the negotiations between member states, however, was any reference to weapons of mass destruction, an omission that I called a disgrace. The impetus for reform had come from the crisis in Iraq. It was hard to believe that more than two years of debate about how the UN should have responded to the problems of WMD in Iraq produced a thirty-eight-page document that mentioned neither.

FROM THE RULE OF THE JUNGLE TO THE RULE OF LAW

"I'll be damned if I'm going to let my son be dragged before some foreign kangaroo court to face judgment," said the judge, whose son had served as a U.S. Army captain in Iraq. It was not an unusual view among American commentators and politicians. The International Criminal Court—established in 2002 to prosecute individuals for the crimes of genocide, crimes against humanity, and war crimes—represented to many skeptics of multilateralism the ultimate act of usurpation of national sovereignty. My surprise was to hear this from a justice of the United States Supreme Court. The judges have a tradition of inviting a guest to lunch with the nine members of the court, and I was delighted to receive the invitation from Justice Stephen Breyer to join them on one of my visits to Washington DC. Over a lunch of salads and sandwiches, the International Criminal Court quickly became the main—and contentious—topic of conversation.

I tried to reassure the irate Justice about the procedures that were in place to stop frivolous prosecutions; that the ICC would act only when there was a credible accusation and the state in question was unwilling or unable to investigate and prosecute the matter. He was unconvinced.

There were echoes in this conversation from the larger debates surrounding international law. Conservative commentators have argued that small states, weak states, need international law and the UN more than the bigger and more powerful states. This is partly true. But the same could be said of a national legal system. Powerful people can sometimes get away with murder. As the rule of law develops, however, such exceptions become harder to tolerate. Sometimes it is formal pressure, sometimes it is informal pressure, that leads to compliance. This can take a long time, but I think we are slowly seeing this happen at the international level.

One of the founding purposes of the United Nations, written into the Charter, is to establish the conditions for justice and respect for the law. Advancing the rule of law at the national and international level was something that I pressed for during my time as secretary-general, and in 2005, the member states unanimously endorsed this position.

As many observers have commented, however, such widespread support for the rule of law in theory is possible only because countries have divergent understandings of what it means in practice. My own understanding is that the rule of law is a principle of governance to which everyone, including the representatives of the state, is accountable, with laws that are publicly promulgated, equally enforced, and independently adjudicated. Those laws should be consistent with international human rights standards. The rule of law also requires fairness in the application of the law, participation in decision making, and transparency. Clearly, not all states yet embody all these characteristics. But all states have recognized the rule of law as a political ideal to which they should aspire.

At the international level, applying the rule of law to the interaction between states is far more complex. Today we lack institutions to adjudicate or enforce the law. The International Court of Justice has jurisdiction only over cases voluntarily submitted to it. There is no international police force with executive policing powers. A problem for any secretary-general seeking to promote the rule of law is how to persuade sovereign states *voluntarily* to submit themselves to the law.

Even before the world became so interdependent, it was clear that a set of rules was needed to regulate international relations. People often forget the extent to which modern life is made possible by international law: it ensures that your mail gets to where it's meant to, that radio frequencies are managed, that ships and aircraft navigate safely. The sort of global society many of us enjoy now wouldn't exist without that network of laws. But it has to be about more than mere convenience for the wealthy. Personally, I see the rule of law as offering a way to broaden access to opportunity and prosperity, and to protect those who are left vulnerable to suffering or exploitation through no fault of their own.

Despite the reservations of the justice of the U.S. Supreme Court and many others in the United States, the establishment of the International Criminal Court represents a major victory for the rule of law in international affairs. After the tragedies of Somalia, Rwanda, and Bosnia, the ICC held a very personal dimension for me. In the negotiations leading to its creation, I quite consciously took positions that I knew would provoke some states, occasionally offering language that other governments or NGOs could use to advance the agenda.

In the end, it was a very close call. I had spoken at the opening of the Rome conference of 1998, convened to adopt a convention on the establishment of an international criminal court, but as the draft was moving toward a vote, I was on an official visit to Argentina. My legal advisor Hans Corell was in the conference room with his team. I told him that if we were likely to get an agreement, I would break off my journey and join them in Rome.

On the day they were supposed to take a vote, India proposed a "poison pill"—an amendment that would have killed the whole process. If the amendment was defeated, that was the last obstacle to be overcome. If the amendment passed, then there would be no court. The existence of the court was on a knife-edge.

I phoned Corell and said, "I'm going to a meeting. The last flight out of Argentina for Rome leaves in an hour and a half. Let me know if we have an agreement."

"Well I don't know," he replied. "Call me in twenty minutes." His call was put through to me twenty minutes later, and Corell held his phone in the air. "Can you hear it?" he asked. The amendment had been defeated and the mood was clearly euphoric.

I sent my apologies to my Argentinean hosts and headed to the airport. I made it to Rome for the signing of what is now the Rome Statute at one of the most extraordinary meetings of my professional life. Not only the activist NGOs but some of the governments that had fought for the ICC were clearly elated. There we were on the platform, with people spraying champagne, saying, "We did it! We did it!"

Beforehand, I had opened the conference in Rome by appealing to the delegates to proceed as if "the eyes of the victims of past crimes, and of the potential victims of future ones, are fixed firmly upon us. It was their cry for justice that had to spur us on to our final destination." Our goal, I said, is a court that would "put an end to a global culture of impunity."

This culture of impunity could not be eradicated with just the formation of the court, but when taking steps to advance its work we must remember what prompted us to act. It began in the burning villages of Rwanda, their paths, fields, and even their churches, strewn with corpses. And the next year, in the bombed-out buildings of Bosnia and the horror of Srebrenica, where upwards of eight thousand defenseless men and boys were shot and dumped into pits. In both cases, the UN and the international community failed tragically to take decisive and forceful action to protect the victims.

These terrible events did, however, shock the world into action. Ad hoc tribunals were set up to bring those responsible to justice and the Rome Statute had now established a permanent court to help end the global culture of impunity.

The parties to the establishment of the Rome Statute have much to be proud of. More than two-thirds of UN member states have, as of 2011, signed or ratified the Rome Statute, tipping the balance in favor of justice. In the face of war crimes, crimes against humanity, and genocide, the default position of the international community is now accountability, not impunity. Where credible allegations of such crimes are made, it is up to those denying the need for international justice to make their case and demonstrate that their own legal response is adequate.

The remarkable success of the creation of the court was the result of strong political will. Further progress will require vision, a strong sense of purpose, and even courage. Take my own home continent of Africa: encouraged by a few African leaders, the African Union in 2011 called on its member states not to cooperate with the ICC in enforcing the indictment issued against President Bashir of Sudan.

But it is not Africa that is hostile to the court, only certain leaders. When I meet Africans from all walks of life, they demand justice: from their own courts if possible, from international courts if no credible alternative exists. The ICC does not supplant the authority of national courts. Rather, it is a court of last resort, governed by the principle of complementarity—it is there to support people and nations in their pursuit of justice.

I am proud, as an African, of our continent's contribution to the success of this great undertaking. African countries and their civil society organizations played an active and progressive role in the creation of the ICC. Thirty of the countries in sub-Saharan Africa have become parties to the statute—the largest single regional block that has joined the court. I am proud, too, that in four of the five cases from Africa currently before the ICC, African leaders have either referred those cases to the court or actively cooperated with the investigations.

In doing so, these countries have sought the support of an international judicial mechanism in the face of their own limited judicial capacity. In the specific case of Kenya, where the ICC's prosecutor has, for the first time, used his own authority to initiate an investigation, he has undertaken his work with the cooperation of the Kenyan government. In all these cases, it is impunity, not the African countries, that is being targeted.

Some people in Africa—and elsewhere—have a genuine concern that our search for justice might obstruct the search for peace. They ask, "How do we convince the leaders of warring parties to make peace if prison awaits them?" Some allege that the prosecutor's work in Uganda and Darfur has delayed or hampered peace efforts. But Rwanda, Bosnia, Kosovo, East Timor—these and other cases have taught me that justice is a partner, not an impediment to peace.

The parallel pursuit of justice and peace does present challenges, but these can—and must—be managed. The prosecutor's discretion in matters of timing is crucial. So is the sensitivity of those mediating conflicts to the legal obligations arising from the Rome Statute. The choice between justice and peace is no longer an option. We must be ambitious enough to pursue both, and wise enough to recognize, respect, and protect the independence of justice.

Further progress also depends on states genuinely exercising their primary responsibility, as set out under the Rome Statute, to investigate, prosecute, and punish those responsible for grave crimes themselves. There must be no going back or lessening of momentum on the issue of impunity in world affairs. Our challenge is to protect the innocent by building a court so strong, universal, and effective that it will deter even the most determined of despots.

Questions of credibility will persist so long as three of the five permanent members of the Security Council—the United States, China, and Russia—refuse to reconsider their position and join those who have taken the courageous step to become parties to the Statute. Others that aspire to permanent membership on the Council also refuse to ratify the Rome Statute. It is my hope that support for the ICC will become a condition for joining any future reformed Security Council.

More than a decade after the Rome Conference, the International Criminal Court has begun its work. It is important to emphasize that the court exercises its jurisdiction only when a state is a party to the Rome Statute and is unable or unwilling to investigate crimes like genocide, war crimes, or crimes against humanity.

In the case of Uganda, for example, the court's help was—initially, at least—welcomed. In Kenya, by contrast, the ICC prosecutor himself initiated an investigation into the violence surrounding the 2007 election. But this was only possible following Kenya's ratification of the Rome Statute in 2005, and this signing and the ensuing investigation was supported by many in Kenyan civil society.

Sudan was a slightly different case. Given the reports of severe atrocities in Darfur from 2004, I asked Antonio Cassese, the former president of the International Tribunal for the Former Yugoslavia, to chair an international commission of inquiry to examine the nature of the violence. He concluded that there had been crimes against humanity, gross and systematic human rights abuses. He was cautious on the question of genocide, which has a specific legal meaning that crimes were committed with the specific intent to eliminate an ethnic or racial group. In addition, he gave me an envelope with fifty-one names that he said might properly be passed to the prosecutor of the ICC.

I went to the Security Council with the report, and told them about the envelope and the list of suspects. "I have not opened the envelope," I said. "And I suggest you don't open it, either. I'm not even going to give it to you. I will send it on to the prosecutor."

The Council passed a resolution formally referring the situation to the ICC, and I sent the unopened letter to the prosecutor, who later issued indictments for the crimes in Darfur following his own investigations. Among them was the president of Sudan.

Critics are correct that most of the early cases are from Africa. But that does not mean that Africa is being targeted. As I tried to make clear at the 2010 review conference in Kampala, which added a definition of aggression to the statute, the ICC is simply needed more in Africa because of the weaknesses of its judicial systems. As these systems strengthen, there will be less need for the ICC. But until then, as we saw once again in the role of the court in Libya in 2011, it provides a useful alternative.

Much as the U.S. opposition to international criminal law resembles an act of faith, there are some advocates of prosecution that put it above any other consideration. "No peace without justice" is a cry sometimes heard in these circles. As we discovered in the tribunals for the former Yugoslavia and Rwanda in the 1990s, criminal prosecution may be used as a substitute for real action. In Yugoslavia it was in part an expression of outrage at Europe's inability to prevent massacres on its own doorstep; in the case of Rwanda, it was, perhaps, an expression of regret at failing even to try.

Yet the idea that all crimes against humanity can and should be prosecuted in international tribunals is naive. In the first place, the ICC statute makes it clear that international institutions should get involved only when national institutions fail. But a more interesting question is whether international involvement can actually undermine hopes for peace. This is the argument that one sometimes hears in the context of peace negotiations: if a leader has an indictment hanging over his head, what incentive is there for him to strike a deal in which he would lose his privileged position?

My own view is that the *threat* of an indictment is an important deterrent against abhorrent conduct, or can encourage a leader to change his behavior. If an indictment is issued too early, however, it can negate such leverage. This was a concern that we faced in Sudan with President Bashir. In Bosnia, it would have been impossible to get an agreement if Slobodan Milošević had been indicted before the Dayton negotiations. Holding off on a possible indictment, however, is not the same as granting an amnesty.

What causes much misunderstanding in these situations is the assumption that, if you are unwilling to prosecute, then you are willing to give amnesties. In 1999, in Sierra Leone, the group demanding amnesty was the Revolutionary United Front, headed by Foday Sankoh. This group was notorious for its use of child soldiers, brutal mass rapes, and tens of thousands of amputations. It was inconceivable that the UN could lend its authority to such an amnesty.

The peace negotiations had reached an advanced stage without my involvement, and I did not want to derail the process completely. But the prospect of amnesties crossed a line. I took the very unusual step of instructing my special representative to Sierra Leone, Francis Okelo, to write into the agreement *by hand* that, for the UN, there could be no amnesty for genocide, war crimes, or crimes against humanity. The incident crystalized my views on the subject, and I later gave similar instructions to all my representatives and envoys engaged in peace negotiations to avoid such situations in the future.

As it happened, Sankoh broke that and other agreements. Military intervention by Britain and Nigerian forces ended the conflict a year later. He was later charged before the special court for Sierra Leone with seventeen counts of war crimes and crimes against humanity, but he had a stroke and died before he could stand trial. As the prosecutor grimly noted, Sankoh enjoyed the peaceful end that he denied to so many others.

As I delivered my Nobel Prize lecture in 2001, I sought a way to link all of our grand aspirations for the organization to something more concrete, more real. And so I spoke of a girl born that day in Afghanistan. That girl's mother would hold her and feed her, comfort her and care for her—just as any mother would anywhere in the world. In such basic acts, humanity knows no divisions. Yet to be born a girl in Afghanistan in 2001 was to begin life centuries away from the prosperity that part of humanity has achieved, and under conditions many would consider inhuman.

Today's real borders are not between nations but between powerful and powerless, free and fettered, privileged and humiliated. The United Nations and its secretary-general cannot right all these injustices, but it is his or her job to speak to all the peoples of the world, and to speak for them when larger forces ignore them.

One of my predecessors in the post of secretary-general, Dag Hammarskjöld, said in 1954 that the United Nations was created not to bring humanity to heaven but to save it from hell. In the aftermath of World War II, with the world divided by a new Cold War and the looming prospect of a nuclear confrontation, his modesty was as ambitious as it was necessary.

Today, however, the UN has to be about more than simply saving succeeding generations from the scourge of war. That concern is only the first line of the Charter. In the lines that follow, it stresses the need to reaffirm faith in fundamental human rights, in the dignity and worth of the human person. The Charter was also a promise "to promote social progress and better standards of life in larger freedom." I took those final words, "in larger freedom," as the title of my most important report on UN reform, which was ably supervised by Robert Orr and Stephen Stedman. In that report, I argued that the UN must continue to play a role in peace and security, but that must be matched by its commitment to human rights and development.

Though the organization remains in many ways a club of states, in all that we do the human being must be at the center. This is an evolution in thinking about the UN, but it reflects transformations that have taken place within states themselves: the rise of democracy and human rights, the acceptance of the Responsibility to Protect.

Throughout all these changes, and of all the difficulties we confronted during my tenure as secretary-general, perhaps the most sustained problem was the management of expectations. This problem was, in part, a difficulty we had in dealing with the media. But it was also a structural issue because in many ways there are two UNs. The first UN is the organization, the Secretariat, headed by the secretary-general. The second UN is the member states. If things go well, everyone is keen to take credit. But all too often it is only that first UN that gets blamed, even though it depends on the second UN for all of its resources and, indeed, its political direction and power to act decisively.

At the same time, the UN needs to be wary of raising expectations about what it can achieve. Within the Secretariat, statements are sometimes issued that create the impression that we expect to save humanity overnight. This can be dangerous and member states are sometimes complicit in this. We learned some of these lessons in Bosnia, when the Council declared safe havens that were not safe. Srebrenica has become synonymous with that disjunction between words and deeds.

We have not always lived up to our own words. But perhaps that is the fate of the UN: to disappoint the expectations of those who see it as the panacea to the world's problems, but to succeed, however incompletely, in giving voice to aspirations of individual men and women struggling in every country to live lives of dignity and opportunity, free of the threat of conflict and repression.

THE FATE OF
THE CONTINENT
Africa's Wars, Africa's Peace

T he Nigerian secret servicemen leaped into the three black Peugeots after they bundled us into the middle car. The driver hit the accelerator so hard that it felt as though we might take off into the night sky. We quickly breached one hundred miles per hour, and as we took the corners, the driver was oblivious to the justifiably anxious reflexes of Lamin Sise, one of my most trusted advisors, who was seated beside me. At every left turn his body was pushed heavily against mine. At every right turn, mine did the same against his. We didn't know where they were taking us, and as the car swung through each harassing curve, something heavy slid in the trunk with the weight of a boulder, hitting one side, then the next.

I didn't want the Nigerian secret serviceman to understand what we were saying, so I now spoke in French. "Where is Nick?" I asked, involuntarily wrestling with the forces of gravity in the speeding car. Nick Panzarino was my bodyguard.

"He's in the car in front," Lamin assured me. It turned out Lamin did not actually know this, or even if Nick had made it into the three-car convoy, such was the pace at which the Nigerians had moved us.

There was a pause in our dialogue as we took in our surreal situation. "He's going rather fast," I said casually to Lamin, noting the stressed speedometer as we blasted through the streets of Abuja.

"Yes, he is," Lamin politely agreed, nodding in the style that one remarks upon the weather. The situation suddenly seemed comic: we were talking in French so we could not be understood, but banally discussing the speed as if we were commenting on the taste of our morning tea.

"What is that in the back?" I asked.

"I caught a glimpse as we were getting in," Lamin said, glancing at me with some trepidation, albeit still with that good-humored twinkle this Gambian always carried in his eyes. "I'm pretty sure each car is carrying a heavy machine gun."

Earlier that night in June 1998, at 9:30 p.m., an unknown Nigerian secret service officer—an agent of the five-year, brutal military regime of the recently deceased General Sani Abacha—unexpectedly knocked on the door of Lamin's Abuja hotel room. "Sir, I'm here to inform you that the Secretary-General is to see Mr. Moshood Abiola immediately," he said. When Lamin came to my room it was clear something was going on.

"Are you here to say good-night?" I asked him, smiling.

"I'm afraid it's no longer a good night," Lamin replied, before telling me what we now had to do.

M oshood Abiola had been imprisoned and in solitary confinement since 1994. Previously he had been a millionaire businessman reveling in the most extravagant of lifestyles, acquired through a long-lasting and close relationship with Nigeria's military governments. But in 1993, there was a short-lived attempt to introduce democracy, and Abiola entered the presidential race. When Abiola looked entirely set to win, the final and full count was never allowed by the reigning military government of President Ibrahim Babangida, even though he had set up the elections in the first place. Abiola backed down quietly, but the vote changed his relationship with the government. He had acquired an unprecedented swell of support from many sides of the ethnic and religious divides that criss-crossed Africa's most populous country.

When President Babangida was ousted from power and replaced by General Sani Abacha later that year, in the midst of Nigeria's deepening financial crisis, the new president dissolved the institutions that had been formed to move the country toward a semblance of democracy—the parliament, the thirty state governments, and every single local council—and declared all political parties illegal. But in the unfolding chaos of Abacha's rule, Abiola stepped forward in 1994 and, on the basis of the thwarted 1993 elections, announced to a huge crowd of supporters in Lagos that he was the legitimate leader and president of Nigeria.

He was immediately arrested and charged with treason and spent the next four years in solitary confinement. During this time, he was denied access to even a radio, saw no one from his family from 1995 onward, was unable to talk to anyone else, and was shown only one newspaper article: a report on the assassination of one of his wives in 1996. The only other reading materials he had were a Bible and a Koran.

Abacha was as illegitimate a ruler as one might have the misfortune to come across—extremely corrupt, and prone to eccentric and self-indulgent behavior on a scale that only Nigeria's crony-capitalist oil wealth could sustain. He loosely promised the return of democratic elections, including to me personally after I became secretary-general in 1997, but persistently reneged on such pledges. Opponents and suspected opponents were arrested, and the ranks of political prisoners swelled, as did the number of victims of politically motivated murders at the hands of his security forces.

But on June 8, 1998, Abacha unexpectedly died. General Abdulsalam Abubakar was installed as his replacement the next day. I had met

Abubakar previously, when he was accompanying Abacha at a summit in Lomé, Togo, in January 1997. He had once served as a UN peacekeeping officer as part of the UN Interim Force in Lebanon, so we had a common past in peacekeeping, which I used to get us talking. I found him reasonable in his outlook and straight speaking, in contrast to the strange, quiet character of Abacha. At one point, when the president left the room, I pressed upon Abubakar the importance of releasing political prisoners. Abacha had only sighed away my repeated calls for greater freedoms and the introduction of democracy, and I hoped influencing his advisors might at least increase the pressure upon the Nigerian president.

But now Abubakar was president, and he, as he later revealed to me, was scared. The country was entirely isolated internationally after repeatedly refusing to change its political course or release political prisoners, and could count on little outside help; it was in a terrible financial position with a cripplingly high debt; Abacha had antagonized the country's many power bases, which had brought growing unrest and violence onto the streets; the military (dominated by the Hausa ethnic group) was used to its privileged position in society and was not going to give this up easily; and while Abubakar recognized the necessity of democracy to ensure the country's political sustainability, a mismanaged and sudden introduction of elections could bring even more instability. Abacha had disingenuously set the date of October 1, 1998, for a transition to democracy, which, everyone agreed, he fully intended to miss. But Abubakar, with his more genuine agenda, was now beholden to this deadline. One way or another, he needed a carefully managed way out of this very difficult situation.

Part of the problem for Abubakar was how to deal with the imprisoned Abiola. If released, he could still upend the political balance in the country if he demanded the presidency as he had before. Such a move would be backed by his mainstay of supporters in the southwest of the country, but almost certainly rejected by the military.

When particularly sensitive meetings were scheduled in my diary—often taking place away from the office and at my New York residence—they would simply be entered in the record of appointments as "Blocked (private) (residence)." A few weeks after Abubakar came to power—on June 22, 1998, at 3:30 p.m.—I had one of these sessions with Nigeria's foreign minister, Tom Ikimi. In the comfort of my living room, he conveyed a message from Abubakar: The president hoped I could help him exploit the current opportunity provided by Abacha's death, Ikimi said, to assist his plan to move Nigeria out of its current predicament. He wanted to return Nigeria to a position of reasonable standing in the region and internationally, to end the country's misrule, and to usher in democracy. But he also wanted to extend the timetable for elections to ease the process of change—and he wanted my public support for this.

Ikimi's style was unrecognizable in comparison to the one he had displayed while serving Abacha. Previously, he had lectured me and others, at length, on how the internal affairs of Nigeria were solely the government's business. That bold front was now giving way to realism: a recognition of the truly interdependent world of which Nigeria was a part. My first thought concerned Abiola. He could not be a casualty of this transition, or it would not be a transition at all. He had all but won the first real attempt at democratic elections, retained significant support, and his imprisonment had caused him to become a symbol for those demanding political change in the country. Continuing to imprison him would mean the antithesis of any progress toward genuine democracy and the rule of law.

"I'm willing to publicly give my approval for the president's plan," I said, as Ikimi's eyes visibly lit up. "But only if Abiola is released." Ikimi looked taken aback. But he replied that if I came to Abuja personally to voice my support of Abubakar's election proposals, then Abiola could be released. I accepted the invitation to visit. I would play whatever small role I could to aid the end of a military dictatorship; particularly in Nigeria, which had suffered enough from military rule, after an exhausting series of coups that had ridden roughshod over the country since 1960.

Due to my schedule, we flew on June 29 to Abuja from Vienna on a plane provided by the Nigerian government. They were clearly keen for us to come, as it was a brand-new and lavishly furnished aircraft, designed for the president's personal use. On arrival I met with President Abubakar to discuss the situation. He reemphasized everything Ikimi had said in New York, and I pushed him to move on his promises, to open up the political system and to bring in civil society, to build the momentum in his favor in order to keep the country on course. He replied positively but said the October 1 date for a transition to democracy was too soon for credible elections. I counseled him that if he postponed the date, he would have to publicly provide a new and detailed timetable and communicate very clearly to everyone why this delay was necessary. I also reminded him that Abiola needed to be released if he was to obtain international goodwill—and mine.

On this Abubakar wavered slightly. He pledged his willingness to release Abiola immediately, but under the condition that he made no attempt to claim the presidency. I could see the general's concerns: if Abiola came out and demanded to be instated as president, it could cause a deep and violent split that, given the fragile conditions, could take the country goodness knows where. Abiola's release was necessary, but it also needed to be a calm process.

I asked if I could see Abiola, to discuss this problem, and Abubakar said a time would be arranged. It was later that night that Lamin heard the knock on his door, and we found ourselves speeding along Abuja's dark roads to Abiola's current holding place. We pulled up at a location near the presidential palace, and sullen guards walked us inside the guest house–like building into a simple, bare room with white walls, where I found him sitting quietly.

After exchanging greetings, I explained that I was in discussions with the president and the junta concerning current developments in Nigeria, and that I was pressing them for his release. He seemed remarkably ambivalent. I asked if he wanted to claim the presidency once he was out, which I told him I was confident would happen very soon. He said he was not sure, commenting that he thought the junta would be afraid if he did. He seemed to be hedging his bets, not wanting to be drawn into a firm answer.

Suddenly, he switched his interest and asked, "But who are you?"

"I'm Kofi Annan," I replied. "I'm the secretary-general of the United Nations."

"What happened to the other one? The Egyptian?" He said, surprised. I had mistakenly assumed that Abiola had been told who was coming to see him and why. All he had been told was that an "important person" would visit. It was amazing the isolation in which this man had been kept—the regime was so used to keeping him in the dark, they maintained his ignorance of anything going on outside even now.

Once he realized who I was, he became more enthusiastic. He also became more explicit regarding his plans. He said he had no intention of claiming the presidency. All he wanted to do was go to Mecca to pray and give thanks. But he emphasized that he would make no commitment in writing. If he did so, he felt this would destroy his reputation. But he said he was willing to give the same personal assurance to President Abubakar.

I conveyed this message to Abubakar the next day, but he was still hesitant. I explained that a free Abiola, who had no interest in upsetting the situation, would be a calming influence on his supporters, not an agitating one. I then told him that I would be announcing in my departing speech to the press that the president had promised me he would release Abiola and the other political prisoners very soon. Whether this speech reinforced his credibility or undermined it would now depend upon him.

In the ensuing press conference, given shortly before our flight out of the country, I did as promised. But I also revealed that Abiola had, indeed, told me that he had no intention of claiming any right to the presidency, further removing any justification Abubakar held for not releasing him and also smoothing the path ahead with Abiola's more hard-line supporters. I was also trying to ease the concerns of those Nigerians who feared Abiola's return.

On our return journey, everything seemed set for Abiola's release. But tragedy struck a week later when Abiola collapsed and died during a meeting with the U.S. under-secretary of state Thomas Pickering. Despite the earnest intentions we had detected in Abubakar, the timing could only be considered suspicious. However, an international team of pathologists established that it was the result of a heart condition, and there was no foul play—other than the fact, I thought, that Abiola had been denied adequate medical care throughout his incarceration. Either way, he was yet another casualty of the systematic violations of a whole range of human rights that are inevitable under personalized and oppressive regimes.

On leaving the country after that final press conference, we found the Nigerians had lent us a very different airplane than the one in which we had arrived. It was old, run-down, and did not look entirely safe. On seeing it, Kieran Prendergast, my insightful and witty under-secretary-general for political affairs, turned to me, laughing through his beard: "Well, you've done what they needed you for. Who cares about you now?" Indeed, within fifteen minutes of taking off, the flaps jammed in a mechanical failure, and the pilot told us that we had to return and change aircraft.

But it was not a false start for Nigeria. Abubakar followed through in the months later. Political prisoners were released, and the military regime's system of oppression began to lift more each day. Elections to the national assembly were held by the end of the year; Abubakar voluntarily stepped down as he always said he would and, in May 1999, presidential elections were held. The result was a reformist African leader, Olusegun Obasanjo, carried into office by popular vote, in a new democratic system that still endures today.

THE CHALLENGE OF AFRICAN GOVERNANCE: BIG MEN VERSUS THE RULE OF LAW

Nigeria's transition is one of many stories indicative of the fact that elections alone are not enough to transform societies into functioning and legitimate democracies. What is needed are, on the one hand, a set of governing institutions and rules, which have to be built up over time, that protect the results of elections and so the rights of people; and, on the other hand, responsible and accountable leadership that serves the people. In short, the transformation of African democracies requires good governance that builds the rule of law, not the rule of force or the rule of one man. Since independence, however, these characteristics have long been in short supply in Africa. Instead, a system of rule whereby power and authority was built around the personality of the leader has prevailed throughout much of this time. It is a destructive form of rule, most commonly brought into being following illegal seizures of power.

Zimbabwe was a prime example of this. In 1965, the white-minority government of Southern Rhodesia (later Zimbabwe) unilaterally declared independence from Great Britain, thwarting the British intent of building a multiracial democratic system as part of the decolonization process. From 1970, Robert Mugabe and Joshua Nkomo led an armed rebellion against the white minority government, with victory for the freedom fighters arriving in 1980. Mugabe took office as prime minister in that year, and then as Zimbabwe's first executive president in 1988—a position that he still holds.

What made Mugabe such an impressive revolutionary leader also made him an autocratic and ultimately dangerous president for Zimbabwe's people. The need for unity, the aversion to pluralism, the distaste for division that the revolutionary experience brings, meant that his rule unfolded in an increasingly autocratic style.

But the perils of this personalized form of rule only became fully apparent from the late 1990s, when he launched a series of aggressive and disastrous land reforms. In the 1980s and early 1990s, Zimbabwe was arguably one of the best-performing countries in Africa in terms of human development. These misguided reforms led to a crippling of the economy and an extraordinary decline in the standard of living and health for Zimbabwe's citizens. But the idea of Mugabe's authority was too entrenched in the political system and in his own mind for there to be any question of his stepping down. Zimbabwe's political institutions were not strong enough to allow any viable means for curtailing his rule or ensuring his removal. Brutal repression increased in Zimbabwe in order to uphold Mugabe's power in the face of unrest.

Pressure from outside, among other African leaders, was slow in coming and feeble. This was largely because of the reverence in which Mugabe was held across Africa due to his heroic revolutionary achievements. Furthermore, he had directly helped the leaders of other freedom movements in the past, such as in Namibia, South Africa, and Mozambique, whose governments were now run by the very same people. In the community of African leaders, he was effectively the foreman of a union of freedom fighters.

The worst feature of this system of rule is that even when the figure in power might seem like a good and desirable leader, such men can, and often do, change. This then leaves the people exposed to dangers from which they have no institutional protection. This was the way it went with Mugabe. His major misdemeanors as a ruler only emerged two decades after he took office.

I personally observed Mugabe's leadership transformation, from a clearly sensible and calculating style into one of irascible, even paranoid, defensiveness. Mugabe's political character, forged in revolutionary war in the Zimbabwean bush, was one that compelled him to hit back when threatened. This was his style. As he grew older, this trait, combined with the escalating criticisms of the outside world, drove an ever-deepening obstinacy in his destructive domestic policies.

I began my time as secretary-general with good personal relations with Mugabe. Even in the midst of the turmoil in Zimbabwe, I saw a value in having this cordial relationship with him—it allowed another potential "way in" for the international community to make him change course. But I may have lost this asset after I commissioned a study on the brutal slum clearances in Harare. Anna Tibaijuka, the head of the United Nations Human Settlements Programme (UN-Habitat), conducted the study, producing findings that were frank and hard-hitting regarding the government's culpability. After that, Mugabe, long wary of British influence in Zimbabwe, accused Tibaijuka of being a British spy sent to Zimbabwe to do Tony Blair's bidding.

Zimbabwe acutely demonstrates the danger of relying on the value of any one man for the health of a country. It is only in the building of representative, responsible, and accountable institutions—with a power, sanctity, and life span greater than that of any individual—that citizens can entrust their collective fate. Leaders like Nelson Mandela understood this. Mandela stepped down without hesitation after one term, citing the very same reason: institutions were always more important than any individual.

In its origin, support for the Big Man system as the solution to African problems derived almost entirely not from a genuine regard for the capacity of such individuals but the requisites of subservience to these autocrats and dictators, for fear of one's status and life. But over time this produced a sense of political culture: these Big Men were how Africa best dealt with its challenges—a conceit pandered to for many years by both Africans and outsiders.

The problems of Africa, however, have always stemmed from a lack of institutions: a lack of the institutional resources necessary to deal with the complex political, social, and economic problems faced on the continent. But irresponsible, unaccountable personalized systems of rule are the enemy of these. Cultivating the authority of a single individual over an entire and diverse population means that any institution that empowers the population's various constituencies has to be blocked or crushed. It means institutions that uphold a system for the peaceful transfer of power between political parties and between leaders have to be eroded or eradicated. Civil society institutions, organizations, and activists independent of the state, and so beyond the control of the Big Man, can never be allowed to flourish. Free enterprise, underpinned by free societies and systems of regulation and law independent of the day-to-day whims of the leader—an essential feature for private sector–driven development— cannot be allowed.

This is the core of why I have long seen Africa's problems as deeply intertwined. The problems of coups, the mismanagement of economies, brutal regimes, the continual violations of human rights, and underdevelopment are all mutually reinforcing. True leadership means institution building: the hard, enduring work of constructing the many forms of government institutions and the independent organizations of civil society necessary for Africa's problems to be met. True leadership means throwing all of one's effort into the mammoth political work of peacefully distributing power between different factions, groups, and constituencies for the common good. True leaders are those who seek to build the power of Africa's people—not their personal power.

But there were few African heads of government who did this in the years after decolonization. This is where colonialism did play an important, destructive role, as it created many of the structural conditions for the politics that followed. This is not to soften African responsibility, which I still emphasize as paramount, but to falsify the suggestion that this system of rule is ingrained in the African psyche and in African culture. Instead, it emerged from the complications caused by externally imposed structures.

The 1885 Congress of Berlin saw the colonial powers divide up Africa into territorial units that made no sense on the ground—partitioning kingdoms, states, and communities from one another, and arbitrarily melding others. Furthermore, the colonial system introduced laws and institutions that were designed to exploit local divisions to enable the strength of the colonial authority, rather than attempts to bridge these divides.

It was these arbitrary boundaries and these divisive institutions and systems of law that most newly independent African countries inherited in the 1960s. The resulting challenge of creating genuine national identities within the colonial-created boundaries gave too much opportunity for the new African leaders to assert the value of their personalities in papering over these divisions. In the absence of any organic unity, some African countries turned to the authority of individual rulers instead of attempting to cultivate political pluralism. The colonial state had not encouraged representation or participation, and neither did the leaders who followed.

Compounding this trajectory in African politics was the continent's revolutionary experience. The struggles for independence, valiant in their purpose, created problems for the politics of the postcolonial era. For freedom fighters, and for good reason, unity was to be prized above all in the fight against colonialism, such was the internal discipline necessary to lead a successful campaign for independence.

This approach to the organization of revolutionary cadres and the mobilization of supporters for a common cause was translated into peacetime politics following these wars. Thus, the very qualities that made revolutionary leaders effective during times of armed struggle often rendered them poor rulers in peacetime. Into the postcolonial state they carried with them the rhetoric of absolute unity beneath their authority. They suppressed even the notion of division.

Thus, revolutionary movements, united in the goal of decolonization, gave way to one-party states, pretending away the divisions of their societies and providing further justification for personalized rule.

The campaign for African democracy is sometimes tripped up by ideas of cultural relativism. The reasoning goes as follows: democracy is a Western value, not a naturally African one. As with views emphasizing the culpability of colonialism, this serves only those who desire the moribund status quo. More important, such arguments are built upon entirely bogus and defunct reasoning.

In fact, in Africa the values of pluralism and collective decision making are ingrained in our oldest traditions, identifiable in the deepest vestiges of African culture across the continent. The traditional means of dispute resolution is to meet on the grass, under a tree, and to stay until a solution agreed by all can be found. In Ghana, we have a saying: one head alone is not enough to decide. In reality, African communities from the village level upward have traditionally decided their course through free discussion, carefully weighing different points of view until consensus is reached. Even in the system of rule by chiefs, the leader still had to govern with the will and support of the people, otherwise the chief could be removed.

The concept of *ubuntu*, a Xhosa word describing a notion that all Africans instinctively relate to, is also highly relevant. It is an element of African humanism, loosely translating into a notion of collective dependence: "I am because we are." It is a philosophy that denotes a sense of an equal share of all in society and in one another, a philosophy that holds at its heart principles that translate easily into notions of liberal democracy.

In my years as secretary-general, I saw the sheer appetite in Africa for political change. But in 1997, it was mostly hidden from view, kept so by the fear of Africa's overbearing rulers and the taboo against open criticism of these powerful men. It only took the slightest act of rhetorical leadership to bring this enthusiasm to the surface. One minor but telling incident was when I was in Gabon at a press conference with mostly African journalists. One of them asked me a grating question: "Mr. Secretary-General, you often criticize Africa and African governments. But is this fair? Why do you do this?"

"I work a lot for Africa and I recognize its hardships," I replied, "but I'm an African and I reserve the right to criticize Africa and Africans. And I will keep doing this." The response from the press was immediate and spontaneous applause. At a press conference this was a very strange thing to witness. But it showed how just touching on this hidden nerve was enough to expose the real desires of Africans for accountable and responsible systems of rule.

Great strides have been made in African governance in recent years, but much more is needed. Progress is deeply uneven. In Ghana, for example, since the repeating cycle of coups was ended, there have been three successful democratic elections, each involving a peaceful transfer of power. It is no coincidence that Ghana is also the only African state to have met both the poverty and hunger components of Millennium Development Goal 1, following its successful implementation of, among other things, strong agricultural reforms. However, in 2009, the Freedom

House Report concluded that only eight African countries were fully democratic, twenty-five partially democratic, and twenty-one authoritarian. A problem is that elections have emerged in some instances as only a veneer of democracy rather than as a genuine feature of political transformation. Elections have been used to perpetuate the rule of the same dictators as before.

Good governance is not built on elections alone, but on accountable and responsible leadership—and institutions that build the rule of law. Responsibility for the future of the continent's political landscape, in regimes built upon by the rule of law over the aggrandizement of individuals, is the responsibility of Africa's people and the demands they make for themselves today. Enduring good governance is not a gift that can be given, but one that must be demanded, made, and shared by the people themselves and as a whole. Agency lies with the people. But as these and other stories show, outsiders can help as well.

Y*ou can't say this. The UN Secretary-General cannot present this to an assembly of African heads of state!"* On June 2, 1997, I was in Harare, Zimbabwe. Assembled in the audience were the heads of state and government from all of Africa, many of whom were in that position only by the grace of arms: coup-plot leaders enthroned simply because of the illegitimate power represented in their military uniforms. A brand-new secretary-general and the first black African to hold the post, I was there to carry a new, and to many a surprising, message to Africa's military governments. As I walked to the lectern, I cast my eye over the crowd and recalled those stressed words of warning regarding the speech I was about to give—poorly formed but, sadly, traditionally conceived advice from one of my senior African aides.

I decided to open the speech directly on the issue that African leaders and diplomats had conspired to ignore for too long: "Armies exist to protect national sovereignty, not to train their guns on their own people,"

I said. "Africa can no longer tolerate, and accept as faits accomplis, coups against elected governments, and the illegal seizure of power by military cliques, who sometimes act for sectional interests, sometimes simply for their own.

"Let us dedicate ourselves to a new doctrine for African politics. Where democracy has been usurped, let us do whatever is in our power to restore it to its rightful owners: the people. Verbal condemnation, though necessary and desirable, is not sufficient. We must also ostracize and isolate putschists. Neighboring states, regional groupings, and the international community all must play their part."

My long-held stance on military regimes goes back to their impact on my home country of Ghana in particular and across the continent generally. Between January 1956 and December 2001, a staggering 80 successful coups d'état took place on the continent, in addition to 108 coup attempts. Africa has many challenges—social, economic, geographical, and environmental. But in my view, and I see Africa's history as bearing this out, leadership is the ultimate cause of the plight of Africa, and the greatest destroyer of leadership and good governance in Africa has been military regimes. The perversion of democratic rule, gross abuses of human rights, and economic mismanagement—the truly great curses of Africa—stem in so many instances from this one infection: the military coup.

Military regimes are collectively the worst-offending examples of poor leadership in Africa. But there are important considerations for the role of leadership in Africa more generally. Many Africans, particularly older Africans, will give you a single, blanket explanation for why Africa has had its problems: colonialism. Many academics will also give you an explanation for why Africa is in the state that it is, often focusing on the structural factors holding it back economically and so underpinning its long-troubled position in the world.

It is true that Africa's short and intense experience of colonialism was destructive and divisive. It is also true that many African countries are landlocked and so denied the vital economic asset of direct access to seaborne trade routes—which many economists emphasize as an essential part of the explanation for Africa's previous poor economic performance as a whole. However, it is inaccurate and, worst of all, irresponsible for Africans to blame colonialism alone. Similarly, if you consider some of the great failures of African development, such economic impediments are not the heart of the problem.

Leadership, and the responsibility of Africans for it, is the lynchpin of modern African history. This is the position that has informed my diplomatic interventions in Africa to this day. Consider my home country of Ghana. Ghana won its independence from Britain in 1957, at which point its per capita income was $390. Malaysia, too, won its independence from Britain in the same year, a country with, at that time, apparently similar prospects for economic development to Ghana's but with a lower per capita income of $270. However, Malaysia went on to construct a framework of parliamentary government that formed the basis for a strong political system under which successful and prevailing economic growth could be fostered. Ghana, by contrast, went on to experience a repeating cycle of military coups, with the first striking as early as 1966, allowing the country only a sputtering process of political institutional development for many decades.

The contrasting impact of these different trajectories on the lives of all men, women, and children in these two countries is now very clear: today Malaysia has a per capita income approximately thirteen times higher than Ghana's. Taking this example, colonialism is practically irrelevant to the debate. The nub of the problem is African leadership and African institutions.

Another example is Madagascar. This island nation is free of the economic curse faced by many African countries of being landlocked and of the threats to economic prosperity that can arise from having unstable neighbors on one's border. In the late 1990s, Madagascar began to take advantage of the United States' African Growth and Opportunity Act, which offered a more beneficial arrangement for African exports. Through the creation of a special export-processing zone, and effective government policies enabling conducive conditions for business activities, almost three hundred thousand jobs were created in a very short time. But when the president, Vice-Admiral Didier Ratsiraka, lost an election, instead of stepping down, he had the port blockaded for eight months to force acceptance of his continued rule. This killed off the export-processing zone, which otherwise may have come to create a striking example of how a very poor African country could take off and break into the world market.

Africa's problems are often portrayed as if they were predetermined, as if the trials it has faced were inevitable, or, if not entirely inevitable, then made so by the colonists. But as the Madagascar story and others like it reinforce, nothing could be further from the truth. The responsibility lies with Africans, their systems of rule, and their leaders. Africa has had the experience it has, most of all, because of the decisions made by individuals and the systems of rule deliberately enacted by leaders and their supporters. Africa, the poverty of Africa, the violence of Africa, is not the inexorable product of its environment but rather the consequence of choices and decisions made by its leaders.

A frican leadership, however, was rarely blamed when I came into office. Colonialism and the economic policies of the outside world, particularly donors, were the sole source of the problem, it seemed. Worst of all, the continued fostering of an anticolonial and outsider-blaming stance was really the servant of a few inglorious individuals in Africa. Typically among ruling cliques, these men had no interest in allowing changes to the moribund status quo that ensured their narrow interests. The function of the overarching debate on the evils of colonialism in Africa was really their tool, thus diverting the people from demands for real progress. It was a backward stance, in all respects.

This is why I sought to use my position to change the debate from early on. In my first year in office, the Security Council requested a report on African issues and how the international community could strive to address the results and causes of conflict in Africa. I tasked a team of UN officials, led by a senior African official, to set about compiling this report, and they put together a document that projected all too many of the same old arguments, with the focus once again on the evils of colonialism and the failures of donors.

I was disappointed with the text, to say the least. The authors had written a report in the same manner Africans had too often adopted when presenting their case internationally. It was an out-of-date, unhelpful, and ultimately dishonest mind-set that needed breaking. But, being an African, I knew I now sat in a prime position to force a change in the African side of the debate. Africans would not be able to dismiss my voice as easily as they could others'.

On seeing the draft of the report, I called in a new team to take over the project and entirely rewrite it. Three new officials took over the lead, including, importantly, a young African, Stanlake Samkange of Zimbabwe, who represented a different mind-set to those of the older African generation. My instructions were simple: to pay the peoples of Africa the tribute of truth, by candidly assessing their challenges and aspirations. The old narrative of colonialism and the failures of donors as the chief target of blame for all Africa's ills was to go, I said.

"It's almost un-UN," commented Under-Secretary-General Karl Theodor Paschke on its release. The Africa Report was direct and frank. This was not how UN reports had been written in the past, and with its release we were shedding a tradition of overt caution in the face of diplomatic sensibilities.

"For too long, conflict in Africa has been seen as inevitable or intractable, or both," I said, when presenting the report to the Security Council on April 16, 1998. "It is neither. Conflict in Africa, as everywhere, is caused by human action, and can be ended by human action." I was applying the new tone of accountability and responsibility that the report sought to invoke. "More than three decades after African countries gained their independence," the report went on to say, "there is a growing recognition among Africans themselves that the continent must look beyond its colonial past for the causes of current conflicts. Today more than ever, Africa must look at itself."

The implication, as clear as I could make it, was that the failures and human tragedies in Africa hitherto were failures of Africans and their leaders, as much as anything else. The report noted the impact of colonialism, but as a historical factor among many, confining it to the periphery in explaining the present. It emphasized the failures of the international community, too, including the UN's failure, in helping the peoples of Africa, the failure of all to help them ensure peace and create the conditions for sustainable development. But it stated these failures as orbiting features of a core problem: internal African politics and African leadership.

Africa was my home, my identity, but I had to be a secretary-general for all regions in the world and all 192 member states, as was the function of my office. That there would be no special treatment or preferential pleading was the message I was determined to put out from the beginning of my tenure.

To accomplish the tasks of a secretary-general, one must work with the entire global community. Most people do not realize that if you define yourself narrowly—such as being concerned only with African issues—then you exclude countries from your concerns and so constrain your own agenda. Those whom you ignore will come to ignore you. But you need *everyone* to participate to get things done in a world such as ours—especially for Africa, where outside help was more vital than for any other region. Why should Latin American or Asian member states help me as a secretary-general working on only African problems? By casting myself as an African secretary-general, surrounding myself with Africans, and prioritizing mostly African issues, I would have actually been less effective for Africa than I was otherwise.

The reaction from the younger generation of Africans, and also from non-Africans, vindicated this method of tough love with my home continent. They welcomed my frank engagement in the discussions of Africa's problems, which did not lay blame unfairly at one source in the old style, a stance they, too, had felt was designed to negate African responsibility. This position earned essential credibility with other governments, particularly the wealthy donor countries, and gave my voice greater presence when I did turn to them for Africa, cajoling them for greater outside assistance. Member states now knew I was as candidly harsh on Africa's failures as I was realistically sensitive to its needs. And they knew I was as serious and intent on issues outside Africa that directly concerned them.

Following the report, progress at the highest levels of international diplomacy was kick-started: a special Security Council meeting of foreign ministers soon convened, endorsing practical solutions recommended by the report; the General Assembly, too, began producing supportive resolutions shortly after; and the Organisation for Economic Co-operation and Development (OECD) began devising new international solutions in partnership with local African efforts. It also contributed attention for impoverished countries, which set one of the enabling conditions for the establishment of the Millennium Development Goals (MDGs) in September, 2000.

As part of the ongoing follow-up discussions on the report, in November 1998 I addressed a summit in Paris. African solutions to African problems was a common refrain at these meetings—and it carried an important element of truth to it. But I knew that to succeed African countries would also have to be supported internationally. There was no way around that. Yet African defensiveness regarding colonialism muddied the waters—it led to the suggestion that development assistance may still be insidious and colonial.

This stance and the cement-firm blame of outsiders led to a position that effectively rejected outsiders while simultaneously pleading for more outside help. I wanted to shift parties away from this dysfunctional position, which was only clouding the real goal: a better Africa for the sake of Africans.

"Yes, we must have African solutions to African problems," I said at the summit, "but the test of those solutions must be in their results, not in their origins. What matters is not who provides the solutions, but whether they provide lasting peace and equitable prosperity." We had to realize the danger of an anachronistic resentment, and focus solely on the purpose of the whole endeavor that we all professed to share. The point was that it was high time for us all—Africans and non-Africans alike—to grow up.

When I delivered the speech at Harare, Africa's heads of state felt deeply uneasy even just to hear my mention of criticism of military regimes. Salim A. Salim, the secretary-general of the Organization of African Unity, commented: "You're the only one who could have said that and gotten away without being lynched! No other African would dare, and we wouldn't have taken it from anyone else."

"Someone had to," I replied.

But Salim was right. There was a power in the role of the secretary-general that was invaluable, that gave you an ability to speak—and be heard—when others were too constrained, whether by convention or coercion. When I spoke in Harare, I knew where my best allies were. I was speaking as much to the gallery as I was to the audience of African heads of state. It was among the former, where representatives of African civil society sat, that the most applause rang out; this was a stark contrast to the deafening silence emanating from many of the African leaders sitting below. By presenting the idea in the words of the secretary-general of the United Nations, I was giving like-minded leaders in civil society a rallying point to gather around, giving encouragement and weight to their own voices.

A year later I heard Frederick Chiluba, the president of Zambia, give a speech to the OAU. He spoke of every game having rules, such as in football, where those who misbehave are given red cards. A red card system should be applied to leaders who came to power through coups d'état, he argued. It would not seem striking today, but at the time it was really quite something to hear an African head of state suddenly criticizing the phenomenon so openly. The genie of open debate was out of the bottle, and things then changed quickly: In 1999 and 2000 the OAU agreed on a series of important declarations rejecting nonconstitutional changes of government. These were then incorporated into the new constitution of the African Union (AU), which officially came into being in 2002. Thus, within the AU was enshrined the principle that no member state could hold membership of the organization following any military seizure of government or unconstitutional transfer of power. A coup meant you would be immediately kicked out as a matter of course. I hoped and expected the UN to follow the AU's lead but that has yet to happen.

We were still going to have coups in Africa, of course. And we did—several. But now there were consequences. The coups in Togo, Mauritania, Comoros, Madagascar, Niger, Mali, and Guinea all resulted in immediate suspension from the AU for these countries, and diplomatic isolation and other sanctions were brought to bear against them. The AU exists to promote regional integration so that the continent's countries can jointly step forward to overcome the challenges ahead. It is an important collective organization for all members, and exclusion from its benefits means something. The impact of this exclusion measure became writ into the calculations of even the most recalcitrant rulers with only the narrowest of interests in staying in power. It was suddenly harder for new juntas to perpetuate their rule.

The impact on the military junta of Mauritania—which seized power in August 2005—was immediately evident. Following this putsch, Mauritania was suspended from the AU, and the regional organization began negotiating sanctions. The junta declared the current government was a transitional measure. Its purpose, they said, was to pave the way for a new democratic system of government for the first time in Mauritania's history. It would be formed as soon as possible in elections in which no one in the military would be permitted to run. We had heard this kind of thing before, so I remained skeptical regarding Mauritania. But in 2007, the junta did, indeed, fulfill this promise and stepped aside to allow elections and a democratically elected civilian government.

Rather than a military regime bent on holding power for all time, the Mauritanian junta seemed to genuinely believe that they had to pass the mantle of power to civilian rule as quickly as possible. African putchists in the old days had always hung on as long as they could, in expectation of little sanction or forfeit. Idi Amin in Uganda, Omar al-Bashir in Sudan, Sani Abacha in Nigeria, Muammar Gaddafi in Libya: they seized power with an empty slate on which to scrawl the timeline of their future rule. The promise of the Mauritanian junta and their follow-through was a stark change, and one we can credit to the new international arrangement crafted by the AU.

In Mauritania, the impact of this progress was spoiled, however. In 2008, there was another coup. It was launched by the same perpetrators of the 2005 putsch, unhappy with the policies of the new president who had dismissed them from the leadership of the military. But to me, this only proved the deeply rooted, malign attitude of the coup-plot leaders, favoring their own position over the political health of the country—

making it even more remarkable that they so cooperatively brought in elections in 2007. The effort of African leaders to implement a system that imposed some sanction on military rulers was making it harder for them to consider perpetuating their rule.

If it was having a serious effect in deterring military rule in Mauritania, which had suffered over ten coups and coup attempts since independence in 1960, then it was having an untold deterrent effect across Africa. In the microcosm of even the flawed developments of the Mauritania case, we were watching the beginnings of a continentwide transformation, improving the chances for a better-governed Africa.

HALF A MILLION RWANDAN GHOSTS: CRISIS IN KENYA

"Mr. President, over one thousand people are dead. It's time to make a deal," I said.

I was meeting privately with Mwai Kibaki, the president of Kenya. My body was exhausted, fatigued by an interrupted recovery from a microbial infection and a fever that had bowled me over a few weeks before. This was almost my last play. The game now had to end. We needed an agreement on the transformation of the Kenyan political system. Otherwise, the country would be unable to bear what seemed sure to come.

It was early 2008, over a year since I had completed my second and final term as head of the UN—a time when I thought my days of hammering out bargains between presidents and prime ministers would surely be over. But I had now been in Kenya for a costly and bloody thirty-nine days in an attempt to mediate a peace deal.

It had all begun with the presidential elections in December 2007, the fourth since the establishment of multiparty politics in the country in

1992. These were held simultaneously alongside parliamentary and local elections—and the stakes were high. But the voting was carried out in a remarkably peaceful fashion. Voting on December 27 contrasted brightly with previous elections marred by bloody fits of local violence. In this peaceful election, many saw Kenya taking another stride forward with an increasingly functioning democracy underpinned by a growing economy. Kenya was sustaining its reputation as one of the more successful of African states.

But when the election result was announced and foul play was called, a dark side of Kenyan society erupted. Beneath the vision of a peaceful Kenya there was a different reality buried deep in its economic and political structures. Twin blades of inequality and crony-capitalist politics had long combined to shear deep grievances, resentment, and desperate competition along Kenya's ethnic contours. Corruption among politicians and the civil service had become a monster in Kenya. Since independence, Kenya was ruled by interchanging ethnic cliques who, copying the self-enrichment of the white settlers before them, used public office to accumulate wealth for themselves, their kin, and their tribe. At a changeover of power, such unfairness seemed to justify a redirection of resources in equal measure to the tribe of the new rulers. Corruption grossly pretended to be righteous, and swelled with every passing government.

That was the situation for the elites at the top. The view from the bottom was of a system built on an immense pile of corruption that crushed the opportunities of ordinary people. By 2007, this corrupt consumption of state and business resources meant little trickled down. The typical Kenyan senior civil servant or CEO, for example, used his position to pay the school fees and hospital bills of around fifty of his kinsmen. This was in contrast to the 55 percent of Kenya's population who now lived on less than a dollar a day. So deep were most people in the pool of poverty that it would take just a ripple in the economy for them to succumb. Only the corrupt distribution of wealth via bloodline and ethnic kinship could provide the guaranteed, sustained means for survival. But in the winner-takes-all dynamic of Kenyan politics, until your tribe had power, you had to wait.

In so moribund a system, corruption was essential to livelihoods across the board. For most Kenyans, life was a bitter struggle through the narrow, fixed avenues cast by the silhouette of tribe. But this was usually a hidden struggle. It was so ingrained in Kenyan life that to most outsiders it was invisible; indeed, Kenyans themselves barely mentioned tribe or tribal affiliation in day-to-day interactions.

This was why, despite the warning signs, few saw what was coming. The long-held preeminence of Kikuyu elites in Kenyan politics meant that, in the run-up to the 2007 election, the opposition campaign positioned itself as geared to overthrowing this inequality. At the local level, particularly among the many poor communities, this political framing of the campaign increasingly developed into a sense of a coming reckoning, of "41 against 1"—referring to the forty-one Kenyan tribes other than the dominant group, the Kikuyu.

The polls put the opposition Orange Democratic Movement (ODM), led by Raila Odinga, of the Luo tribe, far ahead of the Party of National Unity (PNU), led by President Mwai Kibaki, a Kikuyu. This expectation of change, it emerged later, was accompanied not only by a sense of entitlement for the disadvantaged tribes but also a sense of imminent justice on the ground, where the entitled, in their view, would soon have their resources rightfully taken from them. This was particularly so for the Luo, one of the three largest tribes, who had repeatedly been left out of the rotating ethnic hegemony of Kenyan politics that had most benefited the Kikuyu and the Kalenjin.

But on December 30, President Kibaki was pronounced the unexpected victor, and now the thunder struck.

The result flew in the face of the polls and the results of the parliamentary elections, which had put ODM well in the lead. Most were sure the vote had been rigged. The ODM and their supporters declared the election a sham, demanding redress, while the president was hurriedly sworn in at night, at a ceremony attended by a handful of people on December 30. Denying any wrongdoing, he demanded the opposition acquiesce in defeat.

A vast number of Kenyans were in desperate poverty, and their fate was being won or lost in what seemed a cheater's game of tribal musical chairs. The ultimate governor of life in Kenya was not any rule by law but the rule of bloodline—and it was along these same tribal veins that blood now poured.

It started with looting by Luo of Kikuyu businesses and homes—as if in recompense for what they had been denied—and then grew, in an escalating cycle of insecurity and tribe-on-tribe violence that dragged in all of Kenya's ethnic communities. Fear of being disallowed a turn at the feeding station of state resources was met with the equal fear of falling into the deprivation of those barred from it. Anger turned to looting. Looting created insecurity. And insecurity then drove violence, brutality, and, very soon, systematic mass murder. Among other atrocities, there were reports of buses being stopped by gangs armed with machetes, forcing passengers to show their identification cards. These revealed family name and paternal birthplace, thus indicating tribe. If your card gave the wrong answer, you were then beaten or killed.

Before this all started I was in Accra, Ghana. No longer subject to the grueling calendar of a secretary-general, I was visiting my home country for the Christmas period. Like most, I was entirely unaware of the storm brewing in Kenya. Nane reminded me that the Kenyan elections were being held that day. We switched on the television to catch the results. In a short space of time, we then watched the spread of violence across the country, accumulating in intensity all the way. Thirty people were trapped and murdered in a church on New Year's Day; schools were set on fire and whole villages attacked. Murder and rape were wrought on Kikuyu by Luo or Kalenjin, and vice versa. Tribe-on-tribe conflict that ran too deep, some had started to say, for there to be any hope of stopping it. Planes flying into Nairobi were almost completely empty, while vehicles leaving the country were heaving with passengers.

In the images of civilians butchered on the streets and in churches I saw Rwanda and Bosnia. In a country with a majority in extreme poverty but divided across forty-two ethnic groups, the potential for a disintegration into civil war was exposed, and across divides of a complexity akin to Somalia.

Outsiders sensed this, particularly other African leaders. Nobel Peace Prize laureate Archbishop Desmond Tutu flew in from South Africa on January 2 to attempt to mediate between Odinga and Kibaki. But despite the bloody chaos unfolding around them, they weren't ready to talk. The Kibaki camp was too obstinate in its victory, and Odinga's ODM angered that the ascent to power had been denied them. Jendayi Frazer, the U.S. assistant secretary of state for African Affairs, was sent by President Bush to visit Kenya on January 4 with similar intentions, but she, too, met with the same brick wall.

The chair of the African Union at that time was the president of Ghana, John Agyekum Kufour, and he called me over to his house in Accra to discuss the crisis. I agreed with him that he should go to Kenya as chair of the AU to see if he could trigger a break in the deadlock. Due to the Kibaki government's initial public opposition to any external mediation, Kufuor's trip was delayed for several days to ensure his visit was fully accepted by the Kenyan president. Kufour then arrived on January 8, coinciding with the visit of Benjamin Mkapa, Joachim Chissano, Ketumile Masire, and Kenneth Kaunda, the former presidents of Tanzania, Mozambique, Botswana, and Zambia, respectively.

While there, the former heads of state visited the town of Eldoret, where whole communities had already been devastated by violence. Kibaki and Odinga, however, still refused to even meet. But with the violence showing no sign of abating, Kufour managed to get them to agree to a team of African leaders who would come and help broker a solution.

The first I knew of this was on January 10, when Kufour called. "They have agreed to a team of Africans to mediate," he said. "The team I've gotten them to accept is one made up of three: Graça Machel and Benjamin Mkapa. Under the lead of Kofi Annan." After mentioning Mozambique's former minister of education and wife of Nelson Mandela, as well as the former president of Tanzania, Kufor dropped the last feature in. "Will you do it?"

I was well versed in the successes and failures of previous mediation efforts, so I agreed—on the condition that ours would be the only process involved to prevent the parties from indulging in "mediation shopping." I was drawing on my Africa Report from ten years before. African crises needed a full range of instruments for their alleviation, including the interventions of groups of friends and special mediators "to tackle new conflicts before they can expand and escalate beyond control." But the report had also stressed the danger of "rival or competing efforts, once a framework for mediation has been established." This was a common problem, which I had witnessed many times, where faction leaders gamed the situation, seizing on and switching between the opportunities presented by alternative mediators and negotiating plans, dragging out the process in their favor and at the expense of peace. With the obstacles we faced in Kenya, if this happened we would have little chance. The choice was simple, and I wanted it conveyed to the other parties: if we were not the unquestionable leaders of the process, then I wouldn't go to Kenya.

I figured then that it would probably take around two weeks to dampen the tensions and get a breakthrough in the negotiations. I told Kufour that I had to return to my home in Geneva and the office of my foundation to put my situation in order and ensure the way was clear for our mediation.

I was set to leave for Kenya on January 16, but I felt myself coming down with a fever the day before. Having just returned from Ghana, I went to the doctor to check against malaria, but I was told I was fine. Then the next day, in the car on the way to the airport, accompanied by Ruth McCoy, my resourceful and experienced aide at the foundation, my condition deteriorated suddenly. My temperature rocketed and I started shaking with fever. "Take me to the hospital," I told the driver.

I was taken to the emergency room and then admitted to the hospital. They told me I needed to complete a minimum ten-day course of drugs, administered intravenously in the hospital. "I can't wait that long," I protested, "I have to go to Kenya immediately." They said this was impossible. By now the doctor and the whole medical team had gathered at my bedside, and we were engaged in full negotiation mode. "What if I at least rest at home while I organize myself?" I suggested. They said this was also impossible. I had to stay and have the drugs fed intravenously. I stressed that there was no way I could stay ten days. What if I stayed five days, and then took the rest of the high-dose antibiotics orally? They reluctantly agreed, and five days later I was on my way, with big doses of antibiotics in my pocket.

It was not ideal. As a result of what turned out to be a microbial infection, I was in a rotten state. My body was wracked; I could feel the grip of deep fatigue settling in behind the fever alongside the impact of the antibiotics, and I slept for most of the flight. But the time in the hospital had given me some advantages. I was able to continue making a series of calls to important international parties, to ensure full and undivided support for our mediation effort—to the AU; the EU, especially the UK and France; the United States; and the UN, including Secretary-General Ban Ki-moon, who gave me his full support and allowed me to draw staff from the Secretariat. I found more staff at the Centre for Humanitarian Dialogue, including its director, Martin Griffiths. And I brought on board the former legal counsel of the United Nations, Hans Corell. I would be arriving with the fully expressed backing and authority of all the major voices of the international community behind me, so the parties would have to accept my mediation. Furthermore, the situation had become much more violent during this time, making it clear to all that an agreement was essential.

The mediation process of what was now called the Panel of Eminent African Personalities officially began with our arrival on January 22. President Yoweri Museveni of Uganda also chose this day, unexpectedly, to visit Kenya at the invitation of Kibaki. The incumbent Party of National Unity (PNU) camp was against any internationalization of the election dispute. They held power and did not want to change the status quo. So they were trying to bring in a negotiator who would dance to their tune—and Museveni was an ally of Kibaki.

Museveni called me at the Serena Hotel in Nairobi, where I had just arrived. He said he had a peace plan that both the government and the ODM were willing to work with. It was based on their first accepting the results of the elections. He then asked me to come to State House, the residence of the president of Kenya, to meet and discuss the plan.

I had seen too many ploys in my career to be caught by this. It seemed to me that Museveni and Kibaki fancied a scheme that demanded that all accept the election result, and to publicly spin my visit as endorsement of this plan. I made my excuses that I still had to call all the parties before I could make any visits. When I then called Odinga, my suspicions were confirmed. He said there was no chance they would accept Museveni as a mediator, whom they saw as biased toward Kibaki. Nor had they been consulted on this. The Museveni initiative ended there, and he left two days later.

It was estimated that over five hundred people had by then died in the violence, and the atmosphere was fraught across the country. I had no illusions: neither party wanted to deal with the other. But we needed a confidence-boosting measure quickly that would calm the mood and give the impression progress was now being made. Even if they only met in public briefly, this would be a breakthrough that we could sell to the media.

However, neither party wanted to even be seen near the other. The ODM demanded that the PNU admit fraud in the elections, while the PNU demanded that ODM accept Kibaki as president first. It was at the same time that Museveni was meeting with Kibaki that I then went to see Odinga.

"I encourage you to work with your opponent to heal and reconcile the nation," I said. "I'm meeting with the president next. I'm going to ask him to meet with you. If he agrees, I don't want any hesitation from you."

"We won't go to State House to meet him," Odinga replied. "If we do, it will appear as if we are recognizing him as the legitimate president, which he is not."

"I'll tell you what," I said, keen to avoid the firm no that always then becomes a devil to shift. "Let's just get the appointment scheduled, and then we'll worry about the protocol side." Odinga gave an accepting nod. I then saw Kibaki the next day, and told him Odinga was willing to meet with him publicly. I asked him if he would match Odinga's gesture. He agreed. I called Odinga to organize it straightaway.

Once the three of us arrived at Harambee House, the office of the president of Kenya, we met alone in one of the rooms. The country was burning, but they were reluctant to even be there. We sat for over an hour, drinking tea, and they attempted no discussion of a solution. We then walked outside to greet the press and ensure photographs were taken of their shaking hands and agreeing to launch a process of dialogue. I was acutely aware of the importance of this step: it was a confidence-building measure to send a message that the leaders were negotiating and on track toward a solution. I was offering something to quell the desperate atmosphere prevailing across the country.

This was a deliberate mask, however. The truth was they weren't ready to talk. The tension was far too deep. An attempt at negotiations directly between them would just mean personal confrontation. This could kill the whole process. After the handshake, I told them each to give me three names of those who would form their negotiating teams. This seemed to be the only way we were going to get things moving.

The two leaders agreed to launch the Kenya National Dialogue and Reconciliation (KNDR), and the negotiations between their teams began on January 29. In the five days prior to this, I had a chance to reflect on where the process had to go. I already realized the problem was not just one of disagreement between political leaders over an election result: the countrywide violence meant the problem was more fundamental, arising from the makeup of the Kenyan political system and its relationship with society. We needed a process that would address the root causes of Kenya's problems, otherwise any agreement would constitute nothing more than a delay before the next violent crisis. Our job had to be more than just to move the chairs around on behalf of the political elites. The resolution was going to have to come from an engagement with all of Kenyan society. Our mediation needed to be the beginning of a true process of political reform.

In this interim period I also began a series of meetings with representatives from Kenyan NGOs, civil society, churches, businesses, and others, promising them a transparent process in which they would be involved. It was a further calming measure, to encourage the public perception that a process was in swing that was in their interests, not just the politicians'. To all of these parties I promised that any decision or agreement between the parties would be made public as soon as it was signed. Not only did the people have the right to know what was going on, but they had to also own the mediation process if we were going to see reform.

But rearranging chairs was literally how the first negotiation session began on January 29. The plan was that Odinga and Kibaki would come together once more at a meeting to initiate the process between the negotiators. As was standard for such matters, my team arranged the table. I would sit in the middle, with Kibaki on the right, Odinga on the left. But one of the Kibaki team then came in and rearranged the chairs, bringing in the special presidential chair, which he placed in the middle. I walked in to find this scene.

"This isn't a presidential meeting," I said softly. "I'm dealing with two protagonists. Put the chairs back."

"But that's undermining the president," Francis Muthaura, the head of the public service and permanent secretary to the president, argued. Uhuru Kenyatta, Kibaki's minister for local government, then chimed in behind Muthaura, "He never goes anywhere in this country without his chair. And it always sits in the most prominent position."

"This is a political mediation. It's not business as usual," I retorted. "I'm chairing the meeting and they're to go on either side." I knew that if the ODM saw the presidential chair sitting in the middle, they would probably abandon the event. To stop a rebellion from PNU, however, I accepted that the president could still keep his chair, albeit to one side.

The lack of urgency and childish nature of these obstacles were something to behold. This was in the middle of a four-day incident of fighting in the Rift Valley that had left sixty dead. Rumors had spread of hardline PNU leaders ferrying funds to criminal organizations, including the notorious Mungiki, a Kikuyu gang. The Mungiki were now coming out of the slums and into the towns to send a brutal message to those who would threaten Kikuyu. The politicians, meanwhile, were playing with chairs.

After the principals had launched the session, we put it to the two negotiating teams that while there were fundamental differences in their positions, they could at least agree on some basic things: action had to be taken to stop the violence and to address the humanitarian crisis, and measures of some kind needed to be taken to resolve the political crisis in the disagreement between the PNU and the ODM. We also said there were clearly long-standing causes to the nationwide crisis that needed to be examined, followed by recommendations for reform to address them. The parties agreed, and we turned this into a four-point agenda for the entire KNDR process, with the fourth item of the agenda being a long-term reform program for the Kenyan political system.

We took the document outlining the four-point agenda of the KNDR and had it signed and publicly distributed on February 1, as we did with all the other agreed statements that emerged over the coming days. Kibaki was at the AU summit in Ethiopia that day, where he repeatedly attacked the stance of the opposition and only proposed positions that had been rejected outright by the ODM. Our document was a thoroughly basic agreement for talks, but we were continuing with our strategy of building confidence through feeding an image of progress to the press.

Doing anything we could to promote a sense of calm was crucial. The comparisons with Rwanda were not overblown to any that were in the country—far from it. The sense of fear among the public for a looming episode of bloodshed of a similar scale was palpable throughout the mediation process. This fear added further danger: while it gave incentive to succeed in the quest for a political solution, it also gave incentive to prepare for a coming collapse of the country's institutions. Any inflation in this morbid pessimism could itself trigger further violence as groups made efforts to aggressively protect their interests in light of increasingly bloody prospects, creating greater and greater opportunities for antagonism, clashes, and death.

After the reintroduction of multiparty politics in Kenya in 1992, every general election—with the exception of one in 2002 when there was no incumbent running for office—had witnessed some form of political violence. Yet the magnitude and scale of the latest violence shocked Kenyans and the world as a whole. The political violence was of a different character than before, shaking the foundation of the country to a point where it posed an existential threat to Kenya itself. Consequently, the public mood throughout the mediation was one of anticipation, anxiety, and fear of the unknown if mediation failed.

On February 8 an open letter to me was published in a Kenyan newspaper by a chief subeditor. She began by citing widespread fears that I might abandon my mission in Kenya because of the deep intransigence of the leaders involved. She then went on in words that well captured the fearful public mood:

> You have seen the uncertainty that has left Kenyans this vulnerable. I, for instance, feel like a little girl again, begging daddy not to leave her alone in the dark, because a monster will eat her. Annan, you have seen the monster in this country ravage its own. You have seen the degree of violence . . . You and gracious Graca—whom I nominate as the Mother of the Continent—have struck a chord with Kenyans . . . You have made political leaders commit themselves to promote peace. You must not relent in ensuring they keep their word. But being human, you are bound to be fatigued by leaders' doublespeak. We have seen the evident frustration on your face . . . This week, you have steered the talks to delicate waters— the disputed election results. This stage is described as "make or break," which triggers another bout of cold sweat. If the situation prevails, communities might be reduced to just conscripting their school-age children into their militias, to fight for survival. We shall only be driven by base instincts . . . Remember you said that every Kenyan must feel "the cloak of government." Leave us on a solid foundation for real change.

I was moved by these words when I read them, and in response I issued a public statement: I would be neither frustrated nor provoked to leave my work until the job was done. But privately for myself, Graca Machel, and Benjamin Mkapa—as well as for the other members of the overworked team that we were leading—the message only reinforced that we desperately needed real progress to calm the situation before it spiraled out of control.

Yet, despite the heat of the situation, careful and deliberative calculations still had to be made. What the official response to the contested election should be had to be decided. Should there be a full recount or a retallying of valid forms, a rerun of the presidential elections, or a forensic investigation into the results? I had already decided that any kind of rerun or recount of the election was not going to work. There was too much opportunity for further dispute and fiddling of the system. In the violent climate, such a route would also almost certainly make things worse. Nor was a rerun or recount going to solve any of the root causes of the crisis. By now I had come to the conclusion that a power-sharing deal and an amendment to the constitution was going to be the only way to get Kenya out of this bloody quagmire.

But the atmosphere in the meeting rooms and the instructions coming in from Odinga and Kibaki gave no scope for such a deal at this stage. I feared that if we went to the negotiators with the recommendation for a political deal, it would be shot down and killed straightaway. I knew that I could not directly lead them to this choice, proclaiming my preferred route at the outset. These were fiercely intelligent, independent negotiators we were dealing with, suspicious of any solution another might impose upon them. I decided, instead, that the best thing to do would be to take the negotiators through a deductive process. On February 12, I moved the negotiations to Kilaguni Safari Lodge, in the beautiful wild surroundings of Tsavo National Park. In this tranquil new location, as per my instructions, we would weigh together, as a group, the costs, benefits, and risks of each of the options available: a complete rerun of the election; a complete recount; a retally; a forensic audit of the election result; or a political settlement involving a negotiated agreement for power sharing between the parties. For this discussion I brought in Craig Jenness, director of the UN Electoral Assistance Division of the Department of Political Affairs (DPA), to present in expert detail what each option would mean in practice. We then conducted a joint evaluation of these options, with the negotiators taking the lead in weighing the implications.

As I had hoped, when the likely impact of all the options were laid out in stark terms, it was clear that anything other than a deal to share power had little to no chance of calming the situation and resolving the crisis. The other options would take too long, be too dangerous to attempt in such fraught circumstances, or would be too likely to lack credibility in the eyes of the public or the respective parties to the dispute. But the prospect of a power-sharing deal was still daunting to the negotiators—it was alien to Kenyan politics. With this in mind, on February 13 I invited Gernot Erler, a German minister of state, to speak to the negotiators and share his experiences of coalition government, which had come to form a very effective basis for German politics and was a well-established solution there to political crises.

The negotiators then came to an agreement and signed a statement on February 14. It noted that, given "there is a serious crisis in the country, we agree a political settlement is necessary to promote national reconciliation and unity." In addition to this groundbreaking consensus, the statement laid out plans for reforms that included the identification and prosecution of perpetrators of the violence, and also a truth, justice, and reconciliation commission among other judicial reforms—all of which were, in my view, essential to the longer-term process of healing required to recover from this traumatic episode. In the simple February 14 document, therefore, there were not only the beginnings of an agreement for the cessation of the immediate crisis but also the seeds of a major political and societywide reform process.

According to the Red Cross, the death count in Kenya had risen above one thousand by this time, with mass displacement alongside due to the burning of villages and the threat of armed gangs, the looting of farms and homes, as well as widespread sexual violence against men and women. Meanwhile, there was still no movement on what shape the political deal would take, but at least we now had a full agreement on the way out of the crisis: a coalition government. It was a great relief to me, not least because I was sure the other electoral options on the negotiating table would have likely triggered an escalation in the violence.

By now, I had been in Kenya much longer than anyone had planned, and there was still no end in sight. I was physically drained after my heavy course of antibiotics, but there was no chance for any respite. It was like being a hunter: as you attempt to corner your quarry, any lapse in your endeavors may allow it to slip through and escape for good.

By February 25, however, the negotiations were still deadlocked. Patience had been essential in getting us this far, but we now needed more. That morning the negotiators and the mediators, myself included, spent four hours in talks to push for the final agreement on the distribution of power in the coalition, and we got nowhere. By now it was clear what the power-sharing deal required: Kibaki would remain as president; an executive prime minister's position would need to be created, which would be occupied by Odinga; and there would need to be a coalition cabinet shared between the PNU and the ODM that reflected the balance in parliament. But there was no movement on the question of the prime minister's powers. The PNU side, in particular, was holding things back, continuing to project the argument that the power of the president could not be fettered and that the ministries should not be shared.

I was frustrated and decided it was time to throw the PNU and the ODM to the people. So I went to the press and publicly explained that I had concluded the negotiators were "not capable of resolving the outstanding issues." I said it was time for Kibaki and Odinga to conclude the negotiations face-to-face, as it was now their responsibility alone to break the deadlock.

It was a risk, as this move could have triggered an expectation that the talks would fail, inflaming the situation on the streets and in the slums. But the alternative seemed to be no deal at all, which would almost certainly then lead to a much bigger round of bloodshed, and this would take the crisis into the next stage of conflict. I had to scorch the feet of Odinga and Kibaki somehow.

I privately visited Odinga first and then Kibaki. They were not expecting this sudden move, and the prospect of negotiating face-to-face surprised them. Speaking to Odinga, I reminded him that he had all to wait for. If he worked through the compromise now, he would likely be set to become the next president. This message seemed to resonate. It was Kibaki's willingness to compromise on the powers of the president, however, that represented the real obstacle and the chance for a Kenyan peace deal.

In my meeting with Kibaki, I pressed him, explaining I was in regular contact with key members of the international community, Condoleezza Rice and George W. Bush of the United States, leaders from the EU, and elsewhere. "The international community is picking up that this failure to make a deal is because of the PNU's unwillingness to move. There will be consequences from them if this fails."

I also tried to make Kibaki think about the long term, and presented this not as a threat to his rule but as an opportunity for him. "Raila is a younger man, Mr. President. But you are the elder and, right now, you are the president. It is you who has the power to change Kenya. This could be your legacy: a reconciled nation and a reconciled people." He listened in his usual quiet and unemotional way, but replied there were technical issues with a coalition government and questions as to the validity of an executive prime minister in the Kenyan constitution.

"You're the one in charge here," I reminded him. "Save your country. Otherwise you are going to have a lot falling on your head." I studied his face carefully. "Mr. President, over one thousand people are dead," I said in closing. "It's time to make a deal."

The coming meeting between Odinga and Kibaki was our last chance. But I thought we now had it. My public exposure of the deadlock had made it clear that one side was holding things up. If I walked away now without a deal, it would be clear that Kibaki was to blame. He was exposed. Furthermore, I had called the U.S. administration to inform them of what was going on. Condoleezza Rice had then announced that any future relationship between the United States and Kenya depended upon them agreeing to the compromise now on the table. With the deck stacked in this manner, I thought he had to budge.

Kibaki, Odinga, and I then entered into an intense five hours of negotiations on February 28. Other than the three of us, the only people I brought in were President Jakaya Kikwete of Tanzania and his predecessor, Benjamin Mkapa. I wanted them to counsel Kibaki on the Tanzanian system, which also includes a sharing of power between the president and a prime minister. Kikwete, Mkapa, and I had discussed and agreed on this approach the day before, at a meeting in the Grand Regency Hotel. They were now very effective in demonstrating to Kibaki that it was more than feasible for a strong president to operate in such a system, erasing the validity of his last substantive argument against the agreement.

The quarry was now cornered. I had told the leaders that this was the final negotiation, that we would not leave until the deal was complete and we would sign it on the steps outside, in public, as soon as we were finished. Odinga was not going to back out now: this was a compromise to which he was already committed. But for Kibaki the choice was now either shift or walk out alone into the sunshine of derision at his failure to move—in the face of both the Kenyan people and the most powerful actors in the international community.

Kibaki then, finally, agreed to the power-sharing deal. I made sure there was no chance of backing out. I walked them out onto the steps of Harambee House to publicly and immediately announce the deal to the world and sign the document: the Agreement on the Principles of Partnership of the Coalition Government. But it did not feel triumphant. It had taken far too long. As they say in a Swahili proverb, "When the elephants fight it is the grass that suffers." This was what had happened with all the people killed around us.

But with confidence restored, the bloodshed now ended. A process of political reconciliation could now begin, as would the difficult job of healing. Despite the tragic number of people already dead, we had averted a disaster of far greater potential. We had achieved something far too elusive in the history of peacemaking—halting a spiral of violence before too many of either side have little left to lose and live on only for vengeance. The signing of the accord on February 28 brought with it a sense of immense relief across Kenya: Kenyans wished each other "Happy New Year" in reference to the New Year celebrations they had been deprived of by the violence since late December.

The amendment to the constitution in the agreement, approved by the parliament shortly after, was a transitional arrangement that was to lead to a full process of root-and-branch constitutional reform. With that provision my role in mediating the Kenyan political crisis would continue. I had come for two weeks and I would still be working with them four years later. Agenda item four of the Kenyan National Dialogue and Reconciliation process, agreed on by the parties on February 1, was to deal with the fundamental causes of the violence, much of which lay in the political system. Over the months and years that followed, with Nana Effah-Apenteng leading my team on the ground, further negotiations took place to create a new Kenyan constitution. It would redistribute power through a system of devolved government, built also around land reform, a bill of rights, and a permanent reduction in the president's powers. Through this, each constituent county of Kenya and each community, including all its tribal and regional groups, would have representatives with access to a piece of power, negating the destructive winner-takes-all politics of the previous system.

On August 4, 2010, a national referendum was held, and the new constitution, which would change the face of Kenyan politics countrywide, was approved. Working to curb his own authority, Mwai Kibaki also campaigned for the yes vote.

One of the salient features of the mediation in Kenya, and implementation of the agreement thereafter, has been the active and continued engagement of all stakeholders—not only Kenyan politicians and the international community but civil society, religious groups, and the business community. Kenyan society as a whole provided a source of constant pressure on the political leadership. For instance, a commendable role played by the business community was its message regarding the negative consequences of the political crisis on the country's economy—particularly the threat to Kenya if it lost its image as the business center and economic powerhouse of the region. The many facets of Kenyan civil society continue to play an active role in the peace process, helping in diverse ways to ensure the successful implementation of the agreement.

Alongside the reformation of the Kenyan political system, other innovations came out of our mediation. In line with plans set down in the February 14 agreement, on March 4, 2008, the creation of two bodies was formally agreed to: the Commission of Inquiry into the Post-Election Violence (CIPEV); and the Truth, Justice and Reconciliation Commission (TJRC). The TJRC, which began its work in 2009, is mandated to investigate not only the recent violence but the patterns of human rights violations and abuses since December 12, 1963, the date of Kenya's transition to independence. In the TJRC, therefore, is bestowed the understanding that the resolution of the 2008 crisis means confronting the entirety of Kenya's troubled past, not just the recent turmoil. Together with the TJRC, a National Cohesion and Integration Commission was created in 2008 to investigate, outlaw, and eliminate all forms of discrimination in Kenyan society, which have served to create so dysfunctional a system of ethnic inequality. These bodies are manifestations of our attempt to foment root-and-branch social and political change—nothing less than the leadership required to bring about enduring and prosperous peace and stability across the troubled heartlands of Africa.

Another important feature of the reform process, particularly given our emphasis on the importance of affirming and strengthening the rule of law, has been the involvement of the International Criminal Court. The CIPEV included among its recommendations that the prosecutor of the ICC be forwarded the names and information of those suspected to bear the greatest responsibility for the violence. Justice Philip Waki, who led the commission, presented me with the final report of the CIPEV, along with a sealed envelope containing a list of suspects at the highest level, which I would hold and pass on to a prosecutor in a special national court that had been proposed. The recommendation of the Commission was that if the Kenyan government failed to take due steps to hold suspected orchestrators of the violence to account then the envelope should be passed to the prosecutor of the ICC.

By July 2009, it became clear that the Kenyan government was not going to take these steps. As I said then, "Justice delayed is justice denied. The people of Kenya want to see concrete progress on impunity." As demanded by the CIPEV report—which had also been certified and approved by the Kenyan parliament—I then passed the sealed envelope on to Luis Moreno-Ocampo, the prosecutor of the ICC.

After a period of investigation, in December 2010, Ocampo released the names of six prominent Kenyans, including three government ministers, suspected of bearing the greatest responsibility for the violence. In January 2012, the ICC then confirmed that there was sufficient evidence against four of those suspects for them to stand trial. These included prominent figures in Kenyan politics, and the willingness to prosecute suspects of this level, regardless of the outcome, stands as an important marker in Africa's battle with impunity for human rights violations.

In the wake of the Kenyan dispute over the election result and the ensuing violence, the inadequacy of a growing economy and an electoral system alone as a shortcut to prosperity, peace, and stability were once more revealed. If we had brokered only a deal between leaders, our intervention would have been a plaster on a wound that would weep again tomorrow. We had to look, in the truest sense of the word, for a resolution. A peaceful, stable, and prosperous Kenya was one that could be delivered only through responsible, accountable leadership, a culture of respect for human rights, institutions for good governance, the fairer distribution of wealth and power, and, most important, the sanctity of the rule of law. Kenya's future relies on this. Whether it will achieve these things remains to be seen, but it has pointed itself in a direction that all of Africa must take.

Africa Empowered

My role in mediating the violent 2008 Kenyan political crisis, backed by a remarkable international and African support network, was one for which, in some ways, I had spent my entire decade-long tenure as secretary-general preparing. It was perhaps the hardest, most intensive, and enduring of all my interventions in the affairs of another country, and a deal that required me to draw on every aspect of my experience of diplomacy and energy for peacemaking—this time at the heart of my own continent.

As flawed as the commitment of the parties might have been to the Kenyan power-sharing deal, the events following the intervention in Kenya represented a broader turning point, a continentwide change that came from within, conjured from a vision for all Africa. This was a vision that resurrected old dreams for the continent that had been dashed in the aftermath of independence—a vision dedicated to transforming Africa into a place where all people can achieve their aspirations. A future of peace and stability through institutions for good governance; respect for human rights; responsible, accountable leadership; and, above all, the rule of law.

This all came together in Kenya, in an intervention that relied on a deeply changed continent to the one I knew before I took office as secretary-general. The foundations for these changes were laid in the years before 2007, through hard and innovative efforts in African diplomacy by Africans to change the political fabric of the continent. It was a long way from where I had stood and observed the continent in January 1997.

Africa is now on the move. Much has changed on the continent. It is now rightly seen as a place of opportunity, with economic growth strong in recent years. Countries and companies are even queuing up to invest, and, increasingly, the fruits of economic progress are being used to create jobs, raise incomes, and to invest in the future—in education, in health, and vital infrastructure. Good governance is growing, enabling investor confidence and increasingly freeing the ambitions of Africa's people. The eleven years since the Millennium Declaration and the subsequent establishment of the MDGs has been one of the most promising periods in Africa's postcolonial history. Now approximately half the continent is enjoying strong economic growth, as well as rapid improvements in human development. But if African countries are to achieve the new future within their grasp, there needs to be a new focus on the daunting obstacles still to be overcome.

High on this list is agriculture. There are 240 million people in sub-Saharan Africa who do not eat well enough for their health and well-being. Africa is the only continent that fails to grow enough food to feed its own citizens. On average, cereal yields in Africa are a quarter of those of other developing regions—and have barely increased in thirty years. Meanwhile, per capita food production and agricultural labor productivity also remain remarkably low. This is not because of a lack of effort by Africa's farmers but a lack of knowledge, resources, and infrastructure to support their hard work. A uniquely African "green revolution" would have a positive impact not only on food security but also on many of the other challenges facing the continent. It will, for example, reduce poverty, accelerate wider economic and social development, improve health and education, slow migration into Africa's already overcrowded urban areas, boost women's influence within their societies, and provide new opportunities for business.

But there also needs to be a focus on infrastructure and the distribution of energy resources, which have always been two of the main obstacles holding back Africa's economies. Furthermore, considerations of growth need to be held in tandem with concerns for employment, particularly youth employment. If growth does not benefit youth employment, it benefits little about the future. Finally, a bright African future is also one that requires gender balance in all areas of life. An empowered and successful Africa requires all the talents and the fair mobilization of all its resources—it can exist only with equally empowered and successful women.

Africa's people are the central agents, but outside actors have essential supporting roles. At certain times they need to respond with peacekeeping; other times, with intervention or preventive measures and mediation, or through attempts to shape the rules of regional organizations. But in all of this we are seeking a peaceful and prosperous Africa, and one that favors the aspirations of all African men and women.

At the promulgation of the new Kenyan constitution on August 27, 2010, we joined in a crowd of countless thousands in the grounds of Uhuru Park to applaud the referendum result. It was as if we were going back in time with wisdom to our youth. We were finally stepping onto a path we should have taken long ago at independence. Kenya's people had peacefully come together to affirm a new road forward: and they were leading the way for the continent.

While in the crowd cheering the new Kenyan constitution, I caught a glimpse of a face I did not expect to see: Omar al-Bashir, the president of Sudan—a leader recently indicted by the International Criminal Court on charges of crimes against humanity. He had been invited to the event by the Kenyan government? I could not quite believe it, but there he was: an honored guest. His lurking figure at the progressive event was a symbol of the danger Africa lives with today. Huge advances have been made for Africa by Africans. But there can be no complacency. Equally huge challenges remain, and the potential to revert is always there in the background, as Bashir's presence reminded me.

We Africans still have much to do.

REDEFINING HUMAN SECURITY:

The Global Fight Against Poverty and the Millennium Development Goals

M r. Secretary-General, when it comes to condoms, the Pope and I are *one!*" Robert Mugabe fired back this response as he lurched back in his chair and hooked both his first fingers together in a sign of stubborn solidarity. I had just put it to him that much more needed to be done, and urgently, in face of the appalling scourge of HIV/AIDS; and that all African leaders, particularly those with a strong voice on the continent, should encourage the use of condoms. Mugabe at first only shifted uncomfortably in his seat. "Mr. Secretary-General, you shouldn't be talking about condoms."

"Why not?" I asked. "I have even raised it with the Pope." This was true. I had raised the issue with the Pope, and I thought that might open this staunch Catholic's mind. But it was obviously too much for him. He wanted to end a conversation with which he was deeply uncomfortable. His eyebrows furrowed as he raised his voice, issuing his statement of solidarity with the Pope. There was clearly no more he would say on the matter. I was working the diplomatic floor at a meeting of African heads of state, and could not easily show my anger at this response, but I felt a familiar outrage that gripped me every time I encountered this willful obstruction of the campaign against HIV/AIDS.

By the time of that conversation with Mugabe, HIV/AIDS had ceased to be an inevitable death sentence thanks to advances in medicine and antiretroviral drugs. That is, unless you were poor. For those living in countries that could not afford the exorbitant prices set by the pharmaceutical companies, HIV/AIDS did, indeed, mean a certain and slow death.

The scale of the suffering inflicted by this disease is beyond full human comprehension, not least because the impact does not stop at the personal level. During my first term as secretary-general, from 1997 to 2002, HIV/AIDS was creating a cocktail of disasters in the developing world. By some measures, the impact of AIDS was worse than war. In Africa, in 1999 it was estimated that AIDS had killed ten times more people than armed conflict in the same year. By 2000, the disease had created a staggering 13 million orphans worldwide, with 34.3 million people living with the disease on top of the 18.8 million lives it had already claimed.

Worse still, the disease was not just taking away the lives of the people infected; it threatened the future by eating away at the social and institutional fabric of societies. This is because HIV/AIDS' greatest toll was among young adults—and women in particular—the most productive members of society, who also had responsibility for rearing the next generation. It was killing off large numbers of young doctors, nurses, teachers, and other professionals who were essential for economic and social development. It was eliminating the breadwinners of households, leaving what was left of their families and communities increasingly desperate and without even the most basic means for self-subsistence.

The situation was by far the worst in Africa. In 2000, 70 percent of adults and 80 percent of children living with the disease were on the continent, and by then nearly three-quarters of AIDS deaths had occurred there. The economic circumstances were already dire in many parts of the continent, but HIV/AIDS was now threatening to grind any social and economic successes that were emerging back into its soil. But it was far from just an African problem. In Eastern Europe and South and East Asia, rapid rises in HIV infections were occurring at that time. In India, HIV was already firmly embedded in the population, and in the state of Tamil Nadu alone, it was estimated that almost a half million were infected.

The figures were terrifying. I spent most of my tenure as secretary-general in an international environment obsessed with the potential peril of weapons of mass destruction. But in HIV/AIDS, which never received anything like the same level of attention, we had a true WMD—and one that was actively unleashing itself in the world. This demonstrated, far more severely than any other pandemic, the security threat posed by diseases internationally, and the further importance of the UN's Millennium Development Goals (MDGs) as an instrument of self-interest for the rich countries of the world.

More than the statistics, it was the memory of the child victims that stayed in my mind. I had visited HIV/AIDS clinics with Nane, and we had spoken with sex workers and victims of the disease from all segments of society when traveling to countries worst affected by the pandemic. Doing so was not always deemed appropriate for a secretary-general—and not just by the likes of Mugabe. But we could not pretend that these people did not exist or attempt to hide them away.

But before 2000, the world was doing next to nothing about the pandemic. As the economist Jeff Sachs established in an article published at that time, when you broke down the donor figures, it turned out the entire world, in a disgraceful imbalance, was donating a total of just $70 million to fight AIDS across the entire continent of Africa. But like any problem, no matter how severe, there was an opportunity to shift the balance of interest, and intervention, in favor of action—action that would have to focus on changing far more than just the manifestations of one disease.

By 1997, the year I started my first term as secretary-general, I had spent much of my life observing the global development agenda wind its way through a long and grinding journey. It had not come far. Plans for poverty eradication and international development cooperation had spent most of the twentieth century in a stillbirth cycle: laudable imaginings repeatedly crushed by the thrust of power in the international system. For me, it started as a teenage African stepping into adulthood at the advent of decolonization, when all the debates were ensconced in the fervent anticipation that Africans would be finally free to develop themselves. I watched this false dawn, believing, like many of my contemporaries, that we could all play dynamic roles in this exciting future—even as the first coups rolled in and pitiful leadership and institutional decay began to grip the continent.

Later, as a young UN official at the Economic Commission for Africa in Addis Ababa in the late 1960s, my colleagues and I optimistically discussed the continent's economic prospects. We projected heady visions for Africa's regional integration through infrastructure development: continent-spanning communication systems, roads, and rail networks— the necessary fabric for Africa's economies to prosper. Little of this happened. Infrastructure development continued to stall. Travel remained incredibly difficult, so much so that to get from one African country to another, one still often had to go via Europe. While Africa failed to move forward, all the while it was accompanied by a sustained, angry shout from African leaders: the colonial powers were at fault. They had failed to develop Africa, leaving it in this awful mess. But to some of us younger Africans, it was clear that we could not keep blaming colonialism. It was over ten years since decolonization, but while Africa's economies sank deeper, the colonial blame game ran on.

In the 1960s and 1970s, we also watched the UN launch its first "development decades." However, in the rich world it was not with poverty but violence that international attention and political efforts became transfixed. East and West were embroiling themselves in the explosion of civil wars of that time, resulting from the struggles for national power following the retreat of Europe's empires. Among the great powers, which were fueling these civil wars in the hope of securing victory for their favored faction, there was little care for development.

This is not to say that there were not any serious efforts at development for its own sake during the Cold War. The Dutch, Canadian, and Scandinavian governments, for example, devoted serious resources to development in poor countries throughout this period. But in the case of the richest of nations as a whole, particularly among the superpowers and their closest allies, the vast majority of the financial firepower available for spending abroad was not allocated for this. With the likes of Russian-backed Cuban troops openly landing on the coast of Angola, while U.S.-backed South Africans invaded from Namibia—all in the context of the threat of a global nuclear holocaust—few resources were available to improve the lives of the populations of the developing world who were subjected to these wars. The focus was on the politics and the fighting, as if development were a separate and peripheral issue that could be held at arm's length.

The absurdity of this notion was most sharply exposed to me when I came to the Department of Peacekeeping Operations in the early 1990s. The Cold War was over, but development continued to slumber in a separate world to political work. It was clear from the experience of our operations in civil war–torn countries that development was an integral, central part of any successful strategy for addressing conflict. But a real commitment to development at the heart of peacekeeping remained elusive. Military, political, and development matters continued to be treated as distinct areas.

In the Somalia peacekeeping mission, to take one example, the budget available for the military was $1.5 billion. For the humanitarian side of the operation, we set a target of just $150 million, and even this fraction we failed to raise—for a mission with a *humanitarian* goal. In other interventions, member states would lament the lack of local institutional capacity in places like Bosnia, Haiti, and elsewhere, because it sorely hindered their ability to withdraw and leave the place in any semblance of good order. I increasingly responded to these complaints that this was actually our failure: a failure to commit the resources for encouraging locally owned development—an obstinate reluctance to put development at the heart of our strategies for peace. Member states willed the ends but very rarely the means. The world, as ever, was happy to invest in the instruments of violence, but not the resources for peace.

The Cold War didn't just tear the political and social fabric of countries through the proxy wars. It also represented an ideological rift at the heart of the UN. Throughout my UN career before 1989, we would constantly hear the debate between the capitalist, Western view, and the socialist and communist view of economic and social development. As an intergovernmental organization, this made it even more difficult for the UN to enact any kind of single development agenda.

I have to admit that it was very easy to get caught up in those competing paradigms in those days—and we all did at some stage. But I later came to realize that the debate was driven at its heart by an ideological vanity, not a concern for the individuals who suffered the grief and humiliations of extreme poverty. The debate between these visions, between private enterprise–driven capitalism and state socialism, wore on all those years as if in ignorance of the urgency for those who had the most to lose. And what really mattered—the dying, the sick, and the humiliated poor—became lost in the argument.

But even after the end of the Cold War, the UN's development agenda remained in the powerful shade of this debate. In the new world of economic globalization, capitalism was proving the unquestionable locomotive of enormous worldwide change, yet the development agenda was still hindered by this ideological divide. A lingering and deep distrust of business and private capital endured at the UN, even as they became the prevailing reality behind major, tangible advances in development in much of the world.

But an equally limited view formed on the other side: that globalization was a rising tide that would "lift all boats." This led to the deeply mistaken belief among the governments of donor countries that there was no need to provide significant sums of aid, as private investment would fulfill this function. Particularly troubling was the trajectory of change in many places: one hundred countries were worse off in 1997 than they were fifteen years earlier. Globalization was not "lifting all boats"—not by any stretch of the imagination. Instead, the opposite was happening for many. Even worse was the lack of outside help for tackling these colossal problems. In 1996, the proportion of development assistance against gross domestic product provided by donor countries had dropped to an all-time low, and was still shrinking.

By the end of the 1990s, you could only be struck by the legacy of all those years. Over 60 percent of the world's population subsisted on $2 or less per day; over 1 billion people were living on less than $1 per day; illiteracy was at nearly 1 billion; 800 million were chronically hungry—one in seven people on earth—including 200 million children; and 1.3 billion lacked even the most basic health, sanitation, and education services.

Despite these terrible figures on global poverty, there was no sign of urgency among member states to commit even a slight fraction of the resources and effort necessary to face this global tragedy. A profound change was needed. But the fundamental question that had stalked international development for decades remained: how?

On taking office, I realized that we had to be more creative. It was clear that, as things stood, we could not expect to get the resources necessary from the member states. As had been the case for decades, just attempting to persuade heads of government and senior ministers directly of the importance of development, and the terrible state of poverty, had long proved inadequate for stirring their collective concern. It was obvious we needed a new armory of instruments to take this forward. But before acquiring them, I knew we needed leadership of a different kind to renew the UN's mission for development—and to do it in an innovative, energetic way, engaging with all the forces in the private and public sectors able to join the struggle.

From my very first month in the job, I began reaching out to other players on the international scene. The first of these lay in international civil society: charities and other nongovernmental organizations. In developing countries, the UN was finding much of its work to be intimately connected with the varied contributions of NGOs. Many of them had been around for years, of course, but in the 1990s, they began to connect up with one another to an unprecedented degree. Cooperation was often catalyzed by major UN conferences, such as the 1992 Rio Conference on Environment and Development and the 1995 Beijing Conference on Women. These brought together thousands of NGOs, giving them a new level of energy and organization.

I have always said that the UN needs to be a United Nations not just of governments but of peoples, as it is from people, not governments, that all power is ultimately derived. The expansion of robust international civil society during the preceding years represented an opportunity to pursue this aspiration. I was unembarrassed to admit that, in many areas, NGOs were ahead of the UN in what they could deliver. They were the "bomb-throwers," the icebreakers, of social and economic development work, usually with far more on-the-ground experience in their countries of operation.

It was due to the great potential stored in this energy, drive, and dedication, particularly as a sector that was now strengthening its connections internationally, that I very publicly sought to reach out and engage with international civil society and institutionalize this common cause. In the first months of my tenure as secretary-general, I directed all UN entities to establish and formalize close working relationships with civil society, and to create forums for genuine consultation and cooperation.

Our growing string of alliances with this freshly emerged grouping of actors would prove vital to the transformations in the development agenda that were to come. And not just because of these actors' activities in developing countries. Underpinning our common cause was a rational and deeply moral purpose, but the will of most member states was absent. Political leaders within countries are, in many ways, beholden to compromises of multiple constituencies and the many audiences for whom they must perform to sustain their authority. This was why it was often hard or impossible to convince leaders of an otherwise rational course of international action that was in their country's interest. But in international civil society, which represented a network of organizations supported by communities of morally concerned supporters, including many voters within donor countries, there lay the potential to affect those countries' domestic policies.

In expanding our global partnerships for development to international civil society, there was the possibility to tap into and encourage a circle of influence that might move the debate forward worldwide. Indeed, this would prove vital, even to the point where Hollywood actors and rock stars became involved, throwing in their popularity to help make the development agenda a mainstream feature of political debates in the rich world.

In addition to global civil society, the other crucial group of players on the world stage was to be found in business. The state of the world's economy meant that any ideological aversion to allying with capitalism had to be forgotten. Private investment in developing countries had increased from $5 billion in the early 1970s to more than $240 billion by 1997, underpinning major economic and social change in those countries. However, 80 percent of private investment in the developing world went to just 12 countries, with only 5 percent going to Africa and nearly 50 developing countries failing to attract any financial capital at all. Economic globalization was proving extremely powerful, but also powerfully marginalizing. My belief was that, with the right set of partnerships, underpinned by the cultivation of a shared commitment, we could start turning the vast resources and dynamism of business more decisively toward the common good of global development and poverty eradication.

There were natural foundations for an enduring relationship between business and the UN's development efforts. The campaign to eradicate poverty, to raise living standards, and, therefore, to increase personal wealth, presented enormous opportunities for businesses worldwide. International development and poverty eradication themselves created and expanded consumer markets, which can be tapped to extend the boundaries of enterprise. On that basis, business had an inherent interest in being part of the common cause of equitably distributed international development.

I also felt that international business lived in a world of responsibility, as well as opportunity. There were rights, rules, and laws safeguarding businesses and their operations. But there needed to be a forum of accountability that reminded them of their role in safeguarding the rights of others, particularly their impact on the right to freedom from want, hunger, sickness, and an early death. In a globalizing world, where public relations were also global, I felt this was a message they could not easily ignore. From my very first weeks in the job, I began giving speeches to business audiences around the world to sell the message that the UN was open, as never before, for engagement with private enterprise.

On January 31, 1999, I spoke to the corporate and political leaders gathered at the World Economic Forum's annual meeting in Davos. I went there to launch a "Global Compact" between the private sector and the United Nations that aimed to build a broader foundation for globalization based on shared values and principles. From past meetings with leaders there, I had developed a relationship of mutual respect that I believed could be the basis for something more ambitious. I warned of the fragility of globalization and its vulnerability to a backlash from all the "-isms" of our post–Cold War world: protectionism, populism, nationalism, ethnic chauvinism, fanaticism, and terrorism. To safeguard the benefits of a global trade system and the spread of technology, however, corporations had to do more than just engage with global policymakers.

There was—and is—a great deal that they could do on their own, proactively. I didn't want them to think they could use the excuse of dysfunctional governments and trading regimes to delay action. "Don't wait for every country to introduce laws protecting freedom of association and the right to collective bargaining," I urged them. "You can at least make sure your own employees, and those of your subcontractors, enjoy those rights. You can at least make sure that you yourselves are not employing underage children or forced labor, either directly or indirectly. And you can make sure that, in your own hiring and firing policies, you do not discriminate on grounds of race, creed, gender or ethnic origin." This would have to be a two-way street: we at the United Nations would abandon our past prejudices against private enterprise, but in return I believed that global business would have to rethink its role as well as its obligations if we were to put global markets on a fair and sustainable footing.

We also had to build partnerships and expand cooperation within the UN. But the UN's development agenda itself was also divided, scattered across a dizzying thirty-two funds, agencies, programs, departments, and offices. As things stood, there was little hope of any cohesion or single strategic purpose among these organizations. To start rectifying this, I established the UN Development Group in 1997, which sought to bring together all of these strands to deliver a more coherent, effective, and efficient system of support to developing countries. All agencies now had to form a single UN "house" in each country of operation, all under the primacy of the United Nations Development Programme (UNDP) representative. These measures did not solve all our problems. The vast array of challenges in developing countries—from health, sanitation, agriculture, education, and environmental sustainability to infrastructure development—meant that a significant range of actors from the UN and elsewhere were always needed, bringing with them recurring organizational obstacles. But these new measures meant that development was finally ceasing to be a scattered set of endeavors without any shared direction, and was becoming a team effort with a common goal.

The silos dividing UN work were also why we pushed for a transformation in approaches to planning, managing, and implementing our activities in territories torn by civil war, particularly in our peacekeeping operations. It was vital that we integrate development, security, military, and political activity in our interventions in war-torn countries. The motivation was not just the need for an integrated effort in peacebuilding: it was recognition of the intimate connection between economic development and the resolution and prevention of civil wars. Poverty is not the direct cause of civil war, but poverty and failed development nevertheless create the conditions for conflict. It leads to the inequalities between ethnic groups that drive so many civil wars. It further enfeebles state functions that enable governments to respond or preempt violent challenges to their authority. And it produces large numbers of unemployed young men with little future, making them ready recruits for a violent cause.

This is a further reason why rich and poor countries are linked in their interests in international development: civil wars have a security impact far beyond their source. They suck in their neighbors, send thousands of refugees spilling into other countries, create havens for armed groups and terrorists, and they cause the spread of criminal networks and cross-border lawlessness, including piracy. In short, conflicts within states are inherent generators of global insecurity, the causes of which need to be addressed by wealthy and poor states alike.

Another big piece of the international development puzzle lay in the Washington-based financial institutions: the International Monetary Fund (IMF) and the World Bank. Formed at the same time as the UN, these were officially institutions within the UN system, but their prestige and power meant that they operated entirely separately from the UN. With major resources at their disposal and an overlapping interest in global economic issues, they had a crucial role to play in funding, guiding, and effecting efforts at international development and poverty eradication. If there was ever to be any kind of cohesive, global effort to face extreme poverty, then these two institutions would need to be involved.

But in 1997 their relationship with the UN was distant and dominated by bureaucratic turf wars. I knew we could do better. On a visit to Washington, early in the first year of my tenure, I organized a breakfast with James Wolfensohn, the president of the World Bank, and Michel Camdessus, the managing director of the IMF. From that early meeting, we developed a relationship that over the next decade catalyzed an unprecedented level of cooperation among our three institutions.

I did not start reaching out to this wider array of protagonists in anticipation of the breakthrough that was to come in the run-up to the millennium. I was being opportunistic, hunting for any resources I could find in hopes of changing the trajectory and dynamic of international development. But once we began to build this network, pulling all the strands together, as only an institution like the UN could, a new force began to build. This alone was not decisive. Despite the changes we had ushered in, transforming the place of poverty in international affairs required something far more dramatic than just our reforms in the Secretariat. We would have to bring in the member states. But given the history of commitment to international development, it was going to take nothing less than a genuine diplomatic innovation. This would be enabled by, of all things, an accident of the calendar.

It had been expected for some time that the UN would have its own special event to mark the millennium. It was agreed that this would involve a special summit of heads of state and government before the annual meeting of the GA in September 2000. However, other than this, the only guidance from the member states (who, by UN rules, had to choose and mandate the event) was a 1998 GA resolution: "The year 2000 constitutes a unique and symbolically compelling moment to articulate and affirm an animated vision for the United Nations in the new era."

This uncertainty gave us useful leeway in how to fashion the event and the accompanying debate. The traditional role of the secretary-general for such occasions is to arrange the administrative and organizational procedures. But I sensed an opportunity to deploy our moral power as well.

Vaguely designated as being for the renewal of the organization in the new century, the event would have to cover all the major issues facing the UN. But I came to the view early on that poverty should form the core. The year 2000 saw the world with the resources, for the first time, to end extreme poverty. But poverty was still a gaping omission on the collective priority list of governments. The summit represented a rare opportunity to rectify this.

As a first step, on March 27, 2000, I issued a report, *We the Peoples: The Role of the United Nations in the 21st Century*, to be considered by all member states before the Millennium Summit. Reports of such sweep would usually be drafted in the first instance by relatively junior staff members from different departments, after which, for a period of several months, the text would be circulated and amended by other departments, agencies, and representatives of the member states. This process of to-and-fro deliberation and compromise meant that the outcome was almost always the lowest common denominator. Poverty was never going to move forward on that basis. So, instead, I tasked two senior aides from my office on the thirty-eighth floor, John Ruggie and Andrew Mack, to take the lead in producing the report without the departments taking any formal role and without consultation with member states.

Between them and a tight circle from my office, we then produced the document. The member states would decide on any agreement that they signed, but we ensured that the starting point and the basis for any debate was entirely our text.

We knew the report had both to have teeth and to be popularly accessible. Unlike most UN documents, this had to be a text that anyone could understand and engage with, as only popular accessibility could engender the accountability mechanism that would be needed later on. The major development summits and conferences of the 1990s—Copenhagen, Rio, Beijing, and others—had seen the adoption of resolutions that were complex, opaquely worded, and made no real demands on anyone. Hence, while they represented important landmarks in the growing international consensus on development, they saw little substantive follow-up. In *We the Peoples*, however, we set quantifiable and time-bound targets for poverty eradication, and set those targets around clear, simple, and morally undeniable goals.

Another important feature of the report was its endorsement of a more advanced concept of poverty than had been represented at the highest political level up to that time. Poverty is not a monodimensional problem involving just a lack of income. Extreme poverty represents a complex, multifaceted set of phenomena involving the denial of opportunities across many areas of life, causing and reinforcing each other. Part of poverty is a lack of income, yes, but so too is a lack of education, health care, nutrition, access to safe drinking water, the subjugation of women, and environmental degradation. An integral part of the existence of extreme poverty is also the lack of outside assistance for tackling it. *We the Peoples* and the MDGs sought to capture all these.

In the reality of international politics, however, because we had a document that called for major commitments by governments, this made it less likely they would ever agree to it. But there were pressures we were able to make work in our favor. We were reaping the results of our engagement with international civil society. The NGO Oxfam, for example, through its support for the "Make Poverty History" campaign, collected 2 million signatures, which they presented to me in New York during the Millennium Summit. Alongside the Millennium Assembly of UN member states, we held a number of concurrent assemblies: a Peoples' Assembly, in the form of an assembly of international NGOs; a forum of the world's religious leaders; and another for representatives of the various parliaments (as opposed to governments) from around the world. Along with the world's press, these formed a moral forum, to lobby and pressure the governments sitting nearby, which was particularly significant given that many of these organizations had supporters that reached back into the countries of the governments in attendance.

The weight of popular expectation also helped us. The level of adulation and attention accompanying the buildup to the millennium around the world was such that, with a Millennium Summit involving the greatest collection of world leaders in history (it would host 147 in total), the event could only attract intense international scrutiny. The result was a palpable fear among member states that a special Millennium Summit might cause real damage to their credibility if little was achieved. This concern was motivated by the lesson of the fiftieth UN anniversary assembly in 1995. There all the major issues of the world had been discussed but without any agreement to do anything about them, and presidents and prime ministers returned from its pomp and ceremony under a cloud.

But because of how we had fashioned and produced *We the Peoples*, if the member states wanted an agreement, they were going to have to work with the deal on poverty that we had set up for them. There was no other deal available. Combined with the simplicity of the goals set out in the report—on rights to life, health, basic education, sanitation, and food, which no one in their right mind could deny when put to them—this made it even more difficult for the member states to reject our proposals.

There was one further measure we applied to stack the deck in our favor. To be a head of government is to be trapped in the paraphernalia and pressures of office. It is to be in the midst of countless aides and advisors, all the while worrying about the compromises that must be made to appease various domestic constituencies. Many times had we seen this interfere and obliterate agreements based around otherwise rational collective interest. But when you got them on their own, I always found even the most intransigent leaders would typically prove far more reasonable and responsive. At the Millennium Summit we set up three roundtable discussion sessions with the leaders to examine the crucial features of *We the Peoples*. But we also set the requirement that only the heads of state and government would be in attendance. There would be no aides or advisors in the rooms with them. This stripped them of their domestic political padding and the distractions such staff bring to negotiations. The civil servants, advisors, and presidential handlers hated this, but, very tellingly, the leaders loved it.

This tight combination of factors meant that we got the global deal we were seeking. Almost all the features of *We the Peoples* were then endorsed in the Millennium Declaration. The declaration was signed by every one of the UN's 189 member states, with twenty-three other international organizations committing to its targets. Unlike previous great summits, this was not an agreement to certify the balance of power, legitimize conquest, or bolster a concept of the inviolable right of states to run themselves however they wished. This was a pledge by all states to fight the major manifestations of extreme poverty and deprivation the world over. Rather than being explicitly for the power and protection of states, this agreement redirected the principles of responsibility and accountability of all governments toward alleviating and ending the suffering of the world's most downtrodden.

From the Millennium Declaration we would develop the eight Millennium Development Goals. These were finalized in the summer of 2001 after a process of consultation and negotiation led by John Ruggie and Michael Doyle and overseen by my able deputy, Louise Frechette, whose responsibilities included the UN's economic and management agendas. Mark Malloch Brown, the energetic and reform-minded head of UNDP, was then tasked with the ambitious job of implementing and advocating the goals worldwide. In their basic form, the goals are:

- Eradicate extreme poverty and hunger.
- Achieve universal primary education.
- Promote gender equality and empower women.
- Reduce child mortality.
- Improve maternal health.
- Combat HIV/AIDS, malaria, and other diseases.
- Ensure environmental sustainability.
- Develop a global partnership for development.

It is important to note that all these goals, and their subsidiary targets and benchmarks, were expressed and signed up to in some form by major member states in the years before 2000. But these pledges always suffered from a lack of momentum, petered out, or went largely unnoticed.

One of the crucial features of the Millennium Declaration as an instrument of poverty eradication was that it was signed by all nations. It set out the responsibility of the rich nations to provide external assistance, while making that assistance contingent upon an explicit responsibility owned by the developing and poor countries. In short, it was a global deal that established a universal and fully shared duty to deliver development to the extreme poor.

But further setting apart the Declaration from previous pledges to fight poverty, the member states had signed a document binding each of them to a set of concrete, time-bound, and measurable goals. Against these, they agreed, would be a list of quantifiable targets and measures, focused on a deadline of 2015. By signing the Millennium Declaration, therefore, the member states not only made a rhetorical commitment to fight poverty but permitted the birth of a system by which every member state could be held publicly accountable on the world stage. Lending this further power was the simplicity of the goals. Unlike the vast majority of UN agreements and communiqués, these goals could be understood by anyone, from the senior politician in the capital city of the wealthiest nation to the man or woman on the street of the poorest shantytown—and they articulated human needs that were so basic and obvious they were undeniable to anyone who considered them.

Between this universal simplicity and the commitment to a quantifiable set of targets, the member states thus bound themselves within the shackles of an incredibly powerful global idea. Many of them did so unwittingly, I suspect, not realizing the strength of what they had brought to life and expecting it to suffer the same quick death that had overtaken so many other UN declarations. If so, they were to be surprised by what was to come. The MDGs soon became the overarching framework for the entire international development agenda. A decade later, at the September 2010 UN summit, the MDGs would still be at the pinnacle of global affairs, with every development organization dedicated to them, every government engaged, and countless other partners and businesses geared toward their delivery in every part of the planet.

To anyone who reflects back on the agreement, there is no denying its significance. With all the partners that had morally and formally bought into the project alongside the member states, with the common interest of so many otherwise diverse communities around the world, this was more than just a breakthrough UN declaration: it bore the hallmarks of a global social movement.

H ow do you respond to those who say the poor will always be with us?" I asked. I had turned the conversation suddenly. It was July 2, 2005, and I was calling the head of the Anglican Church, the archbishop of Canterbury, Dr. Rowan Williams, to link up before the looming Gleneagles G8 summit. But my real motivation was to ask for spiritual guidance. Once again I had been presented with the view that the campaign to make poverty history was impossible—even ordained by the Bible to fail. The key quotation was in Deuteronomy 15:11: "There will always be poor people in the land."

"To some extent this is based in thinking that the poor are victims of human sin: that there will always be poor people, because there will always be sinners," he replied.

"We shouldn't be complacent," I responded, trying to find a way out of an excuse for inaction.

The archbishop stressed his agreement: "The idea of shared accountability and social responsibility is explained in the Old Testament, and can be applied to the issue of helping the poor. Deuteronomy 15:4: 'There should be no poor person among you.' This is why Deuteronomy 15:11 should be interpreted as instruction that the poor are part of society and should not be ignored, not that we cannot strive to end their plight." I thanked him for this piece of armory that I had never imagined I would need.

The MDGs—putting people irrevocably at the center of development—created an unprecedented enthusiasm, momentum, and collaboration on a worldwide scale. But it did not end our struggle with the old problems of international development, some even as ancient as interpretations of the Bible. It was a reminder that in international development there is and will always remain the danger of the world's slipping back into the unenlightened and narrow-minded views of the past.

Following the Millennium Summit, we sensed the risk that the pledge might fall away if we did not sustain the momentum. Our first step was to firm up the agreement and to formalize its aims. Set against the targets of "We the Peoples" and the eight subsequent MDGs were eighteen subsidiary targets and attached to them were forty-eight further individual metrics for assessing progress toward the goals. I presented these to the member states, telling them that these would form a public "scorecard" for each country over the coming years. To give this further bite, I then invited the heads of state and government to a world summit to be held in 2005, where a global-assessment exercise would be conducted under the world's spotlight on each country's progress toward the MDGs.

But we also needed a strategy for achieving the goals, which the declaration had not provided. This required a team with the intellectual and analytical prowess to chart such a course. In February 2002, I asked Jeff Sachs to lead this endeavor, which became known as the Millennium Project. Sachs's unusual intellect and deep commitment to the cause of poverty eradication made him an ideal addition to my senior staff. It was a complex research exercise, and Sachs pulled together 250 eminent participants across the project's ten task forces, engaging all of the UN system and representatives of all the major UN agencies, while also linking up with on-the-ground efforts across developing countries.

What the Millennium Project demonstrated was that the MDGs were attainable. We just needed the right level of commitment, effort, and, most of all, external assistance. While we had targets and a growing set of plans to make the MDGs a reality, crucial to any success was the ingredient captured in the eighth goal: a global partnership.

This partnership is vital because of the worst feature of extreme poverty: alone, the poor are in too dire a position to help themselves. As Jeff Sachs has explained on many occasions, the basic requirement for ending extreme poverty is to enable the poorest to step onto the ladder of development, which the millions upon millions of the poorest in the world are unable to do alone because of the "poverty trap." This is when communities become caught in a vicious cycle that denies them the minimum level and forms of capital necessary to initiate a process of development.

For any hope of achieving some form of economic development, communities need a combination of several different types of capital, including human, physical, and natural capital. The essential components of these take many forms: healthy individuals free from malnutrition with the skills to productively engage in the economy; asserting women's rights to determine their own reproductive destiny; facilities for commercial activity, such as transport for agriculture or facilities and machinery for other sectors; infrastructure, including transport networks, power supplies, and sanitation and communication systems; healthy soils and ecosystems that sustain human communities; public institutional capacity, in the form of commercial law, judicial and security services, underpinning peaceful societies of commerce and labor; and finally, knowledge, in the form of scientific expertise and skills required to raise productivity and boost other areas of capital. There is also an important role for social capital—the collective value of cohesive community relationships—which, through its networks of trust, enables the sharing of resources between individuals, boosting the power of other forms of capital and also enabling households to survive in times of deepest hardship.

For a community to enjoy any prospects for economic development there has to be a cycle of accumulation of such forms of capital. This requires that the income of each household be of a sufficient size to leave enough left over for both household savings and contributions to the public budget through taxation. These then enable investment in human, physical, and natural capital that in turn sustain business and economic development. What then emerges is a virtuous cycle of capital accumulation, allowing economic growth, in turn strengthening opportunities for increases in household income, and so on.

But among households in communities caught in the poverty trap, what income they have is spent entirely on keeping the household's members alive. This means there is no money available for taxes or savings. Hence, with population growth, the depreciation in the value of assets continues, which leads to an ever-reducing stock of capital in the form of resources and services available in the community. This further reduces opportunities for increases in income for individual households, usually leading to even further decreases in income. Add the impact of diseases, which such households are too poor to protect themselves against or treat, and productivity drops even more dramatically, with the income and capital available deteriorating still further.

The result is negative economic growth and an ever-decreasing level of capital per person. This is the situation for millions of communities around the world, and without help from outside, the situation continues to worsen. The only solution is through the managed use of an external injection of capital into that community to transform the cycle of the poverty trap into one of capital accumulation; significant development assistance from wealthy countries is essential for financing this process.

At the heart of the Millennium Development Goals was an understanding, which today is growing but remains incomplete, of the unique contribution that the empowerment of women can make to achieve the wider aims of poverty reduction, sustainable development, education, good governance, and human rights for all. During my travels to some of the most vulnerable communities in the world—from Afghanistan to India to Africa—I often made it a priority to seek out the schools for girls, microfinance projects geared towards women's employment, and the homes and hospitals that cared for the women victims of HIV/AIDS. I saw the boundless curiosity and eagerness for learning in the eyes of the young girls, the entrepreneurial spirit and sense of responsibility among those engaged in new businesses, and the cruel existence of women carrying a disease that their society often would not even acknowledge. I made it a point to meet with women activists and NGO leaders, ministers and teachers—not just to offer my encouragement and support but also to send a message to their own national leaders that to the United Nations, women would never be invisible.

Of course we also knew that there was no easy path to achieving the empowerment of women—or even basic equality. Gender disparities in education, for example, often reflect social attitudes and cultural practices that will take time and sustained effort to overcome. Early marriage is a stark example. For the poorest households in many countries, marrying off daughters at a young age to secure a bride price is often a practice driven by economic need. Add to that the concern in some societies that the benefits of any investment in a daughter's education will be transferred to her future husband's family. The disincentive for girls' schooling is, tragically, all too common. In countries such as Chad, Ethiopia, Mali, Bangladesh, India, and Sierra Leone, between one-quarter and one-third of girls marry by the age of fifteen—effectively marking the end of their education and the beginning of a life without equality of opportunity.

After the Millennium Declaration, international financing for the MDGs was the big missing piece. I decided that we needed to bring together the world's leading thinkers and politicians on the subject, to devise a political strategy for the way forward in a process that would conclude with a special summit of finance ministers and heads of state and government. In November 2000, I asked Ernesto Zedillo, the president of Mexico, to chair this panel.

The subsequent International Conference on Financing for Development was held in Monterrey, Mexico, in March 2002. This produced the Monterrey Consensus, in which it was formally agreed by over fifty attending heads of state and two hundred finance, foreign, and international development ministers that globalization and privatization alone could not be expected to help the poorest countries, as they lacked the infrastructure and human capital to attract such investment. External government-issued aid, therefore, had an essential role to play in international development, as well as foreign investment and trade. To back this up they issued an enormously important statement, urging "all developed countries that have not done so to make concrete efforts toward the goal of 0.7 percent of gross domestic product as official development assistance."

This commitment to 0.7 percent of GDP was a breakthrough because it represented, for the first time, a decisive financial agreement among developed countries to commit the necessary resources to poverty eradication. Before Monterrey, aid from developed countries had been in decline for many years. In 2002, it stood at barely 0.2 percent of their shared GDP. Monterrey saw the reversal of this trend for the first time since the Cold War. It also brought an unexpected pledge from U.S. president George W. Bush, who decided to join the conference at the last minute. He promised $10 billion from the United States over three years to go into the Millennium Challenge Account, a project designed to increase assistance to countries that had demonstrated their ability to use external funding successfully. Granted, even this new level of commitment did not bring the United States to even 0.2 percent of GDP in overseas development assistance. The United States was still one of the lowest contributors to development in terms of its capacity to pay. Nevertheless, this new move was hugely encouraging. We were nowhere near where we needed to be, but at least we now seemed to be facing in the right direction.

But this did not last long. A few months prior to the Monterrey conference, New York and Washington DC had been struck by the 9/11 terrorist attacks. As a result, preparations to invade Iraq loomed large soon after Monterrey, and world attention fled to that issue, doing enormous diplomatic damage to our attempts to bring about a common and united international focusing of efforts and resources on poverty. While those in the Bush administration were preparing for a military reckoning with Iraq, they were increasingly turning their heads from international development and dividing up the international community as they went.

One of the cruelly ironic features of this change was the fact that international development is a crucial part of the long-term fight against terrorism. While there are no statistical correlations between levels of poverty and the incidence of terrorist attacks in particular countries, failed development and poverty creates inequalities that underpin many of the grievances that drive terrorism. Furthermore, a lack of development undermines a country's ability to sustain effective domestic security forces. It is partnerships with these local forces that in the last ten years have proved the most effective means in tackling al Qaeda globally. International development is a vital security interest for nations of the rich world with any concerns about terrorism.

But in a world consumed with the specter of terrorism, this was poorly understood. Following the invasion of Iraq, members of the Bush administration—though not Bush himself—even turned against the concept of the MDGs. They started refusing to refer to the MDGs in speeches on development and began opposing their mention in UN and OECD documents. Concerned by the commitment required of rich countries by the MDGs there was even a moment when U.S. ambassador to the UN John Bolton attempted to have any mention of the MDGs removed from the draft declaration of the 2005 UN summit, despite it being an event concerned with examining progress toward the goals. Entirely isolated in this endeavor, Bolton was not able to succeed, but this attempt to savage the MDGs at a summit designed to advance them did not benefit the United States' standing in the world.

It is in this erratic manner that the fight against poverty has lurched on ever since. The 2005 G8 summit in Gleneagles, Scotland, hosted by Tony Blair and underpinned by the staunch support of the British finance minister Gordon Brown, was another highlight that later compromised itself. Gleneagles saw a new set of groundbreaking promises, including a pledge to double aid to Africa by 2010. But the G8 has since reneged on this promise.

The vast array of supporters, organizations, activists, and local leaders engaged in development need the financial support and opportunities that only the rich world can provide to multiply the striking results such targeted aid has produced. To mention just two very isolated examples of the impact of targeted aid:

By 2000, malaria was killing over twenty-nine thousand people a year in Ethiopia. In 2005, as part of its campaign to meet the MDGs, the government introduced a program to deliver two mosquito nets to every family at risk, alongside a reduction in the cost of malarial drugs and treatment. This was possible only with donor support, and within three years, deaths from malaria were cut in half. In Rwanda in 2003, access to health care stood at just 7 percent of the population. But a health insurance scheme was brought into place, with the small fee subsidized by foreign aid for those who could not afford it. By 2009, this simple scheme saw access to health care rise to 85 percent.

It is these kinds of projects, replicated across the range of issues and around the world, that could create the sustained, worldwide leap forward in the campaign to end poverty that the MDGs demand. And their enormous and tangible impact on the lives of those affected is impossible without donor funding. But the rich world keeps faltering and has repeatedly failed to fall in decisively behind these activities. While the overall decline in contributions has been reversed since 2000, the developed world has not come anywhere near to meeting its collective promise to dedicate just 0.7 percent of GDP to overseas development assistance—the minimum financial contribution required for any hope of ending extreme poverty.

It is vital, however, also to emphasize that the success of external support is utterly predicated on leadership and the institutional reform efforts of recipient countries. It is not only corruption that can make aid money ineffective or wasteful. It is weak policies, poor leadership, and unaccountable institutions that produce dire results for the lives of the poor as well. In Pakistan, for example, the rate of teacher absenteeism has been 19 percent, and in some places in the world it is as high as 25 percent or more. In Bangladesh, absenteeism rates for doctors in primary health care centers have been reported at 74 percent. As emphasized in a report by the World Bank, absenteeism rates of such severity are not a matter of money—they are an institutional problem that must be resolved through reform and institutional change, which depends upon local leadership and true on-the-ground partners for social progress.

Many developing countries have proven reluctant to undertake necessary reforms to resolve these kinds of institutional problems because such policies can be divisive and politically contentious. (Teachers unions and medical unions can often be powerful players in local politics.) As a 2011 report evaluating success in achieving the MDGs concluded, those countries that are on track for meeting the MDGs are there not because they received the largest amount of aid but because, most of all, they have made the greatest efforts in economic reforms, including in innovations in service delivery.

Responsibility for reform lies with the people on the ground, the politicians and leaders within their own countries. But the failure of donor countries to provide the necessary financial aid when these kinds of reforms are being pursued is perhaps made even more unforgivable by this dynamic. The reformers need to be given every chance. The MDGs are a partnership in the truest sense between the rich and poor. The people within developing countries are responsible, but everyone has a role to play.

Of the countless components to the MDGs campaign and our battle with poverty, one issue—HIV/AIDS—demands special focus. In turning to this challenge, we drew on many of the innovations of the Millennium Declaration, applying them in an intensive form to face down one of the most serious crises of my secretary-generalship.

At 8:50 a.m. New York time, on December 7, 1999, the phone rang.

It was Richard Holbrooke, the U.S. ambassador to the United Nations, on the line:

"We should raise HIV/AIDS as an issue at the Security Council in January."

When I heard this I couldn't help but pause in satisfaction at this news. For HIV/AIDS to obtain the attention that it deserved, and of the right kind, I had believed for some time that it had to be understood as a security issue. It was not just a problem to be packaged away under the label of "health." It was a fundamental security threat of global proportions: just the sort of world issue that the UN, and particularly the Security Council, existed to deal with. But its nature as a disease meant it was of a type never brought to the Security Council before. This was a foolish reason not to act against a threat that had required concerted global attention for years. An obstinate layer of ambivalence in the corridors of power had made leaders apparently impervious to the colossal evidence that mounted every day.

"Well, we have a problem, Richard. You do realize HIV/AIDS isn't seen as a peace and security issue don't you?" I was deliberately baiting him. I needed to establish the level of his ambition. Was this going to be a side issue, a distracting footnote at the Security Council, or was this going to be an opportunity to bring HIV/AIDS into the center of international diplomacy? It would all depend on how the powerful would represent it.

"You know full well that you told me over a year ago that it is a security issue!" Richard replied. "If we take it to the Security Council now, then it's finally going to get the emphasis that it deserves. This is going to be a priority for the U.S. presidency of the Security Council."

The idea was finally in the head of one of the permanent five. A crack in the wall had opened. Better than that, we had Holbrooke leading the charge. I thought the other members of the Council might not be ready to accept this change. But Holbrooke had the force and personality and moral courage, in a manner like no one else, to push the other governments into unfamiliar territory. With the Security Council as a rhetorical partner, there was now a chance for a change in the trajectory of the HIV/AIDS agenda. Holbrooke had been speaking to Nelson Mandela that day, and I remembered my own lesson from Mandela's achievements: you have to have a sense of opportunity.

A year later, a new global level of awareness and willingness to respond to calls to tackle the HIV/AIDS issue had been reached. At this stage, in early 2001, I decided to make this issue a core priority of my office. We were now in a position to make a genuine, life-saving difference. But as with the MDGs, here, too, I realized that the only way to have any hope of pushing forward the HIV/AIDS agenda was through the formation of a global alliance.

The UN had its own agencies tasked with taking on this problem, with excellent leaders who would prove integral to our later achievements against the disease. UNAIDS, run by Peter Piot, was one. With UNAIDS we established the first interagency organization tasked with the essential coordination of all our programs and funding in this area. Another was the World Health Organization, headed by Gro Harlem Brundtland. But our agencies alone were never going to be enough. It was only through a raft of partnerships with NGOs and other advocacy organizations that this campaign could be successfully fought. This was not only because of the scale of the scourge of HIV in the world but also the multiheaded nature of the problem. First, we needed to pursue prevention: to halt and reverse the spread of the virus, requiring education on precautions; information campaigns to raise awareness and the mobilization of young people; and, in particular, measures that would enable mothers to know that they were infected, allowing them to avoid passing the virus to their children through breast-feeding. Second, we had to endeavor to put care and treatment within the reach of the millions of living victims of the disease, to enable access to the drugs and treatments that could totally transform the impact of infection. Third, we needed to pursue scientific breakthroughs, with investment in research for treatments and preventative measures, and, most important, a vaccine against HIV. Given the complexity of the tasks at hand, the solutions were going to have to come from a large number of partners from various sectors. It had to be a truly global alliance.

Just as we sought to build a civil society network for the MDGs, we did so here, but in a more targeted way. The general effort to reach out to partners in business and international civil society in the preceding years meant we had the foundations to be able to do this. With this expanding network, in the following months and years, through a sustained and concerted effort, we were able to achieve two important things: first, in the establishment of a war chest to sustain the complex fight against the disease, in the form of what was called the Global Fund; and second, in the successful campaign to cajole the biggest pharmaceutical companies into dramatically reducing the prices of drugs for HIV/AIDS victims in the developing world.

On April 26, 2001, I gave a speech at the African Union summit in Abuja, Nigeria, dedicated to the subject of HIV/AIDS. In that speech, I issued a public call for the creation of a fund that would form the basis for waging the war against HIV/AIDS. This was the outcome of weeks and months of discussions and suggestions between many parties: NGOs, private foundations, governments, and academics. The overriding call was for a war chest dedicated to sustaining the worldwide campaign against HIV/AIDS, as a lack of resources specifically dedicated to tackling the disease and its effects was considered the chief obstacle to progress. I proposed that there had to be, at a minimum and over a ten-year period, between $7 billion and $10 billion deposited into that fund.

Not long after, we saw the establishment of the Global Fund, designed to finance large-scale prevention, treatment, and care programs in the developing world for HIV/AIDS, tuberculosis, and malaria. The other diseases were included because they ranked on a par with HIV/AIDS in their impact: those with AIDS often died of tuberculosis, and the impact of malaria remained a deep scar across prospects for development in much of the world, particularly Africa.

The Global Fund was perhaps the most important international financing facility for aid established in the last twenty years. Its prominence mobilized donors, and it pooled their contributions, concentrating them into a central, coordinated, and global strategy. It also started a snowball of attention that began to make the subject of HIV/AIDS a reputable one for open and public discussion. That same year, in September 2001, the General Assembly even held a special session to debate the HIV/AIDS pandemic for the first time. This attention was not something the HIV/AIDS agenda had enjoyed before in many public circles, largely due to the sense of embarrassment incurred by the subject's sexual connotations. Finally, this was beginning to change.

The fund immediately attracted philanthropists. Early on, the Bill Gates Foundation stepped forward to donate $100 million. Bill Gates and his wife, Melinda, and I became acquainted over the HIV/AIDS campaign, and they remain some of the strongest supporters of the fight. This is in addition to their uniquely generous contributions to international development as a whole. The fund attracted the support of governments, too. Regardless of the disagreements that would later grow between the UN and the Bush administration on other issues, the U.S. government and George W. Bush in particular became resolute supporters of the campaign. The president immediately pledged $200 million for the fund, while Congress started proceedings to approve $700 million for the next year's budget. Other governments followed, and as early as July the German parliament had already approved a donation of $130 million and the United Kingdom a further $200 million.

Bush would then go further still. He created the U.S. President's Emergency Plan for AIDS Relief (PEPFAR). With $5 billion in funding per year, this was the biggest financial commitment by any country in history to fight a single disease. I spoke to Bill Clinton about the new U.S.

I was educated on three continents, attending universities in Africa, North America, and Europe. My time at Macalester College in Minnesota, United States, was an eye-opening experience of another culture undergoing dramatic changes. In 1960, I joined the Ambassadors for Friendship program at the college, which sent small groups of international and American students out to explore the United States.
Macalester College Archives, DeWitt Wallace Library

On the drums while a student in the United States, 1960.
Courtesy of the author

Setting the record for the 60-yard sprint at Macalester College.
Macalester College Archives, DeWitt Wallace Library

My father, Henry Reginald (H.R.) Annan, in Freemason's regalia. To him, there was no contradiction in being African in identity and European in outlook.
Courtesy of the author

My mother, Rose Eshun.
Courtesy of the author

Briefing President Bill Clinton, Ambassador Madeleine Albright, and Secretary of State Warren Christopher on current peacekeeping operations in the UN situation room. My deputy Iqbal Riza is at Clinton's left. When I took over the UN Department of Peacekeeping Operations in 1993, UN peacekeeping was undergoing enormous changes. Peacekeepers were being sent into dangerous and unstable territories torn by civil war often with limited means and mandates.
Courtesy of the author, photographer unknown

Walking through the streets of Sarajevo with UN peacekeeping officers, 1995. The war in Bosnia was one of the most drawn-out and destructive conflicts for UN peacekeeping in the early 1990s. As secretary-general, I made it a priority that we drew the right lessons from that experience. *Courtesy of the author, photo by P. W. Ball*

With General Janvier, commander of the UN Protection Force in Croatia and Bosnia Herzegovina, flying from Zagreb to Sarajevo before handing over mission responsibility to NATO, in December 1995.
Courtesy of the author, photographer unknown

Being sworn in as the seventh secretary-general of the United Nations, December 17, 1996, by the president of the General Assembly, Ambassador Razali Ismail of Malaysia.
UN Photo/Evan Schneider © United Nations

On a plane above Angola, March 1997. My first international trip as secretary-general was a tour of Africa. As the first sub-Saharan African to lead the UN, putting the continent's enormous challenges at the top of the international community's agenda was a priority throughout my tenure. Shortly after this first visit, I returned again in June, this time with a tougher message for Africa's leaders: to demand their collective rejection of leaders who came to power through military coups.
UN Photo/Milton Grant

In February 1998, I traveled to Baghdad to meet with Saddam Hussein in an attempt to avert another war in Iraq over its weapons of mass destruction program. The negotiations were initially successful, with Iraq agreeing to allow weapons inspectors into palaces and other "Presidential sites." *Iraqi News/United Nations*

With Pope John Paul II, a leading global voice of concern for the poor and a tireless advocate of peaceful resolutions of disputes. I believed the United Nations had to be a United Nations of *peoples*, not just of member states. I worked to open the United Nations' doors to other global organizations, including world religions and other prominent players in international civil society as another instrument for influencing the international agenda on global issues, from tackling wars and disease to promoting development and human rights.
© *Photographic Service L'Osservatore Romano*

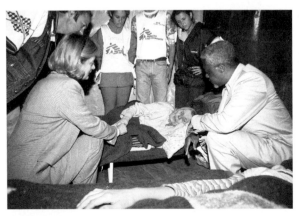

As secretary-general, I made it my mission to put the individual at the center of everything we did. There were few more powerful reminders of the importance of this than speaking with refugees, in this case with a woman who had been forced to flee Kosovo in 1999 in the face of the Serbian campaign of "ethnic cleansing." *UN Photo/Evan Schneider*

During my ten years in office, I got to know Tony Blair, George Bush, and Jacques Chirac well—as leaders and friends—though the Iraq crisis would put our relationships to the test.
UN Photo/Eskinder Debebe

Visiting Ground Zero within days of the attacks of 9/11. I shared my shock and outrage with President George W. Bush and conveyed a universal sense of support and sympathy with the people of the United States.
UN Photo/Eskinder Debebe

Colin Powell lent his unique prestige and reputation to America's case for war over Iraq's weapons of mass destruction. I always admired his dignity and deep sense of duty to his country.
UN Photo/Eskinder Debebe

I began my Nobel Peace Prize address imagining the fate of a girl born in Afghanistan that day and urged the world to unite around the idea that sovereignty should never be considered a shield for gross violations of human rights.

© *Sergey Bermeniev*

After we succeeded in bringing East Timor back from the brink of a savage civil war, the United Nations became responsible for its transition to independence. I asked Sergio Vieira de Mello (to my right) to lead this complex task, and in so doing he brilliantly managed the emergence of a new nation led by the courageous Xanana Gusmão.

© *Sergey Bermeniev*

Wynton Marsalis, a visionary of music and art, became a friend and supporter—though getting a tune out of his trumpet turned out to be a lot harder than it looked much to the amusement of my wife Nane and Luciano Pavarotti.

UN Photo/Evan Schneider

In Darfur, meeting with two women who told me of their suffering at the hands of the Janjaweed militia. Nowhere was the question of intervention more complex or challenging.
UN Photo/Evan Schneider

Nelson Mandela, whose singular leadership qualities and moral courage have been an inspiration throughout my career. As secretary-general, I could always count on his support and—at critical junctures—personal intervention in crises from Africa to Iraq.
UN Photo/Eskinder Debebe

My fearless and loyal friend Richard Holbrooke (standing to Bill Clinton's left), who never hesitated to challenge me when he thought the UN could do better, and never left my side—even at the most difficult moments of my time as secretary-general.
ⓒ *Sergey Bermeniev*

The signing ceremony for the Rome Statute—a signal moment of progress in international law and the fight against impunity for war crimes and crimes against humanity. *UN Photo*

With our children and friends at the Nobel Peace Prize celebration in Oslo—a moment of recognition for the work of the United Nations in every part of the world.

© *Sergey Bermeniev*

agenda on HIV/AIDS at that time. He shared with me a telling insight: "You know what, Kofi? This may be the most important thing he does in his entire presidency." He was right. And by the look on his face, Clinton seemed to signal he wished he could go back and seize the same chance.

In a 2001 speech in Abuja, I addressed the African heads of state and government as directly as I could on this challenge:

"You must take the lead in breaking the wall of silence and embarrassment that still surrounds this issue in too many African societies, and in removing the abuse, discrimination, and stigma that is still attached to those infected. The epidemic can be stopped, if people are not afraid to talk about it."

This wall of silence had been immensely destructive. Mugabe was one of those leaders who remained obstinate in the face of the rational arguments for measures to prevent HIV, partly on religious grounds but largely in embarrassment. Across Africa, methods had emerged to avoid talking about and recognizing the issue. In Uganda, for example, it was covered over with the unpleasant pseudonym "the slim disease."

I was told of one occasion when it was suggested to the then president of Kenya, Daniel arap Moi, that he speak publicly about the use of condoms. His response was: "I am father of a nation. My duty is to keep the people moral and upright. I can't talk to them about being promiscuous!" It was deeply disturbing for me, even to the point of shame, to know my fellow African leaders were so irresponsibly obstinate on so deadly a matter.

Thabo Mbeki, the president of South Africa, was particularly obstructive. Successor to the most impressive of Africans, Nelson Mandela, Mbeki was always going to have a hard time filling those shoes. He made some impressive contributions to life and politics in South Africa and Africa as a whole, providing effective management of the South African economy and playing a proactive role in the conflict-resolution endeavors of the African Union. But he proved incapable of exerting anything like the kind of leadership that was urgently required of him on the issue of HIV/AIDS, and with terrible results. On one occasion, before traveling to South Africa for a conference, I spoke to Mbeki to tell him that Mandela and I thought the three of us should make a public visit to an HIV/AIDS clinic in South Africa to raise awareness of the disease. At first he agreed. But when I arrived in South Africa, it became clear he had no intention of fulfilling this promise. "I don't think we should distract ourselves from the conference" was his only explanation.

At first it just seemed too much for Mbeki. But his position, as head of state of a leading African country, meant that he should not have considered such a reaction a luxury available to him. Worst of all, he refused to recognize the mainstream scientific conclusions about HIV/AIDS: namely, that AIDS is caused by the HIV virus and could therefore be helped through antiretroviral drugs, which he also claimed were toxic. In correspondence to me, he cloaked his reasoning—based on the flimsiest of scientific advice—in postcolonial arguments, alleging racism in the debates surrounding the issue. At a time when neighboring countries were budgeting to provide their populations with antiretroviral drugs—with, for instance, Namibia treating 71 percent of its infected population by 2005—Mbeki was refusing to do the same in South Africa. A team of Harvard researchers later investigated the likely impact of this policy. They found that, at a conservative estimate, Mbeki and the South African government could have prevented at least 365,000 premature deaths if they had not taken this position.

In the buildup to the launch of the Global Fund, the public campaign began to turn our way as we received more and more endorsements from a variety of governments, organizations, and prominent figures around the world. This brought the pharmaceutical companies under the spotlight to a new degree. There was a growing rejection of the big companies' refusal to make their drugs available at affordable prices in the developing world, and this view was now entering the mainstream. In early 2001, my senior staff and I agreed that the time was right to push for significant cuts in drug prices. We had a better chance than ever before for a receptive audience with the drug companies.

This was a very big step. The cost of antiretroviral treatment was such that, at that time, the conventional wisdom in the development community was that the pursuit of antiretroviral therapy for poor countries would never be possible based on simple economics. In this view, prevention and research into a vaccine was the only real hope. But our high-profile advocacy and lobbying for the right of access to treatment in the developing world changed this. We proposed that this was simply a question of will, not economics. Would we help the millions dying when we had the science to do so, or would we not? It was under the shadow of this lingering and hopelessly simple question that Peter Piot, Gro Brundtland, and I arranged a series of meetings with the top pharmaceutical manufacturers, the first in March 2001 in Amsterdam.

As a result of these meetings and the collective process of pressure and engagement worldwide, the pharmaceutical companies began to compromise. This led to a dramatic reduction in the cost of treatment for victims in the developing world. The cost of drugs fell from $15,000 a year to, eventually, just $150 a year, or fifty cents per day. The impact was enormous. As a result of this step, by 2005 countries like Botswana were now able to afford to extend HIV/AIDS treatment to 85 percent of those in need, a dramatic transformation in the life prospects for millions of victims.

Important improvements have been made in the vast struggle to contain and reverse the impact of HIV/AIDS since those early years. In 2010, for the first time, the number of new HIV infections in sub-Saharan Africa began to drop. By the same year, eight developing countries had begun providing universal access to antiretroviral drug therapy across their populations. More lives are being saved from HIV/AIDS now than ever before. Unprecedented advances have also been made recently in research into producing a vaccine, with the possibility of an effective vaccine for humans finally established and, particularly promisingly, the identification of neutralizing antibodies against HIV.

But all this progress, in infection rates, treatment, and scientific research, is under threat from a global fall in funding for the HIV/AIDS campaign. It is estimated that there is currently a shortfall of around $10 billion if these successes are to be sustained. All this hard-won progress depends utterly on the continued supply of major donations, as otherwise it stands to be reversed. By one estimate in the *Lancet*, the British medical journal, new HIV infections could reach a rate of 3.2 million a year if funding is not now increased, as just the activity of keeping the pandemic under control will cost between $397 billion and $733 billion over the next twenty years. The impact of the financial crisis has led to tough economic times and a tightening on donations, but HIV/AIDS is surely an area that we cannot afford to abandon.

Those who argue the MDGs divert resources from the real interests of donor states are sorely mistaken. Such a view reflects a blindness to the world we live in. The walls have come down. The threats faced are those that no single country has the capacity to tackle alone. This is because of the intricate and complex relationship between development and security.

Others have claimed that the MDGs represent little more than a rhetorical flourish that does no good. One activist once even referred to the MDGs as a "Major Distraction Gimmick," and I have heard them referred to elsewhere as nothing more than a useless form of "cheerleading." The implication is that they should be done away with. That would be a mistake.

First, at the diplomatic level, I personally witnessed how the MDGs served to transform the agenda of the world's leaders. Before 2000, social, economic, and development issues had long been a major part of the UN's work. But they were always considered and debated in distinct separation from the other pressing political issues of the times and were never to be expected on the agenda during any urgent negotiations with the secretary-general. By the time I left the UN, this had all changed. Development was at the top of the pile, an entirely appropriate feature of high-level meetings and pressing telephone conversations with heads of state and government. Most important, this has been sustained. The 2010 world summit saw every country justifying its role and charting its progress in pursuit of the MDGs, and all under the gaze of intense international media attention and scrutiny.

The second impact has been in accountability. The MDGs, and their standardized rating system for evaluating progress in development contained in their simple and universally accessible aspirations, have provided a mechanism for civil society in all parts of the world to hold governments to account. This did not exist before, and the universal standard set by the goals has allowed an international community to emerge in transnational solidarity, further empowering people to raise their voices and demand results. The outcome has been a new momentum for good governance in the developing world, with, as Jeff Sachs put it, dozens of governments now forced to "watch themselves in the mirror" of poverty, hunger, disease, infrastructure, and education.

The third major impact of the goals has been to set up a global system for tracking change and enabling comparison. This has allowed vital lessons to be transferred across the international development community of practitioners, activists, and those crying out for assistance. This and the simple and accessible nature of the goals have, for example, allowed a popular appreciation for the enormous benefits wrought by the expansion of capitalism in the East Asian economies, particularly in China. China's poverty rate dropped from 60 percent in 1990 to 16 percent in 2005, demonstrating the value of its economic policies for transforming the livelihoods of the poor. Meanwhile, the failures in other countries, such as Guinea-Bissau, have allowed a clearer contrast and exposure of their situation, focusing attention on those cases so that strategies for changing their fortunes can be devised. This level of comparison and cross-fertilization in the developmental learning process has extended to the microdetail of individual projects also, allowing the transfer of methods, approaches, and technologies among countries and organizations on all kinds of development activities, from the successes and impact of school feeding programs in West Africa to unusual strides against tuberculosis in Nepal.

Fourth is the impact on cohesion. The MDGs are focused on results, themselves centered upon the impact on individuals. This has wiped away much of the friction between developmental paradigms that had previously divided and so impeded international development. It has brought a level of cohesion to international development efforts unheard of before 2000. International development work has always been made up of an array of fractious groups, between ideologically divided NGOs and businesses, with disagreements extending even to the point that institutions like the IMF and World Bank were seen as the "real enemy." The MDGs have ended much of this destructive squabbling. Rather than focusing on the means of development, which were deeply contested, the MDGs focused entirely on the ends of development.

Placing the individual at the heart of the agenda has eroded this debate, forcing a realization of the collective contribution that can be made by the full array of parties. This has allowed a global framework of cooperation, further galvanizing the attention and contribution of other actors on specific MDGs, particularly the private sector. The impact of the MDGs in providing this coherence has not just secured the de-confliction of certain development paradigms, but also the self-mobilization of a new range of contributors to poverty eradication.

The MDGs also come in for criticism in debates regarding development aid. Some are of the view that aid does no good and is frittered away by corrupt governments, or that aid can actually do harm. They quite rightly question the impact of, for example, over $1 trillion of aid transferred this way to Africa over the last fifty years. Between 1970 and 1998, when the majority of these transfers were made, the share of the world's poor people living in Africa rose from 11 percent to 66 percent. The implication is that aid is without value and should end. Trade and private investment should replace it, the argument goes, given these have proved the prime means through which countries have achieved sustained economic development in the modern age.

There are significant flaws in this argument that must be exposed. First, the characterization of aid as without value is based primarily on pre-1990 figures, when most of the total aid sum was transferred. These figures utterly misrepresent the current role of aid. There is a fundamental difference between development aid given during the Cold War and aid given since. Before 1990, most aid money was designed to buy allegiance in the context of the superpower struggle, not international development. Foreign donors showed little interest in the ruling styles of the benefactors and saw no reason to hold them to account for corruption. Aid is now far more closely tied to conditions on its use, such as in the Millennium Challenge Account. The argument against the value of aid might have been a reasonable one if made in 1975. It is more than outdated today.

Furthermore, aid does not necessarily mean rampant corruption; it depends on leadership and the accountability of those leaders. Rwanda, for example, has received significant foreign aid and experienced minimal levels of corruption—the curse of so many other developing countries.

Private investment and international trade also cannot replace aid for most poor nations. Such countries simply lack the features required to breach the threshold of cost-competitiveness in the international economy that is required for investment. Skills and services, infrastructure, an educated workforce, political stability, and other features of social and economic development are required before this can happen, and the only way to get there in most cases is through the effective application of aid in the first instance.

The goal, of course, should be the end to aid. We should be striving for a world where aid is no longer necessary. South Korea is an example of a country that used to be a major recipient of aid but is now a serious donor. This is the example we should be seeking to emulate in all developing countries, and such a result is possible only through aid and then a follow-through of private investment and trade.

The spotlight should not be on aid but on trade. It should really be on the failures of rich countries to remove international trade regulations that stunt the economic ambitions of developing countries. Such policies are entirely at odds with the professed international development agenda of wealthy countries. Subsidies protecting the agricultural sectors of rich countries are most damaging of all, as they make it impossible for developing nations' agricultural sectors to break into the rich markets. The debate should not be on whether we should have aid, but on the appropriate policies to effectively concoct the right mixture of aid, conditionality, good governance, and, most of all, opportunities in international markets—with the latter hitherto a black mark on the community of wealthy states.

Enormous progress has been made in some areas of the MDGs. For example, the target to halve the number of people living on $1 or less per day—lamented as excessively ambitious in 2000—is likely to be achieved, largely as a result of rapid economic growth in the Asian economies, particularly China's. Furthermore, some countries have made significant strides on many of the MDGs. The latest estimates are that nine African countries will succeed in halving the number of people living on $1 or less per day. Yet now that we are approaching 2015 and the deadline of the MDGs, it is clear that most of the global targets will not be met.

The failure to reach the MDGs does not signify a failure of the MDGs themselves; the failure is in our effort to achieve them. The MDGs are not a strategy requiring adjustment or replacement in the face of failure. Instead, they represent undeniable and fundamental rights for all human beings. Therefore, they must remain enshrined as the object of the collective endeavors of humankind. Beyond 2015, any adjustments should not be in the goals, but in the individual targets, taking account of changes and allowing ambitions to be raised accordingly, and in the measures we apply to achieve them.

Furthermore, huge advances have been made in pursuit of and as a result of the MDGs. The ultimate goal is the eradication of extreme poverty, but along the way the goal is also to make things better—to do whatever we can do. The MDGs can continue to do this beyond 2015.

There is a real danger in opening up the MDGs for renegotiation. In my experience, every time you open up a progressive international measure for renegotiation, the result is typically not a progressive outcome but a whittling away of the ambitions. Some may wish, quite rightly, that the MDGs contained more. But we should not risk the hemorrhaging of any of their components.

There are new threats to the MDGs that either did not exist or did not appear in so prominent a form when they were drafted. These include the international narcotics trade, climate change, and the global economic crisis. Consideration for these must be incorporated firmly into the next stage of the war on poverty. The international narcotics trade has taken on a new level of power and ingenuity in the developing world and threatens the reversal of development in the countries in which it takes root. International cooperation to prevent, contain, and erode networks of organized crime is essential for the protection of development in some of the most fragile countries.

Of far more significance, however, is the enormous matter of climate change. The impacts of climate change are already with us, and changes in weather patterns and further rises in sea levels are now inevitable. Support must be given to the poor countries that stand to suffer so that they can respond to these changes and prepare for what is to come.

Without such a globally shared effort, all the hitherto on-the-ground progress in international development could be lost to this threat.

Finally, there is the global economic downturn following the financial crisis incurred by the credit crunch. This crisis is threatening a major and sustained reduction in donor support for international development. The MDGs were launched in an era of increasing prosperity in the rich world, but we should not be fooled into believing that these hard times should necessarily mean especially hard times for poverty eradication. Amartya Sen, the Nobel Prize–winning economist, provides examples from history demonstrating that it is not so much the abundance of resources that is the prime determinant of outcomes for the poor, but the values underpinning their use. During the Second World War, the resources available in Great Britain fell throughout the conflict, particularly in the net availability of food. But (excluding war-related deaths) nutritional health and life expectancy actually *rose,* and did so dramatically, across the population during the war years. Rather than a decline in care and the state of the vulnerable, the deprivations of war spurred new supportive and sharing social arrangements leading to a radical transformation in the food-distribution and health care systems, with dramatic results. The difference was driven by something very simple: a change in attitudes to sharing.

This is a vital lesson to take to the years of economic downturn and the tightening of budgets. For it casts our responsibility in a different light, posing this dilemma not as a question of resources but as a question of our will and our attitude to the sharing of the resources we have.

The ultimate lesson of the story of the MDGs is that we are all responsible.

THE WORLD'S
FAULT LINE

Peacemaking in the Middle East

Y ou give me settlements and I'll give you Arafat," Chris Patten
told Colin Powell. It was 2004, and we were in a meeting of the
Quartet, where the UN, the United States, the European Union,
and Russia had coordinated Middle East policy since I had brought them
together three years earlier. Patten, the EU commissioner for external
relations, was responding to Powell's call for the rest of us to join Washington in isolating the Palestinian leader Yasser Arafat. If the United
States wanted others to sideline Arafat, would Washington insist that
Israel stop expanding settlements?

"That's a very interesting offer," Powell replied in his usual pragmatic manner. Maybe he was wondering whether he could deliver Washington on a deal like this, to say nothing of the Israelis. The issue soon
became moot when Arafat died that November. But I admired Patten for
insisting on a quid for the rather far-reaching quo we were being asked to
sign on to. Decades of attempts to resolve the Israeli-Palestinian conflict
fundamentally came down to this: a recognition by Israel of the need to

end the occupation in the West Bank and Gaza and accept a two-state solution negotiated on the basis of the 1967 borders; and a decision by the Palestinians—and their leader—irrevocably to accept the existence of the State of Israel and surrender the illusion that a Palestinian state could be achieved by stoking Israel's sense of insecurity.

I had heard Washington's mantra many times: "Arafat's the problem." I agreed that Arafat's *behavior* was a big problem. Suicide attacks by Palestinian militias had killed hundreds of Israeli civilians during the intifada that had raged since 2000. I had always taken a clear stand against terrorism, from the Palestinians or anyone else. I refused to accept that it was "legitimate resistance" to blow up Israelis on buses or fire rockets at random toward civilian towns. Arafat was not doing enough to stop these atrocious attacks. Indeed, the apparatus he headed was sometimes complicit in them. In person, Arafat could be compelling—but he could also be completely unreliable. He would casually assert things that he knew that I knew could not be true, and he built a corrupt and confused authority beneath him. I had at times instructed my own envoys to minimize contacts with Arafat to register my displeasure at his equivocation—not easy given the intimate relationship between the United Nations and the Palestinians.

But was Arafat the *only* problem, as Washington insisted? What about Israel's expansion of settlements on Palestinian land and its annexation and isolation of East Jerusalem? These actions violated international law, discredited Palestinians who advocated nonviolence, and ate away at the territorial basis for a viable Palestinian state. Besides, what was the alternative to Arafat? I never forgot that he was the leader who had brought his people to accept the idea of a two-state solution, relinquishing their territorial claim to 78 percent of mandate Palestine, and had signed the Oslo Accords, which recognized Israel. If he was sidelined, the field would be open for Arafat's militant Islamist rival, Hamas. Could anyone seriously want that as an outcome? The Israeli diplomat Abba

Eban famously said that the Palestinians never missed an opportunity to miss an opportunity, but the Israelis and the Americans continually tried to marginalize one group of interlocutors on the Arab side only to find them replaced by an even more recalcitrant opponent.

In short, if Arafat was a problem, Ariel Sharon was too. The Israeli prime minister showed few signs of offering true justice or dignity for Palestinians. He deployed the Israeli army not only to rout out militants but to dismantle the political and security structures of the Palestinian Authority. He had smothered the Palestinians with checkpoints and was building a wall that, whatever its stated security purpose, cut through the heart of Palestinian land on a route that the International Court of Justice ruled illegal. "Good fences make good neighbors," Sharon would tell me. "True," I would reply, "but only if the fence is not built through your neighbor's land."

Instead of debating who were the good guys and the bad guys, I thought the international community had to recognize that the parties were trapped in a tragic logic. They would never be able to overcome their predicament without robust international help. We needed to work together, deploy incentives, and apply real pressure to help both sides to cease self-destructive behavior patterns and negotiate an agreement.

This was easier said than done and raised many dilemmas. What was my proper role as secretary-general? When should I be a quiet agent of dialogue, and when should I resort to the megaphone of public diplomacy? When should I push the Security Council to do more, when should I allow myself to be pushed by it, and when should I be prepared to work outside it—including in an ad hoc grouping such as the Quartet? How should we deal with a democratic government such as Israel's, which, nevertheless, repeatedly violated international law by building settlements, or with militant movements such as Hamas, which resorted to and glorified acts of terrorism but had popular support due to the unsolved grievances of the people? How could we overcome the cynicism and despair fueled by the failure of the peace process itself and make sure that dialogue delivered on the ground?

Still, as secretary-general, I had to confront these dilemmas. The conflict must be solved, since the unresolved plight of the Palestinians and the continued insecurity of Israel are sources of profound moral concern and deep human suffering. There are broader reasons, too. I believe the failure to achieve an Arab-Israeli peace is a core source of frustration and instability in the region. This failure also remains for the UN a deep internal wound as old as the organization itself, given that the Arab-Israeli conflict began at the very inception of the UN—a painful and festering sore consequently felt in almost every intergovernmental organ and Secretariat body. As I told the Security Council before I left office in 2006, the Israeli-Palestinian conflict is not simply one unresolved problem among many. No other issue carries such a powerful symbolic and emotional charge affecting people far from the zone of conflict.

A UN SEAT AT THE PEACE TABLE?

A secretary-general cannot simply turn up and expect to be granted the space to play a political role between the Israelis and the Palestinians. While many other actors wish to see a genuine multilateral approach, the United States is possessive of the file, and Israel does its best to keep others at bay. When I reflected on this early in my tenure, I realized that the secretary-general had been largely absent from every significant step of the modern peace process: the Israeli-Egyptian peace treaty of 1979; the 1991 Madrid Conference; the 1993 Oslo breakthrough; and the Israel-Jordan peace treaty of 1994. During my first three years, I, along with many other world leaders, could only watch during 2000 as President Clinton hosted two summits—one in Geneva with Syrian president Hafez al-Assad, and the famous Camp David talks with Israeli prime minister Ehud Barak and Arafat—in failed attempts to clinch peace deals.

Yet the UN was heavily invested in the issues at stake. It was the UN, after all, that had first given legitimacy (through General Assembly resolution 181, in 1947) to the partition of mandate Palestine into Jewish and Arab states in 1948. The UN's first mediators had been deployed in the region—Count Folke Bernadotte, assassinated by Israeli extremists in Jerusalem; and Ralph Bunche, who received the Nobel Prize for negotiating the armistice agreements after the 1948 war. UN resolutions—particularly Security Council resolutions 242 and 338—were the agreed framework for dealing with the issues left unaddressed by the wars of both 1948 and 1967, on the basis of land for peace. UN peacekeepers were deployed in sensitive border areas, particularly between Israel and Syria and between Israel and Lebanon. UN aid agencies were doing important work on the ground—foremost among them the United Nations Relief and Works Agency, UNRWA, which cared for Palestinian refugees.

But the UN had been politically sidelined. When I observed the moribund debates in the General Assembly on "the Question of Palestine," all the symptoms of irrelevance and even destructiveness were plain. They generated a lot of heat but did not shed much light on who had to do what, when, and how, to achieve peace. The General Assembly and the Commission on Human Rights passed myriad resolutions against the Israelis. Any legitimate criticisms they leveled were often overshadowed by the fact that the member states of these bodies applied standards to Israel that they did not apply to the Palestinians, or to other conflicts—let alone to themselves. This left the Israelis convinced that they could never get a fair hearing from the United Nations.

But the Palestinians had even more grounds for complaint. They were the ones perpetually occupied or exiled. Their lands were being eaten up by settlements, they were seeing Jerusalem gradually isolated and altered, and they were largely unprotected when violence broke out.

Yet the Security Council, with primary responsibility under the Charter for the maintenance of international peace and security, was usually silent. Even when the Council took positions, it did not establish mechanisms to enforce its will. The United States wielded its veto to protect the Israelis even from reasonable international scrutiny and pressure, paralyzing the Council on one of the world's central conflicts.

Neither extreme was healthy, but the split was clear: Israel did not trust the UN and kept the organization at arm's length, while the Palestinians looked to us to uphold their cause yet saw no prospect that we could help to achieve a solution.

I thought this was an untenable position for the UN on the verge of the twenty-first century, as bad for both parties as it was for the organization. Whatever the divisions among the UN membership, I resolved that as secretary-general, I should seek to be an active agent of peace. I realized this depended in large part on whether *all* the players in the region had confidence in me personally, regardless of their views of the organization itself.

REACHING OUT, BUILDING TRUST

With the Palestinians, this came fairly easily. I have strong feelings of sympathy and solidarity with their plight. As a young African, I believed they had been the victim of injustice, and I had identified with their liberation struggle. I had also felt firsthand the sense of loss, injustice, and indignity shared by Arabs, Muslims, and people of goodwill throughout the world over the Palestinian issue when I served as a young UN political officer in the Sinai.

I lamented and condemned the violent outrages some Palestinians committed, and I felt it was the duty of the UN, both on grounds of principle and as friends of the Palestinians, to speak plainly on this matter.

But the "terrorist" epithet was too often used to deny the Palestinians' political identity and obscure the fact that an entire nation was either occupied or exiled. Every Palestinian in the region encounters in his or her daily life the restrictions and denials that arise from the unresolved conflict, summarized in one word: indignity. As I told the Security Council in my last address on the Middle East in December 2006, Israelis need to confront this fundamental Palestinian grievance: "The establishment of the State of Israel involved the dispossession of hundreds of thousands of Palestinian families, turning them into refugees, and was followed nineteen years later by a military occupation that brought hundreds of thousands more Palestinians under Israeli rule." The American public and political system also need to understand that a reflexive and often unthinking support for almost any Israeli action or policy will in the long run serve no one.

But I could easily appreciate the compelling and legitimate narrative of Israelis. Burdened by a uniquely tragic history and alarmed by their perilous geography, Israelis felt themselves surrounded by hostility and only one military defeat away from annihilation. Some Israelis doubted that an agreement with the Palestinians would be achievable because "the maximum we can offer is less than the minimum the Palestinians can accept." Others feared the loss of control that would come with accepting Palestinian sovereignty and were unsure that an agreement would bring the hostility toward them to a permanent end. Many Israelis saw the Jewish claim to *all* the land as stronger than the claim of the Palestinians to *part* of it—an argument I could never accept. But most Israelis were pragmatic enough to look for ways to accommodate the Palestinians and divide the land—*if* Israel's existence and security could be assured.

I had to grapple with the fact that Israelis felt that the UN perpetuated hostility toward them—and they were sometimes right. In my last address in the Security Council on the Middle East, I summed up what I had learned over decades of watching the handling of the issue in the UN's intergovernmental organs. Many may have felt satisfaction in the decades of endless passing of General Assembly resolutions condemning Israel's behavior, I said, but what tangible relief or benefit had this brought the Palestinians? What effect had these had on Israel's policies, other than to strengthen the belief in Israel that the UN is too one-sided to be allowed a significant role in the Middle East peace process?

This statement was the culmination of a decade of reaching out. During my first trip to Israel in 1998, I promised to do my best to usher in a new era of relations between Israel and the United Nations. Israel was the only member state excluded from membership of a regional group, so I called for normalization of Israel's status in the United Nations. I condemned anti-Semitism expressed by member states at the podium in New York and Geneva, and lamented the General Assembly resolution of 1975 equating Zionism with racism. None of my predecessors had said these things—after all, to do so is to criticize the membership itself.

For a good portion of my tenure, I also had a healthy dialogue with Jewish leaders in America. They wanted to influence me, no doubt—but I sought to influence them, too. My best friend among them was California congressman Tom Lantos—a stout defender of human rights, the United Nations, and Israel—who had been rescued from the Holocaust by Nane's uncle, Raoul Wallenberg. Lantos was a rock of support during the Oil-for-Food crisis that we faced in the aftermath of the Iraq War. I also enjoyed ignoring diplomatic protocol by inviting Israeli ambassadors to meals at my house along with diplomats from across the Arab world—they might have been fighting each other, but I was not at war with anybody. These are precisely the kinds of contacts that are possible in a forum like the United Nations.

In later years, Nane and I attended the opening of a new wing of the Holocaust museum at Yad Vashem in Jerusalem and helped persuade other world leaders to come as well. I supported the General Assembly's belated commemoration of the Holocaust in 2005 on the sixtieth anniversary of the liberation of Auschwitz and its designation of January 27 as International Holocaust Memorial Day. As a result, the UN has a Holocaust outreach program—I wish more was known about it. When, in the years after 9/11, I decided to organize a series of seminars through the Department of Public Information on "Unlearning Intolerance" to promote understanding across the divides that seemed to be growing deeper in the world, I made sure the first seminar was on anti-Semitism, because, as I said in my remarks:

> the United Nations emerged from the ashes of the Holocaust. And a human rights agenda that fails to address anti-Semitism denies its own history . . . When we seek justice for the Palestinians—as we must—let us firmly disavow anyone who tries to use that cause to incite hatred against Jews, in Israel or elsewhere . . . The fight against anti-Semitism must be our fight, and Jews everywhere must feel that the United Nations is their home too.

In reaching out to Israelis and to Jews, I often reminded them that UN General Assembly resolution 181 gave Israel its international birth certificate. The United Nations is mentioned no less than seven times in the declaration of Israeli independence that David Ben-Gurion himself famously read out loud in Tel Aviv.

LEAVING WITH LEGITIMACY: ISRAEL'S WITHDRAWAL FROM LEBANON IN 2000

Despite my attempts to reach out, I did not have any illusions about making progress in the peace process with Prime Minister Benjamin Netanyahu, who led Israel during my first two and a half years in office. He had been an Israeli ambassador to the United Nations, and he was gracious to me—I remember him telling me in 1998 at his residence in Jerusalem that his young son thought I was a hero when I went to Baghdad to prevent war with Iraq, since he had been frightened by the gas mask drills the entire country was enduring. But when I urged him, as the stronger player, to be more magnanimous toward the Palestinians in the interest of getting to an agreement, he described me as "Arafat's lawyer." He always seemed to focus on the tactical and expedient, not the strategic or historic.

The time for me to move came when Ehud Barak won the elections in 1999 and became prime minister. He wanted to conclude peace agreements with Syria, Lebanon, and the Palestinians before President Clinton left office in early 2001. Barak had serious intent, but as the subsequent eighteen months unfolded, it became clear that he lacked an understanding of what would truly be required to reach peace, both in terms of what Israel would need to offer and how Israel's politics needed to be managed.

Yet in June 1999, all this lay in the future. I asked Terje Roed-Larsen to become my envoy. As a Norwegian researcher, he had helped broker the Oslo Accords and had then been the first coordinator in the mid-1990s of the UN's work with the Palestinians in the occupied territory. Now, with the consent of the Security Council, I added a political component to his mandate—as special coordinator for the Middle East peace process. Roed-Larsen was creative, energetic, and indefatigable—and knew everyone. In a tough neighborhood, he was at one point or another blackballed by just about everyone. But he usually bounced back.

"Put your ear to the ground," I told Roed-Larsen when I appointed him in late 1999, "and see if you can find openings." He did and reported back that Barak intended to keep his election promise to pull Israel's troops out of Lebanon.

Lebanon is one of the most complex societies in the world. Its stability is at various moments either maintained or threatened—usually both—by its intricate religious and regional variations, its particular relationship with Syria, the impact of the unresolved conflict with Israel and the presence of Palestinian refugees, and a long history of penetration by outside players. All these factors were at play with ever-shifting geometries between 1975 and 1990, when about 120,000 people were killed in Lebanon's civil war.

The war ended with the Taif Agreement, which was designed to abolish political sectarianism and disband militias. Yet Lebanon's confessional makeup remained embodied in the "unwritten" National Pact of 1943, which reserved the presidency for a Maronite, the prime ministership for a Sunni, and the parliamentary speakership for a Shiite.

Israel had occupied southern Lebanon since 1982, when it drove Arafat and the PLO out of Beirut. Hizbollah emerged as a leading Shiite Lebanese group to resist Israel's occupation, with strong backing from revolutionary Iran. Syria—which viewed Lebanon as part of its historic territory—was the de facto guarantor of the security of the country, but as a result penetrated deeply into Lebanese politics. The Israeli-Syrian conflict, while embodied in Israel's occupation of the Syrian Golan Heights, was as often as not played out in the Lebanese theater, manifested in Syria's alliance with Iran and its links with Hizbollah.

Given these realities, it was clear in 2000 that the best context for an Israeli withdrawal from Lebanon would be immediately *after* Israel had reached a peace with Syria. Without this, an Israeli withdrawal from Lebanon would carry the danger of sending the message that Israel was fleeing Lebanon due to Hizbollah's armed campaign, empowering Hizbollah and giving Syria a possible incentive to cause mischief. With a peace deal, Syria would have had an incentive to behave differently and realign its relationship with Hizbollah.

Unfortunately, a March 2000 summit in Geneva between President Clinton and Syrian president Hafez al-Assad failed. Barak had insisted on retaining a thin strip of Golan land on the eastern shores of the Sea of Galilee for security reasons, and when Clinton conveyed Barak's offer to

Assad, the aging Syrian leader turned it down flat. He insisted, as he always had, on a full withdrawal to the 1967 lines and Syrian access to the lake. Barak had not gone all the way in his peace offer. His initiative tragically failed—and with it, the chance to begin a major reorientation in the region.

D ays after the Geneva failure, Barak told me that he would keep his Lebanon withdrawal pledge. But it turned out that he did not want to go all the way here, either. Under pressure from his military, he wanted to withdraw in stages and leave behind security outposts inside Lebanese territory. I told Barak and his foreign minister that if they wanted to coordinate this with me and gain international legitimacy for Israel's actions, I needed a full withdrawal—and I wanted his commitment *in writing*. After much to and fro, Barak wrote to me on April 17 confirming Israel's intention "to cooperate fully with the United Nations" and to withdraw "in full accordance with Security Council resolutions 425 and 426"—the UN resolutions calling for Israel to end its occupation of Lebanon. Egyptian foreign minister Amre Moussa later told me that my insistence on the letter had boosted Arab confidence that I would "do the right thing." This helped give me the space to work with the Lebanese and Syrians effectively, even as I closely coordinated with the Israelis.

I knew that if the withdrawal went well, it would extricate Israel from an eighteen-year presence in southern Lebanon that had become a quagmire, and it would help Lebanon's further reemergence after the civil war. But a withdrawal that went wrong could lead to massive conflict—to say nothing of permanently discrediting me as a regional mediator. As Madeleine Albright said to me at the time, "The UN role in this is a big deal." Since I was in the lead, I insisted that this be respected and asked her and the other big players not to send their own envoys to meddle.

Israel and Lebanon had no diplomatic relations, and under international law only they could agree to the border between them. As a go-between, my job was not to set their border but to determine a line to measure whether Israel had withdrawn in accordance with resolution 425. Drawing what became known as the Blue Line required the UN team to ferret out evidence from archives around the world and was incredibly complicated.

The difficulties were immense. Consider the village of Ghajar—inhabited by Syrian Alawites, in occupied Syrian territory, but right on the border with Lebanon. After 1967 the villagers had accepted Israeli citizenship, unlike other Syrian villagers in the Golan. Yet the village's natural growth over the decades had, it turned out, taken it into Lebanese territory. The Blue Line would have to go straight *through* the village, leaving the northern residents in Lebanon and the southerners in Israeli-occupied Syria. This pleased no one, myself included. Some villagers feared their fate at the hands of Hizbollah. Barak, who remembered conquering the village in 1967, thought "cartography was trumping peace." We secured a Lebanese undertaking that neither the army nor Hizbollah would enter the village—an arrangement that lasted until 2005, when four Hizbollah fighters were killed by the Israeli Defence Forces (IDF) after launching an attack from the north. Ghajar remains an unresolved problem today.

But the biggest headache was the Shab'a farms. The Lebanese claimed that certain farmlands adjacent to the Lebanese village of Shab'a fell in their territory. A map dated 1966 was presented to us by Lebanese president Emile Lahoud, and it showed the farms in Lebanon. Yet it stood gloriously alone, contradicted by eighty other maps—including ten Lebanese government maps from *after* 1966, all showing the farms in *Syria* (and thus within the Israeli-occupied Golan Heights). Even Lebanese banknotes suggested the farms were Syrian.

I asked my staff to check the map presented by President Lahoud. Sure enough, it was from 1966—except for the ink in the area of Shab'a, which was barely dry. We let the Lebanese know that this was a map of "questionable authenticity," and that I would go public if I ever heard about it again.

The Shab'a farms were probably being laid as a political trip wire. Barak's move had taken Syria by surprise and was causing some angst. If Israel's occupation of Lebanon ended, how could the continuation of armed resistance on Lebanese territory be justified, whether by Hizbollah or Palestinian factions? If the Lebanese state regained control of all its territory, would it begin to raise questions about Syria's military and intelligence tutelage of the country?

In the end, we developed a simple way to draw the line between Lebanon and Syria, based on the delineated areas of operation of two UN peacekeeping missions in the area—the United Nations Interim Force in Lebanon (UNIFIL) and the United Nations Disengagement Observer Force (UNDOF) on the Golan. The Shab'a farms were in the UNDOF zone. Israel would eventually have to return the farms—but to Syria, in the context of a peace agreement with Damascus, unless Lebanon and Syria formally agreed that Shab'a was part of Lebanon. To date, they have not done so.

On May 22, 2000, I presented the proposed Blue Line in a report to the Security Council, which endorsed it, just as things were heating up on the ground. The Lebanese had no intention of allowing the occupying force to extricate itself on Israel's terms. Large crowds, including Hizbollah elements, began moving south, entering villages in the Israeli-controlled area. Barak had to rush through his departure—within a week, Israel had vacated almost all positions in Lebanon, leaving mainly at night under cover of Israeli artillery fire.

Throughout the withdrawal, I was in constant contact with both

Barak, who was on the ground near the Israeli frontlines, and Lebanese president Lahoud. With Barak, I pushed to ensure full withdrawal, and he urged that UN posts be established in particular areas. I intervened with Lahoud when actions by Lebanese forces were preventing UNIFIL from carrying out patrols. The withdrawal was replete with violent incidents but never blew up into anything full scale. Both men were former generals, and we managed in the fog of withdrawal to prevent the situation from getting out of hand.

Both sides submitted a host of reservations regarding the Blue Line, particularly the Lebanese. They may not have *accepted* the Blue Line, but I secured from both a commitment to *respect* it. When I certified to the Security Council on June 16, 2000, that Israel had met the requirements of resolution 425, I called it "a happy day for Lebanon, but also for Israel— a day of hope—and a day of pride for the United Nations." And, indeed, it was. There was genuine excitement in Lebanon that eighteen years of Israeli control in the south was over. Meanwhile, Barak told me: "Literally hundreds of thousands of Israelis, especially parents of soldiers, are breathing a collective sigh of relief. The mood is very positive."

My certification to the Council was not without some risk, since many flashpoints remained and loose ends needed to be tied up. However, rather than awaiting the Council's formal endorsement, I visited the region to address those remaining issues. I sensed that the Council would not want to undercut me while I was in the region and would therefore support my judgment that Israel had withdrawn. The Russians took their time to come around, but after some nervous days—I had been in Cairo and Tehran without knowing I had the Council's backing—the gamble paid off. The Council endorsed my report just hours before I landed in Beirut.

While I was seeking to lock in commitments to respect the Blue Line, almost everyone wanted to reopen one aspect or other. Barak was furious that the Lebanese had brought forth new information during the withdrawal that necessitated slight adjustments of the line. These sometimes forced him to move more military hardware than he had envisaged—sometimes more than once, and sometimes only a matter of a few meters. Meanwhile, the Lebanese complained strongly about Israeli violations. The Egyptians were worried that Israel had given a big victory to Hizbollah, while the Israelis accused *me* of having done precisely this by meeting the Hizbollah leader Hassan Nasrallah to urge him to focus on the movement's political and social role in Lebanese society and to cease armed resistance—a message I also gave in Syria and Iran. No one was fully satisfied, but the withdrawal had gone better than anyone was entitled to expect, and I felt I had emerged with all parties seeing me as credible and trustworthy.

In Israel, Yossi Beilin—a pro-peace politician and friend who was always a source of counsel and vision—had led a public movement advocating withdrawal from Lebanon. Beilin proudly presented me with a shirt printed with the words PEACEFUL WITHDRAWAL FROM LEBANON. He felt a major source of tension had been alleviated. I, too, felt at the time that we had come through the worst.

But I understood the Egyptian concerns, which Arafat shared. What message did it send that Israel left Lebanon after Hizbollah "resistance" but no end was in sight for the Palestinians after seven years of the peace process? The lesson was *not* that Israel should have stayed in Lebanon but, rather, that Israel should try *again* for peace with Syria, and even more important, it should move quickly and decisively for peace with the Palestinians.

INTO THE ABYSS: CAMP DAVID AND THE SECOND INTIFADA

Barak certainly planned to move quickly on the Palestinian track. Within weeks, he had persuaded President Clinton to host him and Arafat at

Camp David, without any real preparation. The parties would be brought together to try and resolve the most sensitive problems of the conflict—borders, Jerusalem, refugees, security—issues the two leaders had never properly discussed before. Arafat, who had been left cooling his heels while Barak had showered attention first on Syria and then on Lebanon, was not keen to go to Camp David at all, as he told me in June at his office in the Makata in Ramallah. "We're not ready. In the current state it's bound to fail and we will only have one shot!" He asked me to persuade the Americans not to invite the parties to Camp David. I understood why.

A myth has developed that Camp David involved a generous Israeli offer and revealed that there was no Palestinian partner for peace. I have no doubt that Arafat could have been a more creative negotiator at Camp David, rather than simply awaiting Israeli proposals. I also know that Barak went further than any Israeli leader to date—after all, no Israeli leader had ever put a proposal forward for a Palestinian state of any kind. But Barak was not prepared to contemplate what I believe to be politically essential for any territorial deal: a Palestinian state on the equivalent of 100 percent of the West Bank and Gaza before 1967—22 percent of historic Palestine—with a contiguous state territory on the West Bank, and Jerusalem properly shared. Besides, with the Arab countries excluded from the summit, there was no way Arafat would take risks on Jerusalem, as I told Madeleine Albright at the time. I admired President Clinton for trying, and for not giving up when the summit failed. But it was a mistake for the Americans to side with Barak and point the finger at Arafat for the failure of Camp David. The episode showed the limits of U.S.-only peacemaking and increased calls in the region for more players to be at the Middle East peace table.

Soon, at the end of 2000, the second Palestinian intifada broke out. The parties and historians will continue to argue over how it started—my sense at the time was that there were elements of spontaneity and provocation that sparked the violence, but there were also elements of planning as well. In any case, once the violence erupted, Arafat seemed to ride the storm rather than try to hold it back, while Barak resorted to the harshest of counterproductive measures, humiliating Arafat and using excessive force against the Palestinians. As each side crossed more and more red lines, a hurricane of violence developed that engulfed both peoples and the peace process itself. Much of the fabric of Palestinian life, already frayed by the prolonged and sometimes brutal occupation, was torn apart—and with it, much of the hope for peace on which Palestinian moderates relied. The Israeli peace camp was also left in tatters, as Israelis came to believe that there was indeed "no partner," and turned to leaders on the right. Any modicum of trust between Israel and the Palestinians died.

Albright brought Barak and Arafat to Paris on October 4 and tried to broker a cease-fire, but she was unable to achieve one. The Israelis wanted a cease-fire pure and simple; the Palestinians wanted an international commission under UN auspices to examine the causes of the violence. Moreover, the Palestinians insisted, partly at Cairo's bidding, that a deal should be brokered in Egypt. I was in Paris at the time, and I urged the Americans to move the effort to Cairo, but they declined. I returned to New York, but as things went from bad to worse on the ground, I decided to go to Jerusalem myself.

I sensed a strong expectation in the Security Council that I should do *something*, even if I knew that the Council members could not agree on what. The Israelis did not want me involved. "The prime minister has told me in the most emotional way that Israel will prevent the UN plane from landing at Ben Gurion Airport," Roed-Larsen told me over the phone. I decided I would go anyway—if Israel stopped the secretary-general's plane, it would be their problem. When their bluff was called, the Israelis allowed my plane to land on October 8, and I was received at a hastily put together welcome by the acting foreign minister, Shlomo Ben-Ami.

In my ten years in office, the subsequent ten days of shuttling between Arafat and Barak were among the most improvised, uncertain, and dramatic. While I was on the ground, more than fifty Palestinians were killed, and two Israeli reservists were lynched by a mob in Ramallah. Feelings on both sides were at a fever pitch. Each side was deeply mistrustful of the other's true intentions. Both were talking the language of war.

The longer I was on the ground, and the more back-and-forth shuttling I did, the more vital it became that I not leave without a breakthrough—to do so would have sent a terrible message. I tried and failed to get the leaders to make public appeals for calm and agree to specific measures of de-escalation, and then switched to working with Egyptian president Hosni Mubarak and Bill Clinton to persuade the parties to attend a new summit in Sharm el-Sheikh. The Americans were going to join up with the Egyptians after all.

Arafat did not want to attend the summit with his people under siege from repeated Israeli missile and artillery attacks. He even stopped taking Clinton's calls and avoided giving Mubarak an answer to his invitation. Would he say yes to me? I went to Gaza without an appointment for one last meeting with the Palestinian leader. When I finally got to see Arafat, he seemed back in Beirut: "Barak wants to put me in a corner and make me crawl on my hands and knees. Doesn't he know who Yasser Arafat is?"

I tried to speak as much to Arafat's sense of pride as to his interest—to his heart, not his brain: "Probably you're right. Barak doesn't want you in Sharm. He would be happy if you did not go. But don't give him this pleasure. It would mean he had won. Let world public opinion judge this." I left the meeting without a firm commitment from Arafat, but I upped the pressure by telling reporters that I expected Arafat to be in Sharm.

On the helicopter flight back to Jerusalem, a paper was passed around for the team to offer odds on whether Arafat would say yes. Everyone else was doubtful, but I remember writing "100%." I was sure he was bluffing and he would come. We heard nothing that night, and the team was on edge the following morning at the King David Hotel. I checked first with Sandy Berger, Clinton's national security advisor, and then with Mubarak: "No one called here. I had a quiet night," Mubarak told me. Finally, Arafat came on the line.

"Do I have your answer?"

"Yes," he replied, "I will come."

I called Mubarak back to tell him the news. There and then he said: "You and Solana will attend" (Javier Solana, the former NATO secretary-general with whom I worked closely over Kosovo, was now the EU's high representative for foreign and security policy).

Thus I received my invitation to Sharm, underlining the UN's place at the center of Middle East diplomacy. Solana thought it was historic: "This is the first time in the history of this part of the world that the Secretary-General of the United Nations has been allowed to play a role," he told me. "We have a long life and we need the UN."

I left the pressure-cooker atmosphere of Gaza and Jerusalem for the clear sea, sand, and sky of the Red Sea coast. But the gathering at Sharm el-Sheikh was no less tense for its placid location. Confidence was nonexistent, emotions were running high, and the proceedings were turbulent. At times the gap between the parties seemed unbridgeably wide. Bill Clinton stepped off an overnight flight and straight into action, and worked continuously over twenty-eight hours late into the night and early morning. I had helped get the parties together and worked with Clinton to handle the players at the summit, but it was Clinton who brought home a three-part deal on security cooperation, renewal of the peace process, and a fact-finding committee to inquire into the violence. His stature and negotiating ability really counted.

Barak did not want a committee at all and could only contemplate a

U.S. committee; Arafat wanted a committee under UN auspices, partly to counteract U.S. exclusive ownership of the peace process as a whole. They eventually agreed that Clinton would appoint the committee in consultation with me. The arrangement was a pretty fair reflection of the power realities: the U.S. role remained central, but the UN was now at the table.

In the weeks that followed, Madeleine Albright, Sandy Berger, and I agreed on the names for the commission. The commission chair was former U.S. senator George Mitchell, who later would become Barack Obama's envoy to the Middle East. The Mitchell Report, produced in April 2001 during the early months of the Bush administration, introduced a concept that would rightly become a pillar of peace efforts thereafter—the need for actions on *both* security (by the Palestinians) *and* settlements (by the Israelis) if violence and mistrust were to be avoided and the peace process to make real headway. The report eschewed a narrow "security only" approach, or placing the onus only on one party, which had so often in the past led simply to more frustration and regression.

We had begun to set a new basis for the peace process, but the Sharm cease-fire did not ultimately hold. It was unstitched by the actions of the parties, the provocations and violence of both the Israelis and the Palestinians, and it went effectively unmonitored by the international community. There was a lot more to do if the international role was to be effective. Tony Blair told me at the time that "the intervention of some international authority of some sort" was needed to "impose an agreement"—and even wondered aloud whether I should try to do it, but without willing partner governments in a position of leverage sufficient to ensure compliance with such an attempt, there was no chance of its working.

The peace process was crumbling. Barak faced the prospect of a massive defeat at the hands of Ariel Sharon in elections slated for February 6, 2001. The measures Barak imposed on the Palestinians were severe and far exceeded anything that could be justified by security concerns. In this near-hopeless atmosphere, President Clinton offered on December 23, 2000, take-it-or-leave-it parameters for a final settlement. Barak and Arafat each gave a qualified answer to the Clinton parameters. The United States felt Barak's answer was a "Yes, provided," while Arafat's was a "No, however." So, in their conclusion, the United States squarely blamed Arafat.

With that, President Clinton's years of noble and committed effort ended in unhappy failure.

Even this was not the final word. Israeli and Palestinian negotiators met at Taba, Egypt, in January 2001 to try to finalize a deal before the Israeli elections; on January 27, Taba concluded with the parties recording publicly that they were never closer to reaching an agreement. Despite claiming Arafat was not a partner, Barak was still hoping that a UN-EU summit might be convened to sign an agreement with Arafat, and he and I talked a lot about the idea. But as I watched Barak plummeting in the opinion polls, and saw Arafat launch a blistering attack on the Israelis at the World Economic Forum in Davos, I realized it would never fly. I leaned heavily on Arafat during a two-hour meeting and gathered more than eighty journalists for a joint midnight press conference where he made more conciliatory statements, as he did in an interview with Israeli television, but it was by now clear that no further meeting could be held.

My heart sank when Egyptian president Mubarak recounted a conversation with the recently resigned Israeli president Ezer Weizman, who had been a dovish influence throughout the 1990s. Weizman had said that Barak had failed, and he would join the majority of the country in voting for Ariel Sharon's Likud. Bill Clinton summed it up when we spoke to exchange New Year's greetings. "Labour sees the Palestinians as legitimate," he told me. "Rabin always believed they were people. He always treated them like human beings. The other guys [that is, the Likud] don't see them as a legitimate force." As it turned out, I had managed to win a UN seat at the peace table just as it was being upended. And with Clinton's departure, there was no U.S. president keen to reset the table in a hurry.

FORMING THE QUARTET

It was no secret that President George W. Bush was not going to continue the hands-on engagement of Clinton, but I was taken aback by just how hands-off he chose to be. As the conflict of the second intifada raged in 2001, tearing up so much that had been so doggedly built over the past seven years, he basically watched. It was obvious that at some point a political initiative would be required to quell the violence and get the parties back to the table, and that all the lives lost in the meantime would be utterly wasted. But Bush showed no inclination to intervene, though Powell tried to shift the administration toward engagement.

After 9/11, Bush's instincts to disengage from the Palestinian issue were reinforced—unlike Tony Blair, who realized anew how crucial it was to make progress on Palestine. Bush had a deep personal antipathy toward Arafat. I hosted heads of state at a lunch during the general debate of the General Assembly in November 2001—the first after 9/11. Javier Solana somewhat courageously wandered over to where Bush and I were seated, and casually dropped the suggestion that President Bush take this opportunity to shake Yasser Arafat's hand. "Tell him to shake his own hand," was the inimitable Texan reply. That was that.

On another occasion I even suggested to Bush that he appoint Bill Clinton as an envoy—thinking that Bush could claim credit for any success while distancing himself from any failure. "Thank you for that good advice," he said. This was an unambiguous "no."

I was under no illusion that I could mediate this conflict on my own. So I resolved to keep trying to bring the main international parties together—the United States, the UN, the European Union, and Russia. The Americans held by far the most cards, and we could achieve little without their leadership. The UN embodied the international principles for a solution and had a formidable presence on the ground. The EU could bring real political and financial resources to the table. Russia had a long-standing role in the region. In 2001, I suggested to Powell that he and I, along with Solana and Russian foreign minister Igor Ivanov, should visit the region to pull the parties back from the brink. Our representatives were already working closely together on the ground, and I thought it was time to take it up a notch.

Unfortunately, Powell could not sell this idea to Washington, and in the end I went to the region on my own, while emphasizing that I was working closely with the other three. It was a depressing trip, with Sharon insisting that there should be total calm from the West Bank before he lifted a finger himself to ease up on his army's actions, while Arafat remained maddeningly evasive when I pleaded with him to rein in Palestinian attacks. In Cairo, Mubarak declined my suggestion that he meet with the Israeli leader, joking that Sharon was "too busy eating."

I kept pressing for a meeting of the four key outside players in the region—Russia, the United States, the EU, and the UN—ultimately writing to them in October 2001, and bringing them together in New York for a first official meeting on the Middle East in November. I proposed that we work together and call ourselves the Quartet. Everyone agreed.

I hoped that, through the Quartet, we could help achieve in practice what the UN had so far not been able to do through its own institutions—forge and implement an international strategy for Middle East peace, and help the parties overcome the chasm of mistrust that separated them and the political constraints that held them back. The Quartet was a vehicle with four wheels, but the engine was inevitably "Made in America." This carried risks for my position in particular. But I hoped at least that I could have a hand on the steering wheel, and quite often I did.

At public briefings, the Quartet issued consensus statements, which were primarily driven by requirements of the United States, but I was not shy when speaking at Quartet press conferences in also emphasizing my own independent positions as secretary-general and expressing my own separate opinions. It was a credit to Powell that he was open to working in this way. Others in his position might have balked at the whole idea of the Quartet. Truth be told, Powell probably pointed to the expectations of the Quartet, and the ambitions of other players to get involved in his internal Washington battles, in order to push for a more active U.S. role in the diplomacy.

ARAB PEACE INITIATIVE, PASSOVER BOMBING, DEFENSIVE SHIELD

It was March 2002, and I was in Beirut attending the Arab League Summit. All the attendees were waiting expectantly for Arafat to address them by video link from a besieged Ramallah. There was fear among Arab leaders that Sharon might soon kill or expel him. Suddenly, the screen went blank. No Arafat. No speech. Had the Israelis suddenly attacked his compound, some wondered? Nothing of the sort. Afterward, President Lahoud proudly informed Terje Roed-Larsen that he had personally cut the line. The hatred of Arafat still prevailed in Lebanon, two decades after his expulsion by Israel from Beirut.

If this tragicomic moment reminded me of the many divisions

within the Arab world, including the history of enmity between Arafat and a number of Arab leaders, the fact was that the Arabs found rare unity at the Beirut summit. They embraced the peace proposal of Saudi Crown Prince Abdullah, promising full normalization of relations by all members of the Arab League with Israel in exchange for a return of the 1967 territories and a just and agreed solution for the refugees on the basis of UN General Assembly resolution 194 adopted in 1948. The same group that had famously passed the three noes at its summit in Khartoum in 1967—no to peace with Israel, no to recognition of Israel, no to negotiations with Israel—had come a very long way. If Israel reached genuine peace with the Palestinians, Syria, and Lebanon, the Arab peace initiative meant that Israel's flag would fly in twenty-two Arab countries, and twenty-two Arab countries would fly their flags in Israel. As others have said: the two-state solution could become the twenty-two-state solution. To this day, the Abdullah proposal remains the most compelling Arab offer on the table, offering the Israelis something far larger than a bilateral agreement with the PLO.

But Sharon completely ignored it. Later, when pressed on why they rebuffed this historic opening, the Israelis would cite the reference to General Assembly resolution 194 on refugees—a reference to the "right of return"—as posing unacceptable conditions. This referred to the Arab claim of the right of all refugees to return to their homes, abandoned in the war of 1948 at the creation of Israel—a policy, if enacted, that would swamp Israel with returning Arab refugees and their descendents. Yet the Arab initiative makes clear that there must be an "agreed"-upon solution on this issue. The least the Israelis might have done was make a counteropening of their own. To this day they have not.

The same day that the Arab League reached this historic decision, Hamas decided to send a bloody message about where it stood. A suicide bomber killed 29 Israelis and wounded about 150 others in an attack on a Passover feast. It was a shocking, deeply destructive act that required the strongest condemnation from Arafat if we were not to lose the momentum from the Abdullah proposal. From Beirut that night, I called Arafat four times—the line kept being broken—to urge him to condemn the bombing and show the Israeli public that he truly sought a different path to achieving the Palestinians' aspirations.

This atrocity was the proximate cause of Operation Defensive Shield in April 2002. Sharon launched massive military incursions with the stated purpose of pursuing those responsible for attacks against Israel. Israel proceeded to fully reoccupy six of the largest cities in the West Bank, imposing around-the-clock curfews, and destroying Palestinian security infrastructure that then left the field even more open for militants to launch attacks.

The scenes of horror mounted: the twisted metal and bloodstained wreckage of the Passover hotel attack; Arafat's presidential compound in Ramallah heavily damaged and surrounded by Israeli tanks; Palestinian militants holed up in the Church of the Nativity in Bethlehem encircled by Israeli forces; and the near-total destruction of a Palestinian refugee camp in the center of Jenin. I was appalled at the atrocities that Palestinian militants had perpetrated, with sixteen bombings between March and early May killing more than one hundred Israelis. But the humanitarian impact and the scale of the killing that Israel was inflicting were excessive, leaving nearly five hundred Palestinians dead and nearly fifteen hundred wounded in the same period.

As the violence mounted, the Security Council met almost nonstop. We kept thinking the situation could not get worse, but every day it did. In my addresses to the Council, I condemned terrorism unreservedly but also Israel's excessive use of force and prevention of basic humanitarian assistance to the Palestinians. I sought to apply public pressure on the parties by reminding them not to be carried away by fantasies. I warned Israel that it would be a "miscalculation of monumental proportions to believe that removing Chairman Arafat from the political scene and dismantling the Palestinian Authority would create conditions where Israel can achieve security for itself," and I lamented that the Palestinian Authority "seems to believe that failing to act against terrorism, and inducing turmoil, chaos, and instability, will cause the government and the people of Israel to buckle. They will not."

It was clear that the international community could not break the cycle of violence with cease-fire proposals devoid of any larger political framework—we needed security and politics to go hand in hand. Until that time, in line with Sharon's wishes, the United States had focused only on a cease-fire, through the efforts of CIA director George Tenet and General Anthony Zinni. They were so overconditioning the development of a political horizon that it would never be reached, playing into the hands of those who wanted to intensify the violence and hold back the peace process. My spokesman Fred Eckhard inadvertently summarized the absurdity when he said in response to a journalist's question (on April Fool's Day, 2002, no less):

> The U.S. mediator, General Anthony Zinni, has been trying to get the two sides to begin the Tenet process; which is to lead back to the Mitchell understandings; which is to lead back to the negotiating table. But they're still stuck in the pre-Tenet stage while the violence goes on.

Even George Bush seemed to appreciate that things could not go on as they were, telling me in a telephone call on March 30:

> We've got to understand Israel's right to defend itself. On the other hand, security must lead to peace. So far security is not even leading to security. We are exploring the fundamental nature of Zinni's mission. The situation has overpowered Zinni.

The United States enabled the Council to pass two resolutions—1397, on a two-state solution, which at least noted the Arab Peace Initiative; and 1402, reacting to the violence on the ground, though with nothing binding on either party.

Bush soon publicly called on Sharon to withdraw from Palestinian cities. The Quartet met in Madrid on April 8, 2002. I knew this would be a test for my fledgling foursome, and I was worried we would not be able to find common ground. But the envoys worked through the night before the meeting to agree to a statement, which sent tough and clear messages to both the Israelis and the Palestinians, and gave our full support to Powell before he visited the region—a position subsequently backed by the Security Council.

To my relief and satisfaction, the international community was now at least pulling together, and there was the prospect of a serious political discussion on the way forward. But I had a more immediate concern on my mind: Jenin.

JENIN

Worrying reports were coming in that civilians in the northern West Bank city of Jenin had been killed in large numbers. A Palestinian negotiator claimed that hundreds had been massacred—a claim that later turned out to be false. There were also independent reports that civilians were being denied access to aid supplies and medical treatment by the Israelis, and that the refugee camp had been largely destroyed. Meanwhile, Arafat was hailing the glorious resistance of the people of "Jeningrad."

I did not want to rely on rumors or to condemn anyone until I knew the facts, but I did not want to take a let's-wait-and-see attitude, either.

When the Israelis turned down my request to send an immediate search-and-rescue mission, I instructed my envoy, Roed-Larsen, to take the UNRWA commissioner-general Peter Hansen with him and go directly to Jenin with the media. Roed-Larsen was hesitant: "Jenin is closed. This will blow me out of the political water forever, even if I understand why you think it is the right thing to do," he told me on the phone from his car.

"Yes, I know there is that risk," I replied. "But we have to make choices and there are costs. I'm sorry, Terje, you may have to pay a price. But I will back you." I wanted him to shine a light on what had hitherto been in the dark.

So Roed-Larsen went. He avoided speculation as to whether there had been a "massacre," a word he never used. But he described to the press what he saw, which was "horrific beyond belief . . . It is totally destroyed. It looks like an earthquake has hit it. I am watching two brothers pull their father from the ruins, the stench of death is horrible. We are seeing a twelve-year-old boy being dug out, totally burned."

The same day, I told the Security Council that I believed it should consider authorizing a multinational force in the Palestinian territory, for the benefit of the security and protection of both parties—a suggestion dismissed by the Israelis. I remain convinced that such a force will one day form part of the peace and security solution to the conflict.

Foreign Minister Shimon Peres and Defense Minister Benjamin Ben-Eliezer now welcomed the idea that I should send a fact-finding mission, and the Security Council backed this in resolution 1405. I turned to Martti Ahtisaari—an impeccable Finn with what the Finns call "*sisu*," an untranslatable word combining guts and staying power. The Israelis started to get cold feet when it became evident that he would lead a team that included human rights, humanitarian, military, and police experts. Eventually, it became clear the Israelis would not allow the team in, and I had to disband it.

This kind of episode is played out with some regularity in the Israeli-Palestinian conflict—we saw something similar with the Goldstone report on Israel's and Hamas' conduct during the 2008–9 conflict in Gaza, which occurred after I had departed as secretary-general. There was an important difference—Richard Goldstone was commissioned by the Human Rights Council, not the secretary-general, and the Israelis refused to cooperate with him, citing the bias of the Human Rights Council mandate. But as the Jenin episode illustrated, Israel often also refuses to cooperate with a person with an entirely impartial mandate. The refusal to cooperate with a sober and experienced professional like Ahtisaari was all the more frustrating, because when the dust settled, and I reported later in the year to the General Assembly based on publicly available sources (but not visiting Jenin itself), there were serious violations by the Israel Defense Forces (IDF), but the most extreme claims that there had been a "massacre" turned out to be false.

In the debates over UN fact-finding following certain incidents, there are patterns that recur. When Palestinian civilians are killed in IDF operations, the Israelis say it is a good-faith mistake by an army applying high standards of restraint and care but facing the difficult task of fighting militants in densely populated cities. For their part, the Palestinians and Arabs feel that Israel uses excessive force to maintain the occupation and gets away with it. The Israelis claim they are singled out; the Palestinians claim the Israelis are let off the hook. The secretary-general must consistently and impartially uphold international humanitarian law as it applies to all parties.

There was another situation, a year earlier, in which the Israelis had real and serious grounds for complaint against the UN. In mid-2001, the Israelis gained information that UNIFIL was in possession of a videotape showing the aftermath of the kidnapping of three Israeli soldiers by

Hizbollah. I did not know about the tape, nor did my most senior advisors. Indeed, when we asked, we were positively and absolutely informed by officials in DPKO and UNIFIL that there was no tape. We told the Israelis so, and even took strong exception to their allegations to the contrary.

When the Israelis stuck to their guns, we checked again—and to my dismay it turned out that a director in DPKO knew of the tape, had it in his possession, and had failed to disclose its existence to his superiors. We eventually allowed Israel to view the tape, but the whole sorry episode was a setback in our efforts to build trust with the Israelis. I appointed an independent committee to investigate, which produced a harsh report exposing serious mistakes of judgment and ethics on the matter within UNIFIL and DPKO.

This crisis in our relations occurred around the same time as the 2001 Durban Conference on Racism—a matter largely out of my hands but which Israel viewed as an Israel-bashing spectacle under UN sponsorship, a narrative that clouded the many important achievements of Durban. All this was a millstone around the neck of a UN secretary-general in trying to help mediate in the Middle East.

THE ROADMAP

By June 2002, George Bush had delivered a speech formally committing his administration to a vision of two states. Despite the wreckage of the intifada, both the Arabs (in Beirut) and the United States had now, for the first time, formally signed on not just to peace but to a clear end goal. However, apart from calling for a new Palestinian leadership not compromised by terror, Bush's speech laid out no path to the vision. I had said to Powell a year earlier: "We don't just need a cease-fire, but a timetable for economics and politics, a roadmap, and with monitoring." Many others had similar ideas. After Bush's speech, the view quickly took hold—including with the help of the Jordanians—that we needed a roadmap to achieve it.

The roadmap was not designed to replace a negotiated agreement between the parties. Its purpose was to create the context for those negotiations by rebuilding the confidence shattered by Oslo's failure, while repairing some of Oslo's defects. It is sometimes referred to as President Bush's Roadmap. But it was genuinely a product of negotiation among the Quartet members. Five features gave rise to debate in the group.

The first and most fundamental feature was parallelism. This was my mantra, shared by the EU and the Russians: we believed we would get nowhere if all Israeli actions were contingent on the Palestinians first meeting security benchmarks, and we cited the Mitchell Report in this regard. We sensed that the State Department agreed but the White House did not. Nevertheless, with the UN team making a significant contribution, and after plenty of haggling and difficult moments, the roadmap eventually embodied this principle. In phase 1, the Palestinians were expected to act decisively against terrorism, once and for all, and reform corrupt institutions. But the Israelis also had clear obligations: to freeze all settlement activity, including natural growth, remove the so-called settlement outposts—illegal even under Israeli law—that had mushroomed all over the West Bank under Sharon, and allow the Palestinians to reopen their institutions in East Jerusalem. One obligation was not contingent on the other.

A second key concept was that the roadmap was performance-driven. While timelines were laid down for when the process should move to subsequent phases—including final status negotiations—actually doing so would be dependent on the parties performing. This was important, particularly to the Israelis, since they doubted Arafat's readiness to live up to his roadmap obligations to act against terrorism. But its logical handmaiden was monitoring—the third innovation. A structure was meant to be put in place through which the international community would closely follow each party's action or inaction on its obligations. However, this was always a heavily contested aspect of the roadmap. Despite constant pushing from the EU and the UN, the United States never consented to forming a joint, formal mechanism that could call the parties to account for their failure to act on their obligations. The United States' unwillingness to contemplate empowering a joint platform that could criticize not just the Palestinians but Israel too undid much of the potential of the roadmap.

The fourth new element was the prescription of a clear end goal for negotiations: a two-state solution that ended the 1967 occupation and ensured a real state for the Palestinians and lasting security for Israel. This goal had never been set before at the outset of negotiations. I only wished it could have been stated with far more specificity, drawing on the Clinton parameters with clear terms of reference regarding borders, security, Jerusalem, and refugees. I am convinced that the more specific the international community can be on these issues, the easier it will be for the parties to converge on a negotiated outcome.

Finally, the roadmap introduced a fifth innovation—the option of agreeing on a Palestinian state with provisional borders during the process, as a way station to a permanent settlement. I was never convinced this was a good idea, and certainly the Palestinians did not think so—unless, and only unless, the details of a permanent settlement were already agreed, and this was merely a phase of implementation. Hence, it was referred to as an option. The Palestinian experience with Oslo was that the temporary tended to become permanent—mirroring, I might add, the Israeli fear that a so-called permanent solution might one day turn out merely to be temporary.

Shimon Peres remarked at the time that there was a light (meaning the two-state solution) but no tunnel (meaning there was no agreed way to get from the current crisis to the two-state outcome). The roadmap was meant to shine the light brighter and create the tunnel. But it only had a chance of working if all Quartet members insisted on utilizing its potential to the full and did not allow the parties to wriggle out of their commitments.

It took months to agree on the roadmap, and still months more before it was launched. Washington's rush to war in Iraq stood in stark contrast to the gentlemanly pace of U.S. engagement on the Israeli-Palestinian track, which was only deteriorating the longer it was neglected. I wanted the roadmap released and the parties discussing it already. The United States, most important of all, had proved it was simply unwilling to push forward in the manner that we were. I was frustrated and expressed so publicly in interviews in March 2003, at the lack of ambition to move on the Palestinian situation—especially given that we all seemed to share a common dream of two states but would not take the concrete steps to make it a reality.

AN EMPOWERED PALESTINIAN PRIME MINISTER?

Timing was not the only issue. The United States would not present the roadmap to Arafat. They refused to deal with him or regard him as a partner. On the other hand, it was futile to try to push Arafat out or to presume we could totally ignore the legitimate Palestinian leader. So the UN proposed that Arafat should remain president but appoint an empowered prime minister to control security and finances. These were the two areas on which Arafat had lost credibility, but on which the success of the roadmap hinged. We managed to sell this idea to our Quartet partners.

Getting Arafat to agree was another matter. We first sought Arafat's agreement to the principle before discussing names—even though it was

clear that the prime minister should be Mahmoud Abbas, the senior figure within the Palestinian leadership who had opposed the armed intifada from the outset. Arafat finally relented.

We strongly encouraged Arafat to appoint Abbas, not a Palestinian
businessman whom he had his eye on, and not, as he joked, Lebanon's
billionaire prime minister, Rafiq al-Hariri ("he could bring us lots of
money")! Finally, under heavy pressure, and with the war in Iraq just
starting to his east, Arafat agreed to appoint Abbas. He was sworn in on
April 30, 2003, and the roadmap was formally presented to both parties.
All four Quartet envoys presented it in Ramallah, but the Americans
alone gave it to Sharon. Such was the reality of the game. The United
States was often prepared to share management of the Palestinians but
insisted on preserving its prerogatives vis-à-vis Israel.

Rather than proceeding along the roadmap, Sharon and Arafat
looked for exit ramps. Arafat undermined Abbas, who did not assert his
prerogatives and remained standoffish in political infighting. As Abbas
achieved some early successes, Arafat's jealousy grew. Arafat refused to
cede control over the security services. Abbas soon resigned, and when he
did so, I could feel U.S. enthusiasm for driving forward the roadmap start
to dissipate. We were still a long way from the kind of Palestinian security
performance that would persuade Washington to move on the real political issues. The U.S. obsession with Arafat returned to the fore and remained until his death in late 2004.

WEST BANK WALL, GAZA WITHDRAWAL

Not to be outdone, Sharon also decided to go in a different direction. The
same year that we launched the roadmap, Israeli and Palestinian civil society figures signed the Geneva Accord—a document that proves, beyond

all shadow of a doubt, that an agreement is eminently achievable between sensible people of goodwill on both sides. Jerusalem *can* be shared, sensibly, as a capital of two states. It is *entirely* possible to draw a border that allows most of the Israeli settlers to stay and gives the Palestinians a contiguous and viable state that has the same territory as that occupied in 1967. Security arrangements *can* be found acceptable to both, dealing with threats old and new. Even the highly sensitive refugee question *can* be solved in a way that acknowledges their rights and suffering—including their right of return—but ensures implementation in a way that does not undermine the two-state idea itself. The conflict *can* be ended and two states for two peoples *can* exist side by side in peace.

Geneva and the roadmap put Sharon on the defensive. I sensed that he did not like this agenda and looked for an alternative. He first tried to wriggle out of the roadmap by accepting it with fourteen reservations, which struck at the heart of the concept of parallelism that we had fought so hard to incorporate. There were plenty in Washington who were quite glad to let him do so. With no serious monitoring mechanism in place, Sharon never took action to freeze West Bank settlements. Sharon busied himself with an agenda that involved completing the barrier he was building through the West Bank, withdrawing from the Gaza Strip, thickening settlements in and around Jerusalem, and founding a new political party. These were bold gambits, to be sure, and forever altered the landscape of the conflict. But they brought us no closer to peace.

The name of what Sharon was building embodied the dispute over it. The Israelis termed it a "security fence" because it helped bring to an end the spate of suicide bombings. The Palestinians regarded it as a wall, as indeed it was in the cities of Jerusalem, Ramallah, and Bethlehem where most Palestinians encountered it. I called it a barrier. In fact, the most accurate description of it would be a fence-and-wall barrier. Regardless of what it was called, its construction was clearly politically motivated since it attached large numbers of illegal Israeli settlements to

Israel and cut most Palestinians off from Jerusalem and many from their own lands.

The International Court of Justice ruled in 2004 that Sharon's wall, as they called it, to the extent that it deviated from the 1967 line and went into occupied Palestinian territory, was illegal. The problem was not the barrier itself—Israel could build a wall along its border the same way the United States could build a fence along its border with Mexico. The problem was its route, inside Palestinian lands. The General Assembly asked me to set up a register to record the damage that the wall was causing for Palestinians. The barrier was built with both a security *and* a political purpose in mind. The same was true of Israel's disengagement from Gaza.

When Sharon announced in December 2003 that he intended to leave Gaza, I admit I was surprised. Here was the father of the settlements promising to uproot settlers. He had famously proclaimed that "the fate of Netzarim [a settlement in Gaza] is the fate of Tel Aviv." In explaining his change of heart, he said that the Palestinian population was growing rapidly "in incredibly cramped refugee camps, in poverty and squalor, in hot-beds of ever-increasing hatred, with no hope whatsoever on the horizon"—a powerful description of the impact of nearly forty years of occupation. Israelis often claim that the UN exaggerates the crisis facing the civilian population in Gaza, but perhaps Sharon's own words will convince them. I have not been back to Gaza since, but if this was how Sharon described it in 2005, it must be worse today after years of prolonged Israeli blockade and Hamas rule.

Sharon viewed the disengagement as a tool to rid Israel of a liability while consolidating its hold on key West Bank settlement blocs. He wanted to receive American backing for Israeli positions regarding settlements and refugees in any future negotiations, while further establishing that there was "no partner" for peace on the Palestinian side. He achieved all these tactical victories—but, strategically, the disengagement took both Israelis and Palestinians further away from a solution. It helped to introduce dynamics that made it harder and harder for the Palestinians to stay cohesive as a political unit, played into the hands of Hamas, and left Israelis dismayed at the security consequences of leaving occupied territory.

Whatever my considerable misgivings, I decided that I could not be opposed to an Israeli withdrawal from land that did not belong to Israel. But I was equally clear that this was the "right thing, done the wrong way." We alerted the Security Council that Gaza was descending into lawlessness, chaos, and anarchy—fair warning of what could follow in the vacuum left by an Israeli departure. By acting unilaterally, Sharon undermined the new Palestinian president, Mahmoud Abbas, who had been elected in January 2005 to replace Arafat after his death. Like Barak in Lebanon five years earlier, Sharon sent a worrying message that Israel was more prepared to leave territory when the price of conflict got too high—this time at the hands of Hamas militants—than it was to seek a peace accord with the Palestinian leadership. (Netanyahu did the same in 2011 by rebuffing calls by the moderate West Bank leadership for prisoner releases to the Palestinian Authority, yet releasing one thousand Palestinian prisoners to Hamas in exchange for an Israeli soldier held in Gaza.)

To mitigate these effects, and ensure that a postwithdrawal Gaza would be a viable entity, not a suffocating prison, I wanted to do everything possible to maximize Israeli-Palestinian coordination throughout the process. I also wanted to see that it led us back to the roadmap, not away from it. In the language of the day, it should be "Gaza first, not Gaza last." This required vigorous diplomacy, including from the UN. But by the end of 2004, my envoy Terje Roed-Larsen had left Jerusalem, and in his place I appointed the veteran UN diplomat Álvaro de Soto, who arrived in May 2005. De Soto was used to delicate problems and had done impressive work in peace processes in El Salvador and Cyprus.

Unrelated to this process, Secretary of State Condoleezza Rice called me to propose that the retiring head of the World Bank, James Wolfensohn, should be appointed as an envoy to coordinate the Gaza disengagement. I leaped at the suggestion and urged that he be an envoy not of the United States but of the Quartet as a whole. Wolfensohn was a close friend and passionate about helping the weak and poor. He had unrivaled reach into the pockets of donors and knew the Israelis and the Palestinians well.

Wolfensohn moved mountains to reach a fair and workable framework that would ensure security through the Gaza-Israel crossings, make sure that imports and exports would flow, and enable a proper Palestinian takeover of the greenhouses that Israel left behind in Gaza—even donating his own money for the purpose.

At the eleventh hour, the Americans took over the process and tilted the framework toward the Israelis. I witnessed once again the unhealthy possessiveness that Washington has over the Arab-Israeli peace process, and its reluctance to share it meaningfully with others—even those working toward the same ends. Eventually, however, a new layer of complexity would be added by the decisions of the Palestinians themselves at the ballot box.

Hamas and the Quartet

Few issues in UN Middle East diplomacy caused more controversy than my participation in 2006 in a Quartet position that effectively isolated the newly elected Hamas-led Palestinian Authority government. The

Quartet had backed Hamas' participation in Palestinian elections when we met in my conference room in New York in September 2005. We agreed that a group participation in elections ought not, as a matter of principle, have a militia, but we decided to support President Abbas's strategy for addressing the problem. He wanted to end the militias, and his slogan was "One Authority, One Law, One Gun." He told us he could not disarm Hamas forcibly; instead, he wanted to approach the matter politically, with Hamas inside the parliament, bound by the laws set by the majority, and confronted with the contradictions of its own position.

But when Hamas won the election on January 25, 2006, it became the majority—upending this strategy entirely. Hamas would now form a government and be responsible not only for public services but for the Palestinian security forces. I said publicly that we would work with a duly elected Palestinian government. However, the result was a bombshell for Washington. Rice had acknowledged in September that the Palestinians needed some room for the evolution of their political process. But with Hamas' having won the elections, she seemed determined to close off that room entirely when we met in London five days after the election.

Rice's mood was not made any better when Jimmy Carter, whose Carter Center had observed the elections, reported to the Quartet meeting that the vote had been admirably free and fair—and then criticized U.S. and Israeli policy. I thanked Carter and escorted him from the room so that the Quartet itself could continue discussions, and returned to a frosty glare from the secretary of state. After all, I was the one who had invited Carter to brief us in the first place.

Hamas stood for, and had done, many abominable things in its time. Israelis regarded Hamas as their mortal enemy, and many moderate Palestinians also worried what an unreformed Hamas could mean for their own society. Yet Hamas had now decided to participate in electoral politics and, to the surprise of many, it had been entrusted by the Palestinian people with government. I believe this reflected the failure of

Fatah and the peace process rather than mass Palestinian support for Islamist-dominated politics or the destruction of Israel, a goal to which Hamas was formally committed. Some thought Hamas was sending signals that it was ready to envisage a genuine transformation; others felt the movement was pursuing tactical advantages without changing its strategic objectives.

The Americans wanted the Quartet to agree that all funding to any Hamas-led government should be withdrawn unless it committed itself to three principles: renunciation of violence, recognition of Israel, and acceptance of previous commitments and obligations. I was prepared to sign up to clear standards for Hamas, which I agreed had unacceptable positions. But I respected the vote of the Palestinian people, and I wanted to know whether the Quartet would be prepared to work with Hamas in some way if they made a move *toward* the principles, even if it did not fully *meet* them. Rice largely avoided the question. There was trouble ahead.

I was used to differences in the Quartet, but never before had the divisions been so stark. The United States and the EU were the major donors to the Palestinian Authority and viewed Hamas as a terrorist group. Russia and the UN did not have these restrictions, and the UN had an overall humanitarian responsibility for the welfare of the Palestinians. We tried to secure Quartet agreement on a "common but differentiated" approach—those without restrictions could be the agents for dealing with Hamas as necessary, while those with restrictions could apply pressure. Rice would have none of it: "The fact is we are split and we can't hide that," she said in a Quartet phone call on March 28. When I proposed a Quartet meeting to further discuss the matter, she said: "I am always happy to see you all, but I am not sure there is anything further to discuss in the Quartet."

My immediate concern was to ensure that the Palestinian Authority remained a viable entity. De Soto and Wolfensohn prepared studies showing that if the financial plug were pulled on the Palestinian Authority, it would lead to chaos in health and education services, as well as a large disgruntled security sector whose salaries were not paid. The work of more than a decade of building institutions, however imperfect, could be lost.

The Americans did not seem to mind. Indeed, Wolfensohn and de Soto each warned me that the United States' aim was to bring about the collapse of the Palestinian Authority and Hamas with it. The Israelis had the same view—Sharon's advisor Dov Weisglass told my envoy that it would take "just a few days" for popular protest to force Hamas to meet international demands or fall. Still, it was obvious that donors would not transfer money to the Palestinian Authority if there were no signs of serious Hamas political evolution, particularly as regards its attitude to violence and a two-state solution.

As I told Solana when we discussed this dilemma in an April phone call: "Something we will not be forgiven for is if we are accused of causing the fall of Hamas and a social and economic upheaval in the territories." Fortunately, he and Benita Ferrero-Waldner, who had replaced Chris Patten as the EU commissioner for external relations, agreed. They set up a temporary international mechanism to channel money into key public sector services for the Palestinians, with safeguards to prevent diversion—and it took some persuading to get the Americans to go along even with this. The EU mechanism arrested but could not ultimately prevent the decline of Palestinian institutions. I hoped that a complete collapse could be avoided if the Palestinians could agree on a unity government with a sensible political program. This required Hamas to move and donors not to insist on 100 percent satisfaction.

Some of my advisors felt it was also vital that we have a political dialogue with Hamas to test its intentions, educate its leaders about the responsibilities of both government and the political process, directly convey the international community's expectations, and try to encourage its further political evolution. I had no in-principle objection to this approach, consistent with UN practice everywhere. An essential part of the secretary-general's good offices responsibilities is his prerogative to talk to all players in a given situation and to promote an inclusive approach to political dialogue.

However, my experiences in the region, including with Hizbollah, had made me less than sanguine about the UN's capacity to do this effectively with Hamas—*unless* there was a genuinely agreed international strategy in place about where we wanted to go. Clearly, there was not. I also faced a more awkward reality. A high-level political dialogue with a Hamas government at that time would have shut the UN out with many constituencies. Israel would almost certainly have refused to see my envoy, and the United States warned us in no uncertain terms of where it stood. President Abbas retained his position as head of the Palestinian Authority and the PLO, and it was important to maintain and enhance his position as the leader who stood for a nonviolent approach. I decided that we had to try to work with both parties and our international partners, and that investing our capital on bringing Hamas into the mainstream was unlikely to yield much return and could come at high cost unless there was a stronger basis of international support for it. I was also convinced that, in time, the international position would adjust.

I did not shut the door. I instructed the UN country team that they could have technical contacts as needed to fulfill their mandates. These contacts have been crucial in the years since—particularly in Gaza after the mid-2007 Hamas takeover—to enable UN agencies to deliver their programs on the ground. I also authorized political contacts as necessary. My envoy made telephone contact with the new Palestinian prime minister, Ismail Haniyeh, on a couple of occasions when tensions were high. One of the senior advisors at the office of the United Nations Special Coordinator (UNSCO) was authorized to make contact with the Hamas leadership, beginning a process of quiet political engagement that has matured in the years since, and been utilized by several different parties to address specific problems, ranging from de-escalating violent incidents to supporting prisoner-exchange negotiations.

LEBANON: HARIRI'S ASSASSINATION

While the Palestinian issue dominated my concerns for several years after the Israeli withdrawal from Lebanon, toward the end of my tenure I would also find myself once again at the heart of dramatic events in Lebanon.

For several years, Rafiq al-Hariri, the billionaire Lebanese business-man, by sheer force of personality and immense personal wealth, came to dominate Lebanese politics. Here was a Sunni leader who, to the extent that anyone could, transcended the sectarian divide. As prime minister on several occasions, "Mr. Lebanon" helped to bring the country and its remarkable capital, Beirut, back from the destruction of the war. Indeed, Beirut's revival was inspirational. When I first visited the city as secretary-general in 1998 and inaugurated the UN House in Beirut, I said: "All men and women of hope, wherever they may live, are citizens of Beirut. Therefore, as a hopeful man, I take pride in the words *'Ana Bei-ruti'* (I am a Beiruti)."

Al-Hariri had ties with Saudi Arabia, where he had built his for-tune, and with the West. But he also kept close with Syria, which main-tained some forty thousand troops in Lebanon and whose intelligence chief was probably the most powerful man in the country. The 1989 Taif Agreement had legitimized Syria's military presence as a guarantor of Lebanon's security. But the agreement had also envisaged its drawdown. Through the recovery of the 1990s and into the early twenty-first century, this drawdown never came. Syria justified its hegemony as a counter-balance to Israel's presence.

But once Israel left in 2000, Syria's role in Lebanon seemed increas-ingly driven by ignoble motives, including the maintenance of corrupt Syrian economic and intelligence interests. Syria maintained close ties to Hizbollah, which grew stronger after the Israeli withdrawal, and justified maintaining its "resistance" weapons by claiming that the Shab'a farms remained unliberated Lebanese land. The Lebanese government was not able or willing to establish itself in the south of the country, leaving UNI-FIL (United Nations Interim Force in Lebanon) to keep an uneasy peace between Israeli positions south of the Blue Line and Hizbollah positions north of it.

In September 2004, Syrian president Bashar al-Assad orchestrated a three-year extension of the term of pro-Syrian Lebanese president Emile Lahoud, forcing the Lebanese government to amend a law that set term limits. I always found a step like this a sign of trouble—usually in Africa, where I had taken to excoriating strongmen for overturning constitutional limitations on presidential terms. This move, and the manner of its execution, produced a terrible falling out between Assad and Prime Minister Hariri, who resigned shortly afterward.

Assad's move confirmed my impressions from my earlier dealings with him over the Blue Line. When I first met him in 2000, I described Bashar as "the son of his father and a modern man." By this I meant someone who had the potential to reform his country. More than a decade later, his response to the awakening of the Syrian people in 2011 in protests aimed not at revolution, but reform, confirmed the more troubling suspicion that he was a man beholden to a small group of Alawite security officers and willing to employ any means to retain power. This included a renewed attack on the city of Hama, which had suffered a brutal assault in his father's time and left an estimated ten thousand people dead. As of this writing, Syria is in the midst of the most violent of government responses to the Arab Awakening, with thousands estimated killed by security forces and no end in sight.

Just as Bashar misjudged the Syrian people in 2011, he misjudged the Lebanese in 2004. His intervention against Hariri united Christian, Sunni, and Druze elements in opposition to him—only the Shiites remained overwhelmingly pro-Syrian, including Hizbollah. Assad also misread the international scene. His actions in Lebanon, in fact, succeeded where everyone else had failed in bringing President Bush and President Chirac together after their bitter divisions over the Iraq War. They agreed to pressure Syria over Lebanon.

Chirac had no desire to threaten Assad's regime and had made a point of reaching out to the new president. But he viewed Lahoud's extension as a coup d'état against a fledgling Arab democracy, and against his close personal friend Rafiq al-Hariri. The United States was more motivated by the calamitous aftermath of the invasion of Iraq and its desire to confront any forces contributing to instability there. For his part, Assad seemed determined to insist on his prerogatives in Lebanon, and with no prospect of a peace path with Israel, he tacked toward a deeper alliance with Iran and Hizbollah. All the ingredients were brewing for a showdown.

As Assad prepared to force Lahoud's extension, France and the United States cosponsored Security Council resolution 1559. Russia and China abstained, and the resolution attracted only nine votes, but the resolution was duly passed, and called for the full reassertion of Lebanon's sovereignty and political independence. The Council backed free Lebanese elections, demanded the withdrawal of all remaining foreign (that is, Syrian) forces from Lebanon, and called for the disbanding and disarmament of all Lebanese (that is, Hizbollah) and non-Lebanese (that is, Palestinian) militias.

In time, 1559 would become one of the most controversial UN interventions in the Middle East. Its supporters would say that it embodied the unfulfilled provisions of the Taif Agreement and struck a blow for an embattled Lebanon—certainly, there were progressive forces inside the country who hailed the Council's intervention. On the other hand, the Council's aggressive stance against the Syrian presence in Lebanon stood in stark contrast to its passivity regarding Israel's occupation of Arab land. I would often state publicly that the perception of double standards in the Middle East undermined the United Nations. But more important than this, Lebanon was, as one analyst put it at the time, "a thin reed on which to build a strategy of confrontation" toward Syria.

My initial report to the Security Council on Security Council resolution 1559 stated that no concrete steps had been taken on the resolution, but both the Lebanese and Syrian governments, despite objecting to it, had stated that out of respect for the Security Council, they "would not contest" 1559. Instead, the contestation came on the streets. Lebanon would soon be gripped by a wave of bombings that terrorized the anti-Syrian members of the political elite. The very same day I issued my report, a political ally of Hariri's, Marwan Hamade, narrowly escaped death after a bomb exploded next to his car.

The real earthquake came on February 14, 2005, when Rafiq al-Hariri himself was assassinated in a massive explosion in Beirut. I remember hearing the news after I awoke at the residence in New York and being shocked by its sheer brazenness. The immediate background was chilling. My envoy had returned to New York two days before from a mission to the region, where he had unsuccessfully tried to calm tensions between Assad and Hariri.

At the request of the Security Council, I asked the Irish police chief Peter Fitzgerald—a distinguished officer with past experience in UN peacekeeping operations—to lead a fact-finding mission into the killing. In a dramatic paragraph, Fitzgerald's report recounted that Assad had personally threatened Hariri in Damascus before Lahoud's extension, in a meeting that lasted less than ten minutes. Assad had said he would rather "break Lebanon over the heads of Hariri and [Druze leader Walid] Jumblatt than see his word in Lebanon broken." When I saw Assad in Algiers two days before formally conveying the report, I warned him that the account of this threat might be included in the report. He denied the threat but made no effort to try to have the report changed. Once I submitted the report to the Council, the Syrians asked me to redact this paragraph, which I did not.

Fitzgerald's report recommended that an international independent investigation would be needed to uncover the truth, and the Council established a commission in response. This commission provided an interim conclusion in October 2005 that the crime was "carried out by a group with an extensive organization and considerable resources and capabilities," and that it was almost inconceivable that the assassination plot could have been carried out without the knowledge of the Syrian and Lebanese intelligence services that worked in tandem.

As I finalize these memoirs today, six years later, responsibility for the killing of Hariri and more than a dozen other assassinations in this period is still undetermined. I felt the failure to close the file acutely when, after my retirement, I attended a memorial for Hariri in Paris, and I have had periodic contact with his wife. During the time of the UN's work, certain persons have been arrested and subsequently released for lack of evidence, which has also harmed the process—and a key witness has been murdered. The slowness of international justice can be a problem when the pace of politics is intense.

The United Nations International Independent Investigation Commission (UNIIIC) was eventually superseded by a UN Special Tribunal for Lebanon, which issued a full report on August 17, 2011, including indictments—against four members of Hizbollah. While the indictments are an important step, their implementation is inevitably complicated by the maelstrom of Lebanese politics, and by the fact that Hizbollah today holds a blocking majority in the Lebanese government. Lebanon's stability is hard to maintain in the best of circumstances. It remains to be seen how this issue continues to affect Lebanon's politics in the years to come.

LEBANON: THE CEDAR REVOLUTION AND SYRIA'S WITHDRAWAL

The international outrage that followed Hariri's murder combined with the massive outpouring on the streets of Beirut in the Cedar Revolution made clear that the people would insist on free parliamentary elections, and that Syria would not be able to sustain its military presence. The blocs spoken of in Lebanon today—the pro-Syrian March 8 and the anti-Syrian March 14—take their names from massive public demonstrations at these times.

We achieved a diplomatic breakthrough when Assad informed Roed-Larsen in Aleppo on March 12, 2005, of his plan for a full Syrian withdrawal with a clear timetable. In a meeting in Algiers in late March, I then pressed Assad to deliver his timetable soon and to have Syrian troops and intelligence apparatus out before the Lebanese elections. We received strong support from Washington and Paris—I received many calls from Chirac, Bush, and Rice, personally complimenting our efforts—but I tried not to allow this overbearing interest to sway my work. I found the constant U.S. boosterism ironic given that President Bush had just nominated John Bolton, a Washington figure deeply hostile to the UN, to be the U.S. permanent representative to the UN. This was hardly a sign of support for me or the institution.

There were four bomb attacks in Beirut in nine days at the end of March. The Council's 1559 and 1595 demands were the opposition's manifesto and their conditions for joining a national unity government—free and fair elections, an international investigation into Hariri's killing, and Syrian withdrawal, as well as the resignation of the heads of the Lebanese security services. Eventually, elections were set for May 29, and the UN provided technical assistance to help the fragile state conduct them.

My envoy returned to Damascus in early April to receive the Syrian timetable for a full withdrawal of all troops, assets, and intelligence apparatus by April 30. Assad called me to ask me to delay my next 1559 report until April 26, when his withdrawal would be complete: "It is definite, you can be sure about that," he promised. Rice and Chirac were both upset when I agreed to this request and lobbied me to reverse my decision, but I had the substance I needed from Assad and saw no reason to insist on his face, too. I would keep control over my own reporting—not Assad, but not the United States or France, either.

On April 26, I was able to report that, the same day, Syria had confirmed its withdrawal in writing. I sent a technical team to confirm the withdrawal. They concluded that no visible intelligence presence remained but were unable to certify that all intelligence apparatus had been withdrawn. They had to go back subsequently due to reports that Syrian intelligence elements were still operative—hard to doubt given that many countries would have had intelligence operatives in Lebanon at the time—but they did not appear to interfere heavily in the election.

The momentum on 1559 slowed as 2005 dragged into 2006, primarily because many of the remaining issues were harder to address and required internal political consensus. The Lebanese launched a national dialogue to discuss issues like the presidency and the weapons of Hizbollah and the Palestinians. Hizbollah leader Hassan Nasrallah claimed publicly in 2005 that the movement had more than twelve thousand missiles. But the Lebanese army refused to confiscate weapons caches belonging to those who were still viewed as the legitimate resistance to Israel. Interestingly, however, the national dialogue generated a Lebanese consensus that if the Shab'a farms were returned, territorial disputes with Israel would be over. By implication, this would render obsolete Hizbollah's claim that it needed weapons to liberate Lebanese land.

This opened a potentially interesting way forward. When Ariel Sharon came to the opening of the UN General Assembly for the first time as prime minister of Israel, to bask in the glory of his withdrawal from Gaza, I urged him to consider a further courageous move by withdrawing from the Shab'a farms—even handing them to the UN if necessary. They clearly were not Israeli territory, and leaving them might have weakened Hizbollah's position in the internal debate in Lebanon and strengthened the hand of Lebanese prime minister Fouad Siniora, who headed the pro-Hariri government formed after the May elections. There was strong Israeli opposition to reopening what had been finalized in 2000 when I drew the Blue Line. Yet Sharon seemed to be considering a move when we met in September 2005. If he was, he had not done anything about it when felled by a massive stroke a few months later. Soon after, he was replaced by Ehud Olmert.

There was another way for the Shab'a issue to be resolved: if Syria and Lebanon bilaterally demarcated their borders. But Syria made no move to do this, since it would have further signaled its departure from Lebanon and raised new questions about Hizbollah's weapons. As these somewhat arcane but important issues were being discussed, a full-scale war broke out across the Blue Line.

LEBANON: THE 2006 WAR AND RESOLUTION 1701

I have recounted in the prologue many aspects of my diplomacy during the thirty-four-day war between Israel and Hizbollah in July and August 2006. It brought together almost all the elements that make the Middle East so volatile and was a potent example of the symbiotic relationship between the secretary-general and the Security Council during a major international crisis.

The international split that developed in the Council was captured in one's choice of adjective to describe the goal of international diplomacy—was it an "immediate" or a "durable" end to the violence? Those who used the first appellation thought that the longer the war went on the more Lebanese and Israeli civilians would be killed, Hizbollah strengthened, Siniora's government weakened, and Israel and its Western allies tarnished. I was perhaps the most vocal and visible advocate of this view throughout the war, and many European and Arab leaders and non-Western Council members had the same opinion.

The other camp wanted to give Israel time to "complete the mission" and argued that there could be no stop to the war until the "underlying cause," by which they meant Hizbollah's arsenal, was addressed. Bush and Blair headed this camp, with some tacit Arab supporters who wished to see Hizbollah dealt a blow—along with the Israelis, of course.

While I agreed that the crisis could not be resolved on the basis of a simple return to the status quo, I drew a clear distinction between a cessation of hostilities, which was immediately achievable if the will was there, and the political and security package required for a longer-term cease-fire. I did not see how Israel's bombing Lebanon for weeks on end would cause strategic damage to anyone other than the Lebanese government. I condemned Hizbollah's provocation in starting the war and its barrage of rockets that terrorized Israel, often fired from within civilian population centers. I also condemned Israel's excessive use of massive firepower against targets that often seemed to have little to do with Hizbollah itself.

Within hours of the crisis breaking, I decided to send a high-level mission of three senior envoys to the region. Rice urged me to place the mission within the 1559 framework, including Hizbollah's disarmament, but this could never be a goal achieved during or by Israel's offensive, no matter how long it went on. Even if Israel bombed Lebanon for months, Hizbollah would still be on the ground at the end of it and still part of the

Lebanese government, and both it and its regional backers would have to be part of the solution.

Israeli prime minister Olmert initially told me he probably would not have time to meet the mission, reflecting his hubris during the early days of the conflict that he would not need a ladder to climb down from the crisis. Eventually, he met the mission, and they also visited Beirut. The envoys developed key elements of a package that could secure a cease-fire, including return of the captured soldiers, an expanded peacekeeping force to support the Lebanese government in extending its control over the south, and an international conference to endorse a delineation of Lebanon's international borders, resolving all disputed areas, including Shab'a farms. The subsequent Council negotiations, conducted by the Americans and the French, led to agreement on resolution 1701, which was finally adopted on August 11. I was disappointed that it took a month for this resolution to be agreed to while the fighting dragged on, and felt justified in dressing down the assembled foreign ministers in the Council when the resolution was passed:

> I would be remiss if I did not tell you how profoundly disappointed I am that the Council did not reach this point much, much earlier . . . [The Council's] inability to act sooner has badly shaken the world's faith in its authority and integrity.

But even the adoption of the resolution would not bring the fighting to an end. That task fell to me. I knew from my peacekeeping experience that the language of 1701 calling for an "immediate" cessation of hostilities was not sufficient. I had urged the Americans and the French to insert a date and time in the text. John Bolton, who for all his bravado had never been responsible for a single soldier in his life, ignored this advice.

Eventually, I finalized the cessation directly with Olmert and Siniora. The Israelis wanted another sixty hours, with Olmert assuring me that they would not use this period to take "offensive measures" but to get Israeli troops in a position to "defend themselves" given the vulnerability that any withdrawing force faces. With Rice's help, I brought Olmert down from his sixty hours, and he agreed to a halt at 7:00 a.m. on Monday, August 14. Siniora also delivered his government's agreement, including Hizbollah, to this deadline. I confirmed this in writing to both prime ministers, together with a list of do's and don'ts to define what a cessation meant—essentially augmenting 1701 under my own authority by an agreement with the parties.

D espite Olmert's assurance, Israel went on the offensive in those last three days, including dropping untold cluster munitions that would continue to kill Lebanese men, women, and children long after the guns fell silent. Misleading the secretary-general was not an Israeli offense alone: when I called Bashar al-Assad to urge him not to resupply weapons to Hizbollah, he said quite plainly that Syria did not supply *anything* to the movement. Both he and Iranian president Mahmoud Ahmadinejad gave me their commitment to support 1701. I was under no illusion that this commitment would mean a great deal on the ground. But it was better to have a commitment they could be judged against than not to have any at all. The same applied to the Israelis.

A central element of the 1701 package was a stronger and reconfigured UNIFIL with a much tougher mandate and the right troops. The United States initially wanted to remove UNIFIL and insert a multinational force—something the Israelis had insisted on at the outset of their campaign. I knew this would never come together practically and would not work in Lebanon—and I noticed that those countries urging a multinational force were not the ones ready to provide troops. One thing on which everyone agreed was that it was the responsibility of the Lebanese, not the international presence, to disarm Hizbollah—as Rice acknowledged to me, the United States had not sought to disarm the Taliban, and had let the Afghans lead. The United States eventually accepted that a reconfigured UNIFIL was not only the right choice but the only available one. Washington rightly insisted on the strongest possible mandate, as it was clear that UNIFIL in its old guise could not respond to the situation. The lead would be taken by the French, with other Europeans contributing, but also with non-Europeans in the mix.

There was precious little confidence once 1701 was passed that the cessation of hostilities would hold or that the troops would be forthcoming. The end of the violence simply began a new phase of my work. Getting the troops pledged and on the ground, and ensuring that the Lebanese army deployed south of the Litani River, would be essential if Israel was to pull back behind the Blue Line for the second time in six years.

I pushed the Europeans hard to come up with the credible backbone of a force. To their credit, they delivered—eight thousand troops were pledged in a meeting I held with European leaders in Brussels in late August. To complement them, I reached out to Muslim countries like Malaysia, Indonesia, Bangladesh, and Turkey in a successful bid to supplement the force.

The devastation in parts of Lebanon was immense, and I was determined to get the Israeli air and naval blockade of the country lifted as soon as possible. But the Israelis would not move until assured that appropriate internationals would be in place, while the internationals would not commit until the Israelis moved. Before I had a deal, I gambled by basically announcing that the blockade would be lifted, which generated the momentum necessary. Sometimes I had to risk failure in order to succeed.

Israeli foreign minister Tzipi Livni was particularly upset when I proposed to bring in Malaysia, objecting that they had no diplomatic relations with Israel. I thought this was over the top, and I went ahead—not least because I had specified that they would be deployed to a position not directly facing Israeli troops. The war drove home Israel's vulnerability in an increasingly volatile region and ended with none of its stated goals being achieved. I appointed a German intelligence agent who eventually finalized a prisoner-swap deal under my successor, returning the bodies of the two Israeli soldiers for Lebanese prisoners still in Israel. He subsequently was asked to help out with an Israeli soldier captured in Gaza, in contacts between Hamas and Israel quietly facilitated by the UN. Such necessary negotiations are a reminder that slogans about never talking to terrorists do not survive encounters with the real world—in the Middle East or elsewhere.

Resolution 1701 put new burdens on the United Nations for the security of both Lebanon and Israel, and the region as a whole. I am proud of what we achieved in the months after the war before I left office in December. Despite incidents since, the calm along the Blue Line has held. As I look at our role in Lebanon over the years of my tenure, I can say that we helped get Israel out of Lebanon twice, Syria out as well, supported national dialogue, and strengthened our peacekeeping role.

These were all necessary steps if the Lebanese state was to begin to assert itself. But they were clearly not sufficient to ensure Lebanon's long-term stability. While we have helped stabilize the situation, neither the Security Council's interventions, nor my own, were able to address underlying issues. Lebanese national dialogue generated important areas of consensus but did not lead to significant progress on Hizbollah's weapons. Syria's and Iran's commitment to 1701 was important, but it did not stop their rearming the movement. Our strengthened peacekeeping alongside the Lebanese army has reduced the visibility of armed players in the south, but Hizbollah remains a potent presence and exercises today a kind of veto over the Lebanese government. For its part, Israel did not fulfill its side of the 1701 bargain by moving creatively to help Siniora on Shab'a, and it continued its provocative daily overflights into Lebanese airspace. In my trip through the region after the war and my reporting to the Security Council, I emphasized that 1701 was "not a buffet, but a fixed menu": we had to try to advance on all the issues lockstep and not allow the parties to pick and choose. But if true stability is to be achieved, the answer lies not in peacekeeping or in crisis diplomacy: it lies in the pursuit of a genuinely comprehensive Middle East peace.

Reflections on Peacekeeping and Peacemaking in the Middle East

Every violent eruption with which I had to contend—from the Palestinian intifada and Israeli Operation Defensive Shield to the Lebanon war and constant crises in Gaza—struck a blow at the very idea of peaceful coexistence and mutual security that is essential if the Arab world and Israel are to one day live in peace. Equally, each partially conceived or unimplemented political initiative—from Oslo to the roadmap to Gaza disengagement—eventually discredited the very concept of a negotiated peace for both peoples. The only winners to emerge from this litany of failure have been those who seek to perpetuate the conflict—militants and radicals, whether they fire rockets at or launch suicide bombs into Israeli towns, or subjugate Palestinians in the West Bank while taking their land.

The lessons are clear: the only solutions will be found in politics, not violence; and in comprehensive solutions, not partial approaches.

The challenge facing the UN in the region was—and is—to try to catalyze such solutions, in circumstances where the UN as an institution has traditionally been sidelined from the process. By initiating the creation of the Quartet, I hoped to combine the legitimacy of the UN, the political power of the United States, the financial resources of the EU, and the regional prestige of Russia into an amalgamated diplomatic force—one in which I held the gavel and acted as de facto chair. Doing so helped set a clearer international consensus on what a solution would look like, and what it would take to achieve it. Yet as I have discussed in this chapter, the failure of the Quartet to insist on the basic principles of the roadmap robbed the body of some of its vitality, limiting its ability to shift the dynamics between the parties. I alluded to my own frustration at the end of the Lebanon war, when I told the Council that "the various crises in the region must henceforth be addressed not in isolation or bilaterally but as part of a holistic and comprehensive effort, sanctioned and championed by this Council, to bring peace and stability to the region as a whole."

In the years since I left office, we have witnessed a devastating Israeli offensive in Gaza against rocket attacks and a civil war playing out among the Palestinians themselves. One thing has remained largely constant: the daily creation of facts on the ground by the Israelis. The only ray of hope has been the state-building efforts of the Palestinian prime minister Salam Fayyad, proving beyond all argument that there is at least in the West Bank a Palestinian partner ready to walk the hard road of peace.

Deeply distrustful of Benjamin Netanyahu, the Palestinians are pursuing alternative options for a political way forward—from seeking UN membership for a State of Palestine to increased popular protest against the occupation. The reflexive U.S. reaction against any Palestinian utilization of the UN showed just how charged the issue has become in U.S. domestic politics, and robs the international community of real leverage. After all, what better way would there be to give both parties an incentive to make progress than to acknowledge the importance of the

Palestinian membership application and indicate that it will be taken up and decided, whether affirmatively or negatively, *after* a further effort to negotiate the final terms of a settlement?

If the UN route is closed off, and negotiations lead nowhere, more Palestinian voices will be heard calling for disbanding the Palestinian Authority and returning responsibility for the occupation to Israel—or even for abandoning the two-state paradigm in favor of a one-state alternative. Meanwhile, the Israelis appear to be shifting further to the right, to a point where too many seem incapable of creatively imagining the benefits of a two-state deal for their long-term security, legitimacy, and identity.

Yet only a two-state solution can respond to the needs of both peoples. The international community must at some point, sooner rather than later, take the risk of prescribing the basic parameters on which the parties would be expected to negotiate a final agreement. The Quartet should work to develop these, with the option of subsequently enshrining them in a Security Council resolution. There are risks involved in trying once more to solve the conflict and failing, but the risks of leaving the conflict to fester and explode are higher. We owe it to the Palestinians and the Israelis to help them overcome this tragic and bitter conflict before it is too late.

THE ARAB AWAKENING AND THE FUTURE OF THE REGION

Alongside the region's unresolved conflicts, the Arab world has been held back for decades by the parlous state of its political systems. Regional leaders continually exploited the deep feelings of their people about the plight of the Palestinians to divert attention from the mix of authoritarianism, sectarianism, fanaticism, poverty, and ignorance that grew more potent in the Arab world over several decades. Indeed, one of my regular frustrations as secretary-general was the persistence of bad excuses and red herrings—from the role of Israel to the influence of Iran to the power of America—deployed to disguise the true failings of political systems in the Arab world.

Early in my tenure, I was proud that the United Nations empowered Arab voices to diagnose the problems of societies in the region with far greater insight and credibility than could come from lectures from Western leaders about democracy. In 2002, a fully Arab team of researchers drawn together by the head of the United Nations Development Programme's Arab regional bureau, Rima Khalaf, tossed an intellectual rock into the stagnant waters of Arab public debate with the first United Nations Arab Human Development Report. This report and several successors subjected Arab societies to intense self-criticism and found that three largely homegrown gaps held them back—the freedom gap, the gender gap, and the knowledge gap. Unless Arab societies built political systems based on freedom and democracy, empowered women, and overcame their deficits in knowledge and education, the burgeoning generation now coming of age would face futures of growing frustration and lack of opportunity. Now and then, Arab leaders would grumble to me about the Human Development Reports, but they could not easily dismiss something that came in an Arab voice carrying the legitimacy of the UN itself.

The popular protest movements that emerged in the Arab world in early 2011, offering the region a chance to break the shackles of decades of misrule heaped on centuries of decline, were in many ways the Arab youth's answer to the failings identified in the Arab Human Development Report. It was their way of saying, "We know we're falling behind, and we know why: politics and political tyranny sustained by a false alliance of stability over progress." Ordinary people—particularly the young, who form the bulk of Arab societies today—have shown with eloquence and courage that there is much more to the Arab world than the monarchs, mosques, and militants that otherwise have defined the global image of the region.

A s I write this reflection, one year into the Arab Awakening, I remain optimistic about the changes under way. It would be naive to think they will provide an easy or straight path to a Middle East that is both free and stable. The economic problems and social tensions are acute. Reactionary forces will fight back. Radical forces will try to hijack what is going on. Geopolitics will not stand still. Sectarian and ethnic tensions can easily be inflamed. So we should expect a bumpy ride.

But what is clear is that the main actors who must shape this change need to come from within the Arab and Islamic worlds. Those in Cairo's Tahrir Square expressed universal aspirations but grounded in values drawn from their own societies. Now the challenge is for Arab societies to find a new consensus for their political systems and cultural values. But the UN will inevitably be involved in many ways—witness the Security Council's role regarding the intervention in Libya; the organization's diplomatic efforts there and in Yemen; the work of its human rights spokespersons to speak out against Assad's brutal crackdown in Syria; or its continuing work to help countries like Tunisia and Egypt navigate their transitions. As it did with the Arab Human Development Reports, the United Nations must do what it can to empower those in the region who are committed to debating these issues profoundly and pursuing real change responsibly.

The movement for legitimacy and accountability long denied Arab peoples is not about Israel, Iran, or the United States—perhaps the first time in decades that rulers and reactionaries have been denied the chance to blame those outside forces for a stagnation far more homegrown than imposed from outside. For too long, the region had largely been politicized only by the Arab-Israeli conflict and the misdeeds of Israel and the West. The Arab Awakening has repoliticized the Arab street about the futures of their *own* societies.

THE WARS OF 9/11

Terror, Afghanistan, Iraq, and the United Nations at the Brink

AUGUST 19, 2003

I was half a world away when the call came. Iqbal Riza, my chef de cabinet, rang after locating Nane and me on a small island in Finland where we had gone for a short holiday. A massive bomb had struck the UN headquarters in Baghdad, resulting in many casualties, he told me. Amid the confusion in the immediate aftermath, no one had been able to locate Sergio Vieira de Mello, my close friend and special representative, who had gone to Iraq following the U.S.-led invasion to lead our mission there. Other members of his team were known to be dead and injured—just who and how many was still unclear.

As we made plans for my immediate return to New York, Riza urged me to be careful and to travel with only the greatest discretion, not knowing if a wider campaign against the UN was under way. Al Qaeda had long before named me as one of their targets for my role in what it saw as the dismemberment of Indonesia, Asia's largest Muslim nation, following the independence of East Timor, and they had singled out Sergio for the same reason. After I asked Sergio to lead the UN return to Iraq, Riza and I had spent a great deal of time with him discussing the complexity of a role that was in equal parts necessary and poisoned from the outset.

As we knew he would, Sergio had tackled the challenge with his unique mix of courage, energy, sensitivity, shrewdness, and commitment to the UN's highest principles of civilian protection. A broken Iraqi society, on the one hand, and an ignorant and high-handed American occupation unaware of Iraq's complexities, on the other, was the welcome that had greeted him on arrival three months earlier. The day before the bombing, I called Sergio from Finland. During my holiday, I had decided that he needed to come out of Iraq for consultations at UN headquarters so we could make a sober assessment of our role in Iraq. He cheerfully agreed but insisted that from New York he travel on to Rio to visit his mother and also get a few weeks' break from the burdens of leading our efforts in Iraq. I said fine, and we ended our call joking and laughing, and signed off with our usual greeting: "Courage!"

When I arrived in New York at the end of what felt like an endless journey, Riza picked me up at the airport and confirmed our worst fears: Sergio, Nadia Younes—his chief of staff and my former chief of protocol— and nearly two dozen other colleagues were considered to have perished. I had spent the flight asking myself: Why did this have to happen? Could it have been avoided? Could I have done something different to protect them? Should they have gone in, should they have stayed? I rehashed the arguments over and over again—and I thought of my colleagues and the families they left behind.

A war that I had tried to stop with every fiber of my being had now taken the lives of two of my closest colleagues, along with some of the most brilliant and dedicated UN staff ever to serve the organization. None of them had believed in the war itself but saw it as their personal and professional duty to come to the aid of the Iraqi people already being convulsed by the beginnings of what would turn out to be a decade of civil war. And now they had been murdered—in an act of terror that forever changed the UN's sense of risk and vulnerability for our missions in the field. Of course, UN diplomats, peacekeepers, and humanitarian workers had lost their lives in the line of duty before, but to be targeted, in this way, in this country, by the enemies of an occupation that we had sought in every way to prevent, was the cruelest of fates.

On the day of the bombing, I had to respond by reminding the world of our larger mission in Iraq. I could not allow the United Nations to be intimidated by terrorists, and I issued a statement denouncing the attack and recommitting the organization to helping the Iraqi people emerge from war and occupation. Within weeks, it became clear that Iraq was being plunged into an indiscriminate and unspeakably brutal war zone, without room for those not engaged in armed combat. By the last week of September it was clear the risks to our people could no longer be justified, and I ordered the evacuation of all remaining UN staff from Iraq. An epitaph written for Sergio and Nadia in the days after their death captures the sense of loss, anger, and their enduring commitment to the mission of the United Nations that will always stay with those of us fortunate to have served with them:

Sergio and Nadia lived lives of sacrifice and substance. Their deaths both shame and mock the armchair warriors, the television talk-show mudwrestlers, the pontificators, the manipulators and the simplifiers. Their deaths are a reminder that imperium, no matter how benign its intent, is never altruistic, and calls forth its own responses. And their lives are a reminder that it is just possible to do some small good in this rank, sorry, blood-drenched world.

Steven Erlanger, journalist and friend of Sergio
and Nadia, *New York Times*, August 24, 2003

T he shattering damage done by the U.S.-led invasion of Iraq was of course not limited to the loss of 22 UN officers on August 19, 2003. In the course of the decade following the invasion an estimated 115,000 Iraqi civilians died in the ensuing anarchy and civil war; more than 10,000 coalition soldiers were killed or wounded; some 4 million people were made refugees or were internally displaced; social, economic, and environmental devastation; the standing of the United Nations as an institution and an agent of global security gravely harmed; the promise of multilateralism so ardently sought in the aftermath of the end of Communism blighted; the Middle East peace process set back another decade or more; the vital priority of creating a stable Afghanistan unable to foster terror and instability blithely discarded; Al Qaeda strengthened rather than weakened; Sunni-Shia differences in the Arab world transformed into a murderous schism; the vital and noble principle of humanitarian intervention tainted by its association with aggression and domination; and last, the global standing of the United States, a founding member of the United Nations and long-standing pillar of international order, tarnished by identification with the worst of the abuses, tragedies, and chaos that war brings in its wake.

IRAQ AND THE UNITED NATIONS

In the six years from the end of the first Gulf War in 1991 until my election as secretary-general, Iraq became transformed from an example of the international community's acting lawfully in pursuit of the highest aims of the UN's founders to an albatross around the organization's neck. The sense of global accomplishment following the liberation of Kuwait by a multinational alliance formed to defeat an aggressor state was soon replaced by exasperation over Baghdad's evasion of its cease-fire obligations and deepening concern about the plight of the Iraqi people.

The UN mandate had been to reverse the invasion of Kuwait, nothing more, and the prudence, discipline, and judicious assessment of the risks of war had led the administration of President George H. W. Bush to stick to that mandate. At the same time, this left Saddam Hussein in power, the predatory leader of a brutal, tyrannical regime that demonstrated little evidence of intending to comply fully with the demands of the international community. My predecessor, Boutros Boutros-Ghali, offered me only one piece of advice as he left office at the end of 1996, and it was prophetic: "Watch out for the question of Iraq," he said. "It will become very important."

Given its twenty-year record of aggression abroad and repression within, Saddam Hussein's Iraq was a familiar issue for the United Nations by the time I took office in 1997, and a number of my senior team had long been directly involved in managing the international consequences of Baghdad's policies. None of us had any illusions about the nature of the regime. Iqbal Riza, my chef de cabinet and closest advisor, had served as deputy to Olaf Palme, the UN's envoy during the vicious and devastating Iran-Iraq War from 1980 to 1988. He had witnessed firsthand the effects of Iraq's use of chemical weapons on civilians and earned the lasting enmity of the regime leadership by insisting to the then secretary-general, Javier Peres de Cuellar, that Iraq's use of these weapons be exposed to the world. My senior Arab advisor, Lakhdar Brahimi, a former foreign minister of Algeria, had negotiated the Taif Agreement to end Lebanon's civil war, and had also dealt with the Iraqis in various other negotiations. Contrary to the perceptions and prejudices of some member states, my team was well versed in dealing with the intransigence and venality of the Saddam regime.

My own experience with Iraq dated back to the days immediately following Iraq's invasion of Kuwait, when I was asked by Secretary-General Perez de Cuellar to travel to Baghdad with my friend Viru Dayal and negotiate the safe passage of the nine hundred UN staff then based in Iraq and Kuwait. This turned out to be the easy part. In addition, there were some twenty-two hundred Westerners in Iraq whom the regime began to deploy as human shields, and my team began working closely with Western ambassadors to secure their release. What few people realized was that in addition to the UN and Western civilians, some five hundred thousand Asian and African nationals were also stranded in Iraq and Kuwait—people who were free to leave but had neither the means nor the organization to do so. Going beyond the original purpose of our mission, this became our main focus and, working with the UN Disaster Relief Organization, we eventually negotiated passage to Amman, Jordan, and then an air-bridge from Amman to Asia by which the majority were able to go home.

Following the liberation of Kuwait, the Security Council, determined to ensure that Saddam would never again be able to threaten the region or the world, passed a series of resolutions that would impose on Iraq the most draconian disarmament and sanctions regime in the history of the United Nations. The Council made clear that Iraq would have to verifiably disarm itself of its weapons of mass destruction, and implemented a dual policy of extensive economic sanctions and intrusive weapons inspections. While the main objective was to ensure that Iraq was disarmed of all weapons of mass destruction, the sanctions mostly hurt the people as opposed to the regime. Few at the time imagined that twelve years later, the sanctions would still be in place, with Iraq still defiant and the world still focused on the threat Saddam posed. The expectation was that Saddam would acquiesce rather than endure the misery and suffering of his own people. The sheer obstinacy—and enduring survival instincts—of Saddam's regime had been grossly underestimated.

A fundamental gulf was revealed, however slowly and painfully, between the instruments of the international community and the realities of power in Iraq. Even as sanctions crippled the economy of Iraq and resulted in widespread malnutrition among its children, Saddam's grip on the country was strengthened—as any opposition was weakened, and the limited sources of wealth increasingly became concentrated in the hands of regime loyalists. A "Republic of Fear" was enabled inadvertently, but relentlessly, by the regime's most fervent enemies—the Western members of the Security Council.

As the sanctions persisted year in and year out and misery spread throughout Iraq, the Security Council realized that unless it did something to alleviate the suffering of ordinary Iraqis, the sanctions regime—already leaky and undermined by smuggling condoned by Western powers wishing to limit the damage to Iraq's neighbors—would collapse entirely. This was the rationale behind the creation of the Oil-for-Food Programme that was established by resolution 986 in 1995 after five years of negotiations by my predecessor Boutros Boutros-Ghali with Baghdad, and which for eight years provided food and medical supplies for some 26 million Iraqi civilians. All the while, however, a cat-and-mouse game had been playing out between Iraq's leadership and the United Nations about how and when to secure the disarmament of Iraq's weapons of mass destruction.

In resolution 687 of April 1991, which established the terms of the Gulf War cease-fire, the Security Council demanded that "Iraq shall unconditionally accept, under international supervision, the destruction, removal or rendering harmless of its weapons of mass destruction, ballistic missiles with a range over 150 kilometers, and related production facilities and equipment." It also required Iraq to make a declaration, within fifteen days, of the location, amounts, and types of all such items.

To run the new inspection and disarmament programs, the Council turned to Rolf Ekeus to head the United Nations Special Commission (UNSCOM)—responsible for inspection operations inside Iraq—and also to Hans Blix, then the head of the International Atomic Energy Agency (IAEA). They were two experienced and scrupulous Swedish diplomats and disarmament experts. With great persistence and discipline, these two men succeeded in destroying an extraordinary amount of prohibited weapons, all the while retaining the trust and confidence of the entire Security Council—not an easy task. Just how exceptional they were soon became clear when Ekeus retired and recommended to me an Australian diplomat, Richard Butler, as his successor.

Despite reservations about Butler on the part of friends such as Madeleine Albright and Nabil El-Arabi, the Egyptian ambassador to the UN, I decided to appoint him. That was a colossal mistake and one of the worst appointments I ever made. The Iraqis, of course, continued to maneuver and manipulate and with Butler, alas, they found the perfect foil. Despite a record of expertise and experience in disarmament, he soon appeared to prefer diplomatic bluster and television appearances to the hard and painstaking work of steering the Iraqis to compliance. His increasingly evident bias against both the Iraqis and key members of the Security Council, including Russia and China, soon turned him into the Achilles' heel of the UN's attempts to disarm Iraq through peaceful means.

Even though it was my appointment, the chairman of the UNSCOM formally reported directly to the Security Council. But Butler's mistake was to view the United States, and not the UN, as the overseer of the disarmament process. After one particularly egregious session in the Security Council, with Butler treating the other members of the Council like small-time mayors, I called him into my office and warned him that any senior UN official who chooses to serve just one member of the permanent five members of the Council soon loses the support of the others. Worse, I warned, such an approach would undermine the Council's cohesion, hindering its ability to function as a decision-making body. On a more personal note, I also added that once his credibility with the other members of the permanent five was shredded, the United States would then have little use for him, and they would withdraw their support for him as well.

Over the course of 1997 and 1998, a series of inspections led to confrontations with the Iraqi authorities. One of my concerns was the impact of the Iraq sanctions on the UN's standing around the world. The international community's engagement in Iraq was heavily militarized, given the no-fly zone, the periodic threats of bombings, and the intrusive inspectors. Also, Iraq was not allowed to develop its infrastructure and its oil resources were managed by the UN. However misplaced a view, this was widely seen—in the developing world in particular—as a case of the UN picking on a weak country with Security Council resolutions a cloak for great-power bullying. The question leaders across the Middle East and beyond continuously asked me throughout the years from 1997 to 2003 was simple: if the UN can impose such draconian measures on a government to force compliance with UN resolutions, why has it not done the same with Israel? One of the arguments the Americans were making was that Saddam had not implemented UN resolutions. But Israel was in similar noncompliance with UN resolutions over the territories it had occupied since 1967. This inconsistency incensed many parties.

In November 1997, I personally stepped into the Iraq quagmire for the first time. I knew full well that my interventions would be met with suspicion and maneuvering on all sides, but I was equally certain that there was a vital role to be played. I appointed three senior diplomats, Lakhdar Brahimi, Emilio Cardenas, and Jan Eliasson, to go to Baghdad to engage the Iraqis. Baghdad at this time was clearly determined to re-engage the UN at a senior level, namely with me as secretary-general, and it had made its negotiating position clear: it was not seeking confrontation; it had implemented all Security Council resolutions without receiving adequate respect for its sovereignty, integrity, and security; and that one member state—the United States—was using UNSCOM for its own purposes.

Later in November, as pressure was growing on UNSCOM to amend its practices and possibly change the composition of its inspection teams, U.S. secretary of state Madeleine Albright called me to urge that all such appeals for the alteration of UNSCOM's work be rejected and that all key decisions be left to the Council and UNSCOM. "It's important for your stature that you do not bend," she said, adding that she spoke as "a friend." "We must retain the independence of UNSCOM." With the latter point I agreed entirely, but I suspect we had different ideas on what "independence" meant in this case.

What became increasingly clear was that Butler's management and leadership of UNSCOM was, in fact, a gift to Saddam—allowing him, with a growing body of evidence—to claim that he was all for disarming and cooperating with the international community, but that UNSCOM's approach made this impossible. This was entirely untrue, of course, but what Butler and his backers in Washington and London failed to understand was that the further they pushed him to do their bidding, the more he undermined his own position and that of his inspection organization.

In late 1997, it was clear the United States had lost patience with the inspections process and was agitating for military action or full Iraqi compliance. UN inspectors under Rolf Ekeus, a shrewd, meticulous, and persistent Swedish diplomat, had been in Iraq for some seven years and had in that period destroyed more weapons of mass destruction than the coalition had during the entire Gulf War. This record of success, however, was achieved despite—and not because of—the regime's attitude toward the inspections. By this time, Iraq had identified a new reason to resist cooperation; namely, the national security and dignity of its presidential sites—vast complexes of buildings and parks designed for Saddam and the senior leadership of Iraq. Of course, this resistance flouted resolution 687, which had made clear that there could be no exceptions to the demand for immediate and unconditional access to all sites. I knew Saddam had to open these "presidential sites" and palaces, as stipulated by resolution 687, but I also felt deeply uneasy that the world could go to war over this issue—any deaths arising from this relatively trivial matter seemed utterly needless. I believed there was a way to win full compliance without unnecessary humiliation for the Iraqis.

On February 13, 1998, as consultations with the permanent five members continued and I decided to send a technical team led by Staffan de Mistura to Baghdad to map the presidential sites prior to my own arrival, I received a call from Albright. She was clearly getting worried about the idea of a special, high-level UN mission to Baghdad following the technical visit and pleaded with me not to travel before a permanent five consensus had been reached. As this had always been the basis for my trip, I stressed my agreement. But then she insisted that by sending a technical team to Baghdad I was somehow accommodating Iraqi demands. If anything, I corrected her, I was calling their bluff. If the Iraqis considered the presidential sites to be critically sensitive locations this was their chance to delineate where they began and where they ended, putting a stop to the games that were being played around them.

The next Monday morning I received calls from Clinton and Albright within an hour of each other. They had clearly decided that it was the day to send me a tough message—not least for domestic political reasons. I could sense that Clinton had just been given an overall briefing of the Iraq problem, because he began with an overview and then got to his point of saying that he wanted a diplomatic solution as much as I did, but that it had to be principled and have integrity. I assured Clinton that that was precisely the point of my initiative—to ensure the continuing lead of UNSCOM in all inspections under its executive chairman. But, by adding new diplomats to each of the teams we could give the Iraqis something that represented respect for their own dignity, but which in no way impeded the effectiveness of the inspections.

Albright, as always, went straight to the point: "Everyone here is concerned about whether you really got the message about how firm we are," and I replied, "Absolutely, I know the stakes and the mood in the nation and the other party." I explained that the solution was simple: the new inspections team would be headed by an UNSCOM commissioner and would be staffed by permanent staff of UNSCOM and IAEA, and directed by Butler, the executive chairman of UNSCOM. Additional members of a diplomatic background would be appointed jointly by myself and Butler. Unconvinced, Albright resorted to the kind of warning with which I would soon become familiar: "We won't hesitate to say that a deal with Iraq was a lousy one if that proved to be the case."

I resolved to go to Baghdad and on the Sunday before my mission, Albright came up to New York and met me at the residence of the secretary-general to give me her "red lines," her final demands that all sites must be accessible, and for multiple visits, without time limits. None of these were a surprise or a problem for me, and I also knew that the purpose of her visit had as much to do with internal U.S. politics as with the mission itself. For the Clinton administration that meant, on many occasions, needing to seem tough with the UN. She even asked if I would go "even if we wouldn't want it." I told her that I would be going to Baghdad with a strong consensus from the Council that Iraq must return to compliance—but I would also be preparing my own negotiating points. I had to remind her of my role as secretary-general, answerable to 191 other member states and of our duty to seek peaceful resolution of disputes.

On arrival in Baghdad, I was met on the tarmac by foreign minister Tariq Aziz and some two hundred journalists from around the world who had been allowed into the country by the Iraqis to highlight the talks. I was then driven to a large white guesthouse where my team and I prepared for the next days' talks. Sitting amid the splendor (however kitsch) of Saddam's houses, I could not help thinking of the waste and abuse of it all, and how an entire generation of Iraqis had been denied the opportunities of prosperity, dignity, and freedom for the sake of one man's grip on power.

I knew that what the Iraqi regime sought was a sense of dignity and respect throughout this process. This was not so different from the

Chinese tradition of emphasis on not losing face. I had learned from my own experience of negotiating with Iraqis and from the advice of aides such as Lakhdar Brahimi that such dignity could be a matter of life and death—however trumped up or manufactured it might seem to be in Western eyes. To those who would ask why Saddam should be shown any respect or dignity—and that achieving mutual trust with a tyrant was an affront to his many victims—I could reply only that this was my task. As long as the international community was committed to an inspection regime requiring Iraq's cooperation, how else were we going to obtain it?

We then entered negotiations with the Iraqi team led by Aziz. From this meeting, which lasted until two in the morning, I had a sense that we would be able to agree on a resumption of inspections. But it was clear that only one man could authorize it: Saddam. We were left in the dark about whether—and when—a meeting with Saddam would take place. Shortly before noon the next day a cortege of cars suddenly appeared to take me to meet with him. When we entered one of his palaces, I found that he had changed out of his usual military fatigues into a navy-blue suit—an indication it seemed of his understanding of the need to show at least the outward signs of diplomacy.

We sat down together on the lush, gold-rimmed seats of a reception room. He was careful and correct in his manners and anchored by a deep and confident calm at all times. He was almost serene, exhibiting in his personal character the untouchable status he had long held in Iraq.

My objective was clear: to obtain Saddam's agreement to a resumption of inspection by giving him a ladder to climb down from his position of defiance. In the absence of any way to force him to concede, I set out to build a basis for agreement by appealing to his sense of pride in building Iraq into a modern state and the need to protect it from further harm. I opened by seeking to appeal to his sense of responsibility for the fate of his country—including his vanity as a leader. I recounted the wars Iraq had been through and said, "Mr. President, you are a builder. You have spent years building and rebuilding Iraq following war." I stressed my recognition of how far they had come in rebuilding their society after so much destruction—which of course he had been responsible for. Then I urged him to avoid all of this progress being set back over a dispute over palaces. "You say you have no weapons in the palaces," I said. "In that case, open the doors and let the inspectors go and see for themselves." Halfway through the conversation, he said, "Excuse me; I have to go and pray." Once I was alone with his interpreter, I turned to him and asked: "Am I getting through to him?" "Yes," he replied, "Yes. Yes." He was clearly relieved, hoping that this would avoid another war.

When Saddam returned, he thanked me and praised my courage, adding that "I know powerful people did not want you to come." Stating that he trusted me, he authorized his team to complete the draft agreement and we received his approval by midnight. Before saying good-bye, I urged Saddam not to push each issue or dispute to a crisis point but instead to call me to discuss his concerns so we could avoid a repetition of this incident. He looked at the phone at his side, and then at me, and said, "That thing, I never touch it." He was clearly concerned about more than whether the phone could be tapped.

The agreement secured Iraq's commitment to providing "immediate, unconditional, and unrestricted access" to UNSCOM, providing we followed a set of special procedures when accessing eight presidential sites to address Saddam's requests for dignity and respect by including diplomats, and not just technical experts, in inspection teams.

On my return to UN headquarters in New York, I emphasized to the press that this was a case study in what diplomacy backed by force could achieve—that you show force in order not to use it. "You can do a lot with diplomacy, but with diplomacy backed up by force you can get a lot more done."

When I took some questions from the assembled reporters I learned my first, hard lesson about the nature of public diplomacy—and the uses and abuses of my words. In answer to a simple question about the deal with Saddam, I stated what I thought was the obvious and replied that he was a man I could do business with—as I evidently just had. Of course, looking back today, I can see how this could be misconstrued not only as approving of his character but also as a lack of skepticism regarding Iraq's commitment to upholding this agreement and the tyrannical nature of his regime.

Just as the means had to be diplomacy backed by the credible threat of force, the ends were clear: Iraq's full compliance with all Security Council resolutions, the disarmament of Iraq, reintegrating its people into the international community, securing the stability of the Gulf region, and ensuring the effectiveness of the United Nations as a guarantor of international peace and security. No secretary-general has the luxury of choosing whom to engage with to achieve these objectives—in the case of Iraq and elsewhere.

Sitting down with leaders such as Saddam—or Bashir of Sudan or Gadhafi of Libya—is a responsibility you cannot shirk given what you're trying to achieve. You need to deal with those who can make a difference, those who can stop the bloodshed. You have to talk to the leaders, and get them to find a way to end the killing. Otherwise, how do you accomplish it? I also believed that such leaders could be engaged on a range of levels and motivations, however selfish, that I could turn to the benefit of a broader mission for peace. If you don't try it you won't ever know. You have to test it. The stakes are so high that you do not have the luxury of saying. "I'm not going to talk to this guy. I'm not going to shake his hand." By doing that you may be condemning thousands and millions to their deaths or further persecution. I'm trying to get them to do the right thing. I may fail—but I have a responsibility to try, to test it.

To the Security Council, which I met with shortly after the press conference, I was explicit about the risks. Reminding them that I had conducted the mission with the full authorization of the Council and that I had restored full and unlimited access for UNSCOM and strengthened its position with the Iraqis, I placed the onus of execution squarely on the Iraqi authorities. "I am under no illusions about the inherent value of this or any other agreement. Commitments honored are the only commitments that count . . . This agreement tests as never before the will of the Iraqi leadership to keep its word . . . If this effort to ensure compliance through negotiations is obstructed by evasion or deception, diplomacy may not have a second chance." I knew that what Iraq craved most—dignity and respect—could be demonstrated by a well-prepared set of negotiations that would result in a degree of mutual trust.

What was also critical was that the Iraqis be given a sense of light at the end of the tunnel; not, as critics complained, because any of us were soft on Saddam or wished to give him a way out, but because we knew that such an intrusive inspection regime required an incentive for Iraq to cooperate. Otherwise, why would they continue to allow a degree of scrutiny without precedent? And of course casual talk at that time in Washington of never lifting sanctions on Saddam, no matter what, did not help matters. The United States and its allies were entitled to state this position as a matter of national interest. However, they could not expect to have a United Nations committed to the peaceful disarmament of Iraq to simply play along. Nor could they have been unaware that this gave Saddam the excuse to tell the rest of the world that the game was fixed no matter what he did. We needed the inspections to work toward resolving the ongoing crisis with Iraq. Until then, the Gulf War would not truly be over.

The Council unanimously endorsed the memorandum of understanding (MOU) I had negotiated with Saddam. Even Butler went on television to say that if the agreement was faithfully implemented by Iraq, it would provide the basis for UNSCOM to carry out its work successfully. That, of course, had been the premise of negotiations all along.

My mission to Baghdad early on in my tenure demonstrated the possibilities available to a secretary-general if one was willing to intervene when diplomacy through other avenues had failed. The agreement bought us six further months of inspections—although they would prove difficult and acrimonious almost from the beginning.

M atters came to a head in early August 1998. UNSCOM was characterized by a growing impression of unaccountable and undisciplined inspections. Butler called me on the afternoon of August 3 to brief me on his meetings with Tariq Aziz that day. The Iraqis had clearly taken a strategic decision to force the issue: they had told Butler that he must tell the Security Council immediately that Iraq had been disarmed; that it did not possess any more weapons of mass destruction; and therefore a decision on sanctions could and should be taken. When Butler replied—correctly in this case—that he was unable to do so absent further verification, Aziz ended the conversation with the warning that "Either you go to the Council and tell the truth—that we have no more weapons—or we will not meet with you or your technical staff again."

Tariq Aziz was once again taking his country to the brink by declaring that Iraq was fully disarmed and demanding that UNSCOM state that forthwith or lose the regime's cooperation. Butler, of course, was not able to do this—but his position had been weakened further by increasing allegations, including from within UNSCOM itself, that the mission had been used by national intelligence agencies for information gathering unrelated to its disarmament mission. The Iraqis seized on this and won support from Russia in denouncing UNSCOM, and Butler in particular as untrustworthy.

When the Iraqis then issued a new set of demands about the makeup, location, and basic function of UNSCOM—essentially requiring it to be totally reconstituted—Albright and Sandy Berger together called me to insist that this was an attack on the UN and as "the face of the UN to the world," what mattered was my reaction, not the Council's. It was my memorandum of understanding with Saddam that had been violated, they stressed, and unless I "hit the Iraqi statement out of the park" in the Council's next meeting, as Berger put it to me, the United States would act on its own. My immediate instinct was that my public reaction should be in reinforcement of the leading role of the Security Council, as was its proper function, but this argument went nowhere with the U.S. representatives. I now saw, and not for the last time, what my interventionist approach to the role of secretary-general had done: even though I was the servant of the Council, the reality around the world was that my voice in some quarters would now carry more weight in this moment of crisis than the statements and resolutions of a distant and impersonal club of great powers in the form of the Security Council.

My answer to the standoff was to acknowledge that we had undergone a seven-year process, and we were still without prospects for an outcome that either side would accept. I therefore proposed a comprehensive review of the UN's relationship with Iraq, including the role of UNSCOM. While Washington opposed such a move—it would amount to "bargaining" with Saddam they insisted—the broader Council, including the UK, understood the value of engaging the Iraqis in a process whereby they would come back into compliance and we could set out on a path to conclusion, rather than permanent crisis. Ambassador Jeremy Greenstock, the UK permanent representative to the UN, was authorized in October by all members of the Council to engage with Tariq Aziz on the terms I set out. What they kept going back to, however, was the fundamental distrust between Iraq and UNSCOM. The standoff continued for another month. There was even a renewed attempt by Greenstock to convince the Iraqis that through a new Security Council resolution the path to an end to sanctions would be made clear.

A year's exhaustive diplomatic efforts to achieve Iraq's peaceful compliance with the demands of the Security Council were about to come to an ugly—and messy—end. On an official visit to Morocco, I was awakened at 3:30 in the morning of November 11 by a phone call from Mohamed ElBaradei, the director-general of the International Atomic Energy Agency. UNSCOM was withdrawing its staff from Baghdad, he told me. From Butler himself I had heard nothing and so I called Albright to find out what the Americans were planning with Butler. She was able only to confirm that the United States was withdrawing dependents from Jerusalem, Tel Aviv, and Kuwait City, but what she clearly wanted to know was if I would be making a statement in response to UNSCOM's withdrawal.

The United States had in the meantime been coordinating their response with the UK and France in order to achieve maximum impact from the Butler announcement. Half an hour later, while I was reviewing our options with Elisabeth Lindenmayer, my close and trusted special assistant, Albright called me back to ask if I had received a statement in my name drafted for me by the United States, the UK, and France condemning Iraqi intransigence, and whether I would issue it. I told her as politely as I could at 4:30 in the morning that I was perfectly capable of having my own statement drafted and would issue one if I thought it appropriate—and that it would be in my own words. I was still furious about Butler's deeply unprofessional behavior and I was in no mood to accommodate his masters. I had a far more serious responsibility now: by withdrawing the UNSCOM staff precipitously without informing me—and knowing that it could be a trigger for military action—he had placed in grave danger the lives of nearly four hundred UN staff doing vital humanitarian work. Of course, Butler thought he would force my hand on withdrawing the other UN staff, but I refused. Even though the inspectors would leave, the UN's humanitarian workers stayed in Iraq until the 2003 invasion, alleviating the suffering of the Iraqi people and carrying out their mandate.

Previously that year, on August 5 and October 31, Iraq had halted cooperation with UNSCOM, and each time we had walked them back. Now, in November, after Butler removed his inspectors without consulting us at UN headquarters, U.S. planes were ready to take to the skies, intent on bombing targets across Iraq in punishment for noncompliance. In response to this threat, on November 13, I immediately called in the

Iraqi ambassador to tell him that I would be sending Saddam a letter calling on him to readmit the inspectors—and this time the Iraqis reacted promptly and sent a reply within twenty-four hours accepting my request. When I received it, I called Berger right away—who was furious. "Kofi, I've got to tell you frankly. We literally had our planes in the air. We stopped this and we're taking an enormous risk if once again you and we are embarrassed by noncompliance by the Iraqis." I assured him that I agreed, and that I had made no promises on the lifting of sanctions—something I neither wanted nor was in a position to do. In closing, however, he requested that I back the United States if Iraq were to break its renewed pledge. "I've no doubt that it will work for one week—I'm concerned that in three weeks he will again restrict access and we'll be humiliated." Once again, Saddam miscalculated and soon gave the United States and its allies the justification for launching Operation Desert Fox, which on December 16 ushered in four days of bombings.

Throughout the preceding year's negotiations, whenever the military option was floated, I would ask the question: "After the bombing, then what?" I never got an answer—not from Washington, not from London. And, of course, the four days of bombing did nothing to advance the disarmament of Iraq. In fact, Desert Fox ushered in a four-year period without inspections and without a dialogue with Iraq about its place in the international system, even as sanctions continued to devastate its people and hand Saddam the ultimate propaganda tool—to be able to blame the West, and not his own misrule, for the misery of his people.

9/11, AFGHANISTAN, AND A NEW WAR

On the morning of September 11, 2001, I was at my home, the residence of the secretary-general on the East Side of Manhattan, when Iqbal Riza, my chef de cabinet, called to tell me of the first plane striking the World Trade

Center in downtown Manhattan, some three miles from the headquarters of the UN. Insisting that I stay at the residence, Riza took charge of evacuating the building and managing the immediate response. What then followed, the second plane in New York and two further planes targeting Washington, was more shocking than we could have ever predicted. In the course of the next few hours, nearly three thousand people were killed from more than a hundred different countries making it an attack not merely on the United States but on "humanity itself," as I said on that day. As Nane and I, like millions of others around the world, watched the unfolding horror on our television screen, we felt a deeply personal sense of grief and sympathy for our fellow citizens of a city that had become our home as well. In response, the UN then became a center for the outpouring of support and sympathy for the United States. In the Security Council, an extraordinary diplomatic drive swiftly produced two resolutions unanimously: One reaffirming the inherent right of self-defense of the United States against the Taliban in Afghanistan, which had harbored and supported Osama bin Laden and al Qaeda; the other creating a new counterterrorism body under the Council, which was to coordinate the global response to a menace that had taken a new and terrifying form.

Three months later, on receiving the Nobel Peace Prize for our efforts to revitalize the United Nations—and, in the words of the citation, making "clear that sovereignty cannot be a shield behind which member states conceal their violations"—I began my acceptance speech with the image of a girl born in Afghanistan and spoke of the twenty-first century as having been entered through a gate of fire. I wanted to honor the memory of those who had perished on 9/11, but also set the confrontation with terrorism in the broader context of the challenges facing the international community, including the human rights of the Afghan people and their prospects for peace and development.

After the Taliban was swiftly toppled in late 2001, the question of who was to govern Afghanistan, and how, had to be answered. Here, the United Nations had valuable experience, and a superb diplomatic troubleshooter perfectly suited to the role of forging a new government in the form of Lakhdar Brahimi. "The UN is left alone in Afghanistan with no real support from anywhere," Brahimi had told me in a dispiriting conclusion in mid-1999 when he was my envoy for Afghanistan. I had appointed him in 1997, early in my tenure, to see if the UN could bring peace to the ravaged and internationally neglected nation. But after two years on the job and a series of fruitless efforts, he saw absolutely no prospect of ending the war.

Back then we had repeatedly raised the alarm to the UN membership of the serious consequences of what was happening in Afghanistan. For instance, I warned the General Assembly in a November 1997 report that the external players

> must also be held accountable for building a fire which, they should be aware, is unlikely to remain indefinitely confined to Afghanistan. Indeed, that fire is already spreading beyond the borders of Afghanistan, posing a serious threat to the region and beyond in the shape of terrorism, banditry, narcotics trafficking, refugee flows, and increasing ethnic and sectarian tension.

Among those playing with fire were the Pakistanis, who remained ambivalent about the international cooperation process that we had established in the "Six plus Two" contact group (involving the six nations bordering Afghanistan as well as the United States and Russia), and Pakistan continued their support for the Taliban, fearing the alternative of a pro-India government.

While we had predicted in 1997 the worsening of a cocktail of regional problems created by the civil war in Afghanistan, I had never imagined that this fire would erupt in New York just a few miles from UN headquarters, on a bright September morning four years later. When it did, and the Security Council authorized an international coalition to remove the Taliban regime by force of arms, the outcome of the military confrontation was never in doubt. Much less clear was how to put Afghanistan back on its feet. After a quarter century of war, a decade without a nationally agreed-upon government, and an international military campaign, how would the country be governed and rebuilt?

A consensus quickly emerged that the United Nations had the legitimacy and credibility to convene the Afghan factions. As everyone turned to the UN, I turned once more to Brahimi.

Our prior efforts at the UN in attempting to broker peace in the Afghanistan civil war now proved useful. Following the military defeat of the Taliban, representatives of the key sectors of Afghan society were already convened at the negotiating table. An umbrella—the Geneva Initiative—had been created for dialogue on the future of Afghanistan between the former king's supporters (known as the Rome Group) and the Pashtuns and Hazaras, who opposed the king and were backed by Tehran (the so-called Cyprus Group). This work produced no immediate results, as UN diplomacy often does not, but it was far from wasted, as UN diplomacy seldom is.

After I reappointed Brahimi as my envoy to Afghanistan in early October, he tiptoed carefully through the many groups and interests concerned, doing what people very often fail to do in these situations—listening, carefully, to everybody. Some grumbled that we were moving too slowly. Colin Powell's mantra was "speed, speed, speed." He was concerned that if the political process fell far behind the ongoing military operation, a vacuum would be created. He even told me in mid-November that "something is needed to put a fire under Mr. Brahimi, rather than relying on the level of energy he has hitherto exhibited." On other occasions, the Iranians or the Russians or the Pakistanis would ring me and complain that they were not being sufficiently consulted or had some other objection to our diplomacy.

But these objections soon faded. Once Brahimi had consulted adequately—including with a kitchen cabinet of outside experts whom he had remained in close touch with through the years—Brahimi moved with speed to fashion a diplomatic process to support the UN lead, and a political process among the Afghans to help them chart the way forward for the country.

There was a lot of discussion and debate on the shape of a postwar UN presence in Afghanistan. Kosovo and East Timor were the most recent blueprints for UN interventions to stabilize a traumatized society— countries where we had almost assumed the responsibilities of a sovereign government. But these were small territories with relatively homogeneous societies and benign security environments, where the population backed a strong UN intervention to help their transition to independence. We could not apply our little experience from these operations to Afghanistan. We had to tailor an approach suitable to a vast, ethnically factionalized, poor, and almost ungoverned nation, with a long history of resistance to outside rule, and which would continue to be a battleground between Western forces and al Qaeda elements. Brahimi was acutely sensitive to the deep-seated hatred of foreign occupation in Afghanistan, and feared that the wrong strategy would play into the radicals' hands.

We decided that the UN could be the midwife for the birth of an interim Afghan government as the first step in an agreed process of transition, and should provide discreet support to the Afghans in building better governance from an extremely low base. But we would have no pretensions to run Afghanistan. Any UN political role had to be based on a genuine Afghan national consensus, and UN agencies should work to put the Afghans in the lead in rebuilding the country. I spoke of a "homegrown" solution. But it was John Renninger, a senior officer in the Department of Political Affairs, who coined the term that would come to characterize the UN approach: the "light footprint."

It was also clear that security would be the essential platform for postwar political, economic, and social reconstruction. I did not favor sending UN peacekeepers, as they would take far too long to deploy and would operate in an environment where there would not yet be a proper peace to keep. We recommended to the Security Council that a multinational force was required to provide an international security presence in the main cities to ensure security and give sufficient space for the political and security transitions. Eventually, an all-Afghan force would be the logical security guarantor.

But it was the regional diplomacy as much as the architecture in-country that would determine the success or failure of our efforts. The role of Tehran and Islamabad as the hitherto main backers of the Northern Alliance and the Taliban respectively, would be essential for the outcome of the inter-Afghan negotiations. Could their rivalries be sufficiently reduced, and their influence over groups in Afghanistan be used to positive effect? We paid close attention to both. The other key actor was, of course, the United States, by far the most powerful player, and I worked as closely with Colin Powell as Brahimi did with his U.S. counterpart James Dobbins.

After a frenetic round of bilateral consultations, I convened the "Six plus Two" group with each member fielding its foreign minister at a meeting on November 12, during the opening of the general debate of the General Assembly. The meeting took some careful handling, but afterward we were able to announce a consensus in support of the creation of a "broad-based, multiethnic, politically balanced, freely chosen Afghan administration representative of [the Afghan people's] aspirations and at peace with its neighbours."

Shortly thereafter, the Security Council supported my proposal to convene a meeting of representatives of the various Afghan groups to chart the political transition.

At the end of November 2001, a conference was organized in Bonn with the main participants, including the leaders of the Northern Alliance that had formed to fight the Taliban, the leaders from the Rome and Cyprus processes, and the Peshawar Conference, which had all been formed in previous negotiations. Brahimi also added that each of these were welcome only if they had at least one woman in each delegation.

The Northern Alliance was now working out its own divisions even as it was gaining dominance over the Taliban on the battlefield. Its representatives did not want the Bonn conference to reach a final outcome, preferring instead to play a long game in which the spoils of power would be decided among them at a later date. Equally challenging was the fact that the largest ethnic group, the Pashtuns, were only partially represented—an unavoidable flaw at the heart of Bonn. There were heavy differences over security and power-sharing issues—indeed, the political and ethnic geometry of Afghanistan was uniquely complex. There were many inherent and unavoidable flaws embedded in the Bonn process, but simply getting the Afghans to Bonn was an achievement.

I sent a message to the Bonn conference appealing to the Afghans to seize the opportunity, and German foreign minister Joschka Fischer opened it. I continued to support the effort through constant calls to the leaders with influence on the parties. In Bonn, we cordoned off the conference venue to outsiders. This no doubt frustrated the couple of dozen nations that sent observers, including the Americans, but it allowed the team to orchestrate their intervention with one party or another, whenever needed, around the clock. After an all-night session, Brahimi clinched what became known as the Bonn Agreement.

Bonn was not a final peace agreement, and it did not establish a permanent government for Afghanistan—neither objective was possible or even desirable given the hasty convening and imperfect representation. We ensured that the agreement instead had the capacity for course corrections and adjustments built into it in readiness for unfolding developments. Bonn laid out a series of steps with target timelines, with each step designed to make the governing authority more representative and legitimate than the last.

According to the Bonn Agreement the immediate target was to establish within two weeks an interim authority headed by the Pashtun Hamid Karzai. Within six months, an emergency *loya jirga*—an Afghan tribal council—was to be held under the auspices of the former king. Within eighteen months, a constitutional *loya jirga* would meet to adopt a new constitution for Afghanistan. Two years after the emergency *loya jirga*, there would be nationwide elections.

Crucially, and worryingly, the Afghans decided to defer the question of disarming the militias and warlords. But they did agree to invite a UN-mandated international security force to Kabul, with a view to its later expansion to other urban centers. They also agreed to withdraw all military units from Kabul and other centers where the force deployed. Despite the fait accompli of having captured Kabul, we managed to secure from the Northern Alliance an agreement to withdraw from the capital and to participate in a multiethnic interim authority under a Pashtun head—albeit in exchange for a strong position inside the interim authority.

For all its imperfections, which we acknowledged, the agreement was a remarkable achievement in such a short span of time. When Brahimi called to brief me on the final outcome, I remembered that one regional foreign minister had said to me just six weeks earlier that any UN conference would be a "very long process" and warned me not to "waste your time." I had often wondered until that moment if he was right. But we were all deeply conscious that the hard work was just beginning.

In March 2002, the Security Council mandated a United Nations Assistance Mission in Afghanistan (UNAMA). Consistent with our approach, the mission would try to put the struggling Afghan state in the lead, with individual nations responsible for providing security and supporting the Afghans to reform and rebuild their armed forces, police, and judiciary, as well as combat Afghanistan's trafficking of opium. The UN would instead provide discreet support for the political dialogue necessary to sustain the transition; the running of elections; the preparation and endorsement of a constitution; the protection of human rights; and the delivery of humanitarian aid.

The Bonn process, initiated by the final agreement of the conference in December 2001, is a modern example of the unique convening potential of the United Nations, the skillful discharge by an envoy of the secretary-general's good offices role, and the effectiveness of UN political action when supported by the Security Council. The same could be said of the successful convening of the *loya jirga* six months later and several other steps in the transition that the UN helped to facilitate on the ground, culminating in the constitutional *loya jirga* of December 2003. All these developments were much better than could have been reasonably hoped for.

B ut Afghanistan was hardly an unadulterated success story. If Bonn showed the potential of the UN's peacemaking role, the realities we confronted over time, both geopolitically and on the ground, were sobering reminders of its limits.

These became apparent early on. When I visited Kabul in January 2002—the first world leader to leave the confines of Kabul Airport after the war—the goodwill toward the UN was palpable, as was the overwhelming desire of an exhausted people, above all else, to put a quarter century of war behind them. Tony Blair had stepped forward, courageously I thought, and agreed that the British would lead the first international deployment into Kabul, spearheading the forty-five-hundred-strong International Security Assistance Force (ISAF) authorized by the Security Council. The deployment went far more smoothly than any of us expected, and during my visit I heard increasingly vocal demands from Afghans for the expansion of ISAF to the rest of the country.

This was something we could never achieve. If the politics had struggled to catch up with the military side in late 2001, we now faced the opposite problem: the security reality began lagging behind the formal political transition. The inability to close this gap became the greatest threat to the transition itself.

We would return to this theme time and again in our reports to the Security Council, but to little avail. While the U.S. State Department appreciated the need for a comprehensive strategy to reconstruct Afghanistan, the U.S. military pursued a narrowly focused military campaign against al Qaeda—and, as it turned out, began to divert resources from Afghanistan to prepare for an offensive against Iraq. This soon absorbed most diplomatic and military energy, too.

On the ground, the warlords became the security contractors of the United States, and in turn resisted the power of the central authority. I am not suggesting it was easy to ignore the warlords—the UN itself came in for criticism that they had a prominent place in the 2002 *loya jirga*. But whereas ISAF was seeking to collect their weapons and reintegrate them, the United States was recruiting them to fight the war on terror. Meanwhile, the Pakistanis helped the Americans to chase al Qaeda—but Pakistani intelligence secretly supported Taliban elements both in Afghanistan and in the tribal areas of Pakistan.

In time, it became apparent that a serious course correction was needed. In autumn 2003, we proposed a Bonn II conference. This was designed to examine the shortcomings embodied in the original Bonn agreement, particularly regarding the issue of the representation of all the major sectors of Afghan society, to turn around what was by then a deteriorating security situation, and to speed up reconstruction. This, most important of all, was also the opportune time to reach out to those Taliban who wished to join the political process at a time when they were at their weakest and most amenable to a deal. But, fatefully, we could not get the support we needed, including from our U.S. partners, for this proposal to be realized.

President Bush had told me in October 2001, "During the presidential campaign, I said I would not use the military for nation building, and I intend to keep that pledge." It was an unwisely narrow approach to a deep-rooted problem, and embodied an illusion that Afghanistan could be stabilized on the cheap. It took several years before the United States stopped paying the warlords. It also took five years for the Europeans, who had been excessively cautious in their readiness to deploy, to strengthen their security commitment. It was only when President

Obama came into office that these issues were fully and properly examined afresh, but by then it was very late in the day. As the United States and its allies are making clear their plans to leave the country by 2014, history looks very much as though it will repeat itself, leaving the people of Afghanistan once again pawns in games, great and small.

CHRONICLE OF A WAR FORETOLD

Before the 2003 invasion of Iraq it was always assumed that Saddam's lack of full cooperation was because he refused to give in to the demands of the United States and the United Nations and was determined to retain Iraq's WMD program. It would turn out that the Iraqi regime, despite all its games, did actually fully disarm its WMD capability in the years between 1991 and 2003. Tariq Aziz, Saddam's long-serving foreign minister, once asked a senior member of the UN's inspection team, UNSCOM, "You know why we never can allow you to certify that we've rid ourselves of our weapons of destruction, don't you?" The UN official replied incredulously that this was the entire purpose of the inspections, and that once free of the stigma, Iraq could come in from the cold. Aziz replied, "The Persians and the Jews." For Saddam, in other words, sustaining the fear that he possessed WMD was all about deterring Iran and Israel, two countries that he considered mortal enemies. The Iraqi regime under Saddam neither wanted to appear unarmed nor suffer the humiliation of appearing to capitulate in full to the demands of the international community—and this was a game they may have been able to continue to play for many more years if it had not been for September 11.

On September 11, the threat perception of the United States and the United Kingdom changed dramatically, and their response would change the world. A new inspection commission, the United Nations Monitoring, Verification and Inspection Commission (UNMOVIC), had been established in December 1999 to replace UNSCOM, with a new head in Hans Blix, the former director general of the International Atomic Energy Agency. For the first two years, however, the inspections issue lay largely dormant in the Security Council. Soon after the United States presidential election in 2000, at the urging of the Bush administration, the focus of the Security Council returned with a fierce momentum to the issue of forcing Saddam's compliance. Within weeks of the attacks of 9/11, foreign leaders were expressing their concern to me that the United States would set its sights on Iraq and Saddam, with the Indian prime minister Atal Bihari Vajpayee telling me in mid-November that an attack would "destroy an anti-terrorist coalition which was still very fragile." And in January, George W. Bush delivered his State of the Union Address, which described Iraq as part of an "axis of evil." To many, the war was already in motion.

It was clear that a new resolve had taken hold in Washington—a determination to see Saddam disarmed definitively. In late February, I met with two senior British diplomats and warned them that if the United States were to extend its war against terrorism to Iraq, many member states, including some European countries and Canada, would require the Security Council to authorize any action. A few days later, one of them came back to see me to caution me that the United States was determined to have the resolutions completely obeyed, or to "have the regime out." When I responded that Saddam had a habit of miscalculating, he replied that "either they will get rid of the capability or they will get rid of him."

But what was also clear even to the most ardent opponents of military action was that the current strategy wasn't working: the sanctions could never be made "smart" enough to spare the Iraqi people from continued suffering; nor were they robust enough to ensure with certainty that Baghdad wasn't finding ways to rearm in contravention of its obligations to the Security Council.

On the other side of the debate, the French, the Chinese, the Russians, and the Germans became over time evermore determined to prevent the unilateral use of force by the United States as something they considered fundamentally inimical to the international system and the role of the Security Council in peace and security. Over the following year, the negotiations for a new resolution gained speed with both sides insisting on their own interpretation of what was acceptable. I began to host a regular series of private lunches for the ambassadors of the permanent five members to seek a strong dialogue, if not actually an agreement that would have to be sought at the head-of-state level.

In early September 2002, I received a call from Joschka Fischer, the German foreign minister, who expressed his concern about the path we were on. I let him know that, based on my conversations with a range of leaders, there was a growing unease about the impact preemptive action taken by one state would have on international law. "What precedent does it set?" I emphasized that support given by the United Nations for military action would bestow both legitimacy and legality on anything done with respect to Iraq. Later that month, George W. Bush came to the General Assembly and made a powerful statement about Saddam's violations of multiple resolutions of the Security Council. My answer in my own address to the Assembly was that there was no alternative for the legitimate use of force than through a united Security Council and that there was still time to seek a peaceful way out. After the meeting, I spoke with Tony Blair for whom the process of negotiating a new resolution wasn't so much about achieving the disarmament goals. To him, above all, it was a test of the UN in the eyes of the United States: "a critical moment for the UN to persuade the U.S. that the UN has the wherewithal to be effective and relevant in the future."

As negotiations over a resolution to authorize the return of UN inspectors to Iraq intensified, suspicions grew on all sides that this had a lot less to do with Iraq's alleged weapons of mass destruction than the question of who would be the supreme arbiter of the legitimacy of the use of force in the international system. Specifically, the debate revolved around the one or two resolutions that would be needed to justify the use of force in the event that the Iraqis—as most expected—would fail to fulfill their obligations. Who would determine when they did fail to cooperate? And who would determine the consequences—one state or the Security Council as a body? As the United States pushed to assert its dominance over this process, France and other members of the Security Council pushed increasingly against it.

A key question arose around the degree of "automaticity," namely, whether a material breach of the terms of the new resolution would result in the automatic endorsement by the Council of the use of force. President Chirac of France made clear to me, in a call on September 28, that France was prepared to use its veto to prevent such an outcome. Colin Powell then began an intense round of negotiations with his French counterpart Dominique de Villepin, and called me on October 4 to say that he was seeking "a bridge between them and us on automaticity." He added that he had told de Villepin that it was no good for the two sides "to throw hand grenades at each other," and that it was vital to find a solution that preserved "their equity and our equity."

By mid-October, my own position was becoming more and more difficult to balance: I was increasingly caught between the strongly divergent interests of the most powerful members of the Council. On October 11, Colin Powell called me to remonstrate: "You're taking the French line with two resolutions, my friend." A week later he warned that "we have not given up our right to act with like-minded friends if necessary." I was not taking the French line, of course; instead I was holding to the position that we needed an outcome backed by a united Security Council as the best solution. The same day, Foreign Minister Igor Ivanov telephoned to state Russia's position: "If the resolution is aimed at strengthening the operation of the inspectors, we are ready to work constructively with them. But if it is aimed at creating a legal framework for military operations, it is unacceptable to us." The divisions in the Council that had appeared after the brief unity following 9/11 had now turned into deep disputes between the parties' negotiating positions.

At the end of October, Powell, in one of his many requests for me to convey how strongly Washington was wedded to its position, said that "what everybody needs to understand is that this is the best way to avoid war . . . If the French keep playing games," Powell continued, "they will get exactly what he is trying to avoid."

He concluded by saying: "We're losing patience here and we have an election coming." Over the next week, the focus was on achieving strong support for the resolution, and over the course of many calls, even Syria was persuaded to vote in favor, so that on November 8, resolution 1441 was passed unanimously. There was a genuine sense of achievement in the Council that day, a belief that through tough negotiations, the member states had found a formula that would preserve the prerogative of the Council while making clear to the Iraqis that time was running out on their games and obfuscations. I was, however, mindful of the seriousness of Washington's purpose. On the eve of the vote, I spoke to Powell and in an exasperated voice he warned: "What you're going to have to figure out is to get to the Iraqis somehow—and I am not sure anyone can get to Saddam—and tell him that we're not looking to see how much he will be fooling around, but if he has made a strategic choice for cooperation. If he thinks he can rope-a-dope the inspectors again, he's in for a shock."

I made my own view clear on the question of "automaticity"— whether resolution 1441 contained provisions for an automatic response with military force in response to the establishment of a material breach of the resolution by the Iraqis. As I established in my statement after the vote: "What is important is that there are no triggers in this resolution, and the Council will be back to review what the inspectors bring them . . . How this crisis is resolved will affect greatly the course of peace and security in the coming years in the region, and the world." The next day, I met with President Bush and praised him for taking the multilateral route. In private, he was as tough-minded as ever, but his response indicated that he also understood that resolution 1441 did not include provisions for the "automaticity" of military action. He stressed that any consequent military action would be "swift," but emphasized that "if Saddam stiffs Blix in any way we'll go back to the UN. Even if it's over a paper clip. Seriously." He then reflected on the situation in more emotional terms: "You, I, and others have the obligation to free people where we find that they are being tortured and killed . . . It brings tears to my eyes when I think about what the Iraqi people are going through."

Soon Saddam was back to his intransigent modus operandi, even as UNMOVIC and IAEA inspectors were beginning their inspections. The Iraqi submission of a "full and complete declaration," which they delivered with much fanfare in a twelve-thousand-page document turned out to be neither. The United States, just before Christmas, then began to hint at how widely it would define a further "material breach" on the part of Iraq. This received the predictable response from Paris and, on January 20, French foreign minister Dominique de Villepin stated that under no circumstances would France allow the Council to authorize war with Iraq. It had already been planned that the United States would soon formally and fully make its case to the Council that Iraq was in material breach of the Council's resolutions, and lines were clearly being drawn by the French in preparation for this. The disparate British attempt to secure a second resolution—something Washington never believed it needed— was coming apart. In the region, major countries were already beginning to worry about the aftermath of a war in Iraq. When I spoke to the Saudi foreign minister Prince Saud at the end of January, he warned that there was "potential for tremendous chaos in Iraq." It would be a "windfall for the terrorists," he added, since they could "go in and plant roots."

Washington's decision to send Powell to make the case to the Council and the world on February 5 was bold. What it did without question was underline the centrality of the United Nations as the indispensable forum for the management of global peace and security issues. As I heard Colin set out the evidence as the Americans saw it, I was impressed with his delivery but I was most concerned about the substance. He did not produce any evidence of the "smoking gun" variety, despite effectively claiming to possess such evidence. Worse, I was not alone in thinking that Powell himself did not appear as though he entirely believed his own case. He seemed to be saying it purely for raisons d'état. While the other Security Council foreign ministers delivered their own prepared statements in response to Powell at the official meeting, it was during the lunch I hosted for the members of the Council afterward that the most penetrating debate took place.

The German foreign minister Joschka Fischer started by stating that there was "total unanimity that Iraq must disarm and must do so proactively." I added that the inspectors now had a clear set of tasks and, while the Security Council had its resolutions before it, it "may have to come to a time when the Security Council will have to decide on a material breach and will have to decide on the serious consequences." I added that "the time may come when we have to take some tough decisions based on what the inspectors say."

The tension between Colin Powell and Dominique de Villepin was evident for all to see. In an impatient, exasperated tone, Colin asked de Villepin what exactly he had meant in his statement earlier in the Council about providing more help for the inspectors. De Villepin then launched into an extensive monologue about the alternatives to conflict and the fact that Iraq was but one of many proliferating countries, and noted that "we should find a different way than military action—we do not believe that military action can be so virtuous as to create democracy in the Middle East." He continued by stating that the UN had to be central to any next step, as "no country could win the war and win the peace as well. I do not believe we can go to war based on suspicions and evasions. I am asked how long a delay should be acceptable in terms of the inspections. I ask how long will it be to regain the peace? I ask, how will this affect terrorism, how will this affect other proliferators? We are facing other issues: North Korea, Iran, Middle East." De Villepin closed by saying that France would not accept "automaticity."

I could see Colin balancing his frustration with Dominique with an admiration for his eloquence and the way he had set out the case against war. He replied sharply: "I did not ask about the use of force. I asked about what you meant about adding to the number of inspectors."

At this point, Russian foreign minister Ivanov intervened to separate the issues into the question of WMD; the nature of Saddam's regime; and what he called "emotions." He added in an aside that while the president of Pakistan, Pervez Musharraf, was in Moscow for the first bilateral summit in thirty years, he was not sure if there were more al Qaeda in Pakistan or Iraq (this then triggered the Pakistani foreign minister's launch into an impassioned defense of his country). Fischer sought to bring the sides together by appealing to Ivanov to use the Russian influence with the Iraqis, noting, "Igor, you are working with them." Ivanov replied that they had also worked with Milošević, to which Colin replied, "Igor, you need to find some new friends. It's over."

In a moment that brought the gravity of the moment firmly into to the room, Colin asked to speak again. He started by saying that "my credentials are solid with this group. I have looked here for a peaceful solution, and there is still time for a peaceful solution. We all await the report on the fourteenth, and it will tell us if there is progress or something else. Nobody wants war; the United States does not want war; the president does not want war; I do not want war. I believe I can say in fairness that I know more about war than anyone in this room. I've lost friends in war; I've fought in two wars; I've commanded wars. The last thing I want is another war. You know how I am characterized in the press, as a 'reluctant warrior' or a 'dove.' I have no problem with that label."

Colin continued: "However, I don't accept the premise that wars always lead to bad results. Yes, the unavoidable and unintended consequences have to be considered carefully, as in the case of the legacy of the wars in Afghanistan. However, other conflicts have different lessons— lessons of good—coming out of them."

At this point, Joschka Fischer interjected: "And we are the best example of that."

Colin concluded: "If it comes to conflict, and the United States finds itself in a position to lead a coalition, under UN authority, or a coalition of the willing, the U.S. understands the obligation it has, the prospects of turmoil and unintended consequences, understands fully the responsibility to leave the area in a better state. If conflict comes, we will not look away, and Iraq and the region will be better off. However, our preference remains peace, not war."

I have recounted this exchange in detail because it captures, as few other moments do in that year of extraordinary drama and diplomatic maneuvering, the depth of passions, and the way in which the question of Iraq became about something far larger: the foundations of peace and security, and the place of the United Nations as the sole legitimate authority to endorse the use of force except in cases of self-defense. Over the next month, I was in nearly daily contact with the leaders of a dozen countries or more, including Tony Blair, George W. Bush, and Jacques Chirac. On February 21, I was in Paris as part of a tour of European capitals and called Bush to give him my own unvarnished assessment of the mood there. I pointed out that the leaders and peoples of Europe who were demonstrating in large numbers had no interest in the survival of Saddam Hussein, but rather were concerned with the way the use of force was being contemplated. Bush, in response, made clear to me the prism through which he had come to see the challenge. He said that "Saddam Hussein is a brutal dictator who tortures his people, and he is a threat to the United States and the world. Without Saddam, the world will be a safer place." He added that U.S. military action would bring about the "liberation of Iraq."

On February 24, France, Germany, and the Russian Federation issued a joint memorandum to be circulated among the members of the Security Council on the Iraq situation. "The combination of a clear program of action, reinforced inspections, a clear timeline and the military build-up provide a realistic means to reunite the SC and to exert maximum pressure on Iraq." On March 5, the foreign ministers of France,

Germany, and Russia met in Paris and announced that they "would not let a resolution pass that would authorize force." Two days later, during one of my regular briefings with Blix and ElBaradei, Hans told me that the Iraqis had stopped destroying the missiles under UNMOVIC supervision. It seemed to be clear by then that the die was cast.

On March 10, I spoke at a conference in The Hague and made clear in response to a question that the Council faced a momentous choice and that an attack on Iraq without Council authorization would be in breach of the Charter. Chirac, on the same day, stated explicitly that France would veto a resolution that would automatically lead to war, explaining that he did not believe war was the means to the disarmament of Iraq. On the same side as France were other strong allies of the United States, including Mexico and Chile. The Mexicans made clear to me during numerous calls that they were under immense pressure from Washington to support the action. For them, however, something far greater was at stake. As Luis Derbez, the foreign minister of Mexico told me in a call on March 13, they simply could not support "a decision allowing unilateral action and the authority to go to war." Reflecting on the history of his continent, he added that he had told Powell that Mexico could not "allow the UN to justify toppling a government."

Time was running out, however, and with or without the UN the United States and its allies were on a course for war. On the eve of the Azores Summit, a meeting among the United States, the UK, and Spain, Blair called me to say that he could not "see a way out of the impasse." The day after, following a call from Colin Powell stating that the United States had made the decision to invade, I authorized the withdrawal of all remaining UN personnel from Iraq, and three days later, the invasion began. War had come to Iraq, once again.

The decision by the United States and its allies to proceed with the invasion of Iraq without Security Council authorization was a defeat for all of us who had sought to ensure that Iraq's defiance of the United Nations was met by a united and effective response. But it was a vindication, too, of principle over power. Members of the Council, including close allies and neighbors of the United States, had insisted on the prerogative of the United Nations Security Council to decide under international law whether a member state was in material breach of the Council's resolutions, and what the consequences should be.

Amid the exhaustion and exasperation, the sense of countless hours of diplomacy spent in vain, and an impending gloom about the consequences of a unilateral war, the United Nations had stood up for itself, and its founding principles. It would matter little to the world—and to the people of Iraq—in the months and years to come, but far worse would have been a rubber stamp for a war fought on false premises. From such a misjudgment, the road back to credibility and legitimacy in the eyes of the world would have been far harder.

INTO THE STORM: IRAQ AFTER THE INVASION

On March 20, 2003, the United States and its allies invaded Iraq, bringing an end to more than a decade of attempts by the United Nations and the international community to secure the disarmament of Iraq consistent with its obligations under the cease-fire terms of the first Gulf War. Years of intense, fraught, and ultimately futile diplomacy were replaced with a massive invasion of a sovereign state without the authorization of the Security Council. The initial relief at the swiftness of the collapse of the Iraqi regime was soon replaced by scenes of looting and general lawlessness that left Iraqis uncertain and increasingly fearful of their future.

Four days into the war, Jeremy Greenstock, the British ambassador to the United Nations, came to see me to begin the work of closing the breach between the UN and the coalition. The next day, I invited the ambassadors of the five permanent members of the Security Council to a working lunch, resuming the dialogue we had maintained throughout the run-up to the war, now in the context of an active conflict. For all the acrimony, I was struck by the pragmatic atmosphere in the room, and the desire, particularly on the part of the Russian and Chinese ambassadors, to find a basis for working together again in the wider interest of the international community. Everyone had an interest in ensuring a successful postconflict environment in Iraq. No one wanted to see long-term damage to the United Nations, or a deeper geopolitical divide.

At the UN, we soon focused on the ways in which we could contribute to securing a better future for the people of Iraq, like so many other victims of war and tyranny in need of our assistance. This was not an easy call. Among a large number of member states—and many of our staff—there was a view that the UN should not in any way be seen to be endorsing the invasion, or helping implement an occupation that followed an unsanctioned war.

This was the paradox about the much-vaunted "vital role" that Blair and Bush avowed would be made available to the UN. In fact, we did not seek a "vital role," nor in the end did we receive one. What I determined in the days after the invasion, after a great deal of consideration, was that we had an obligation to the people of Iraq that went beyond whatever feelings of betrayal or disapproval any one of us might have. The Iraqis needed our help and, as the United Nations, we were duty bound to answer the call. It was neither realistic nor desirable for the United Nations to shy away from a role in such a complex, and consequential, postconflict arena.

I had asked Sergio Vieira de Mello to lead our mission because I believed his distinguished field experience—from the Balkans to East Timor—would ensure the strongest possible contribution by the UN to the stability of the country while retaining our independence from the occupying powers. Having arrived too late to stop the U.S. representative in Baghdad, Jerry Bremer, from issuing two disastrous orders on the disbanding of the Iraqi army and the de-Baathification of the Iraqi state structure, Sergio focused his efforts on securing as wide a political consensus as possible for the future governance of the country. In this mission, despite severe limitations on his powers, his freedom of maneuver, and his influence over the key decisions of the coalition, he succeeded greatly. By carefully and patiently listening to all sides in the fracturing Iraqi mosaic—and earning the trust of the Shia religious leader, Ayatollah Sistani—he helped form what became the Governing Council, the first genuinely Iraqi expression of a post-Saddam government.

The bombing on August 19 that took Sergio's life and that of twenty-one other colleagues was the vicious response from the terrorist groups determined to thwart any attempts—including those by the United Nations—to secure a peaceful postwar environment in Iraq. A month after Sergio's death, another suicide bomber struck near the UN headquarters in Baghdad. The attacks were clearly not going to end. Following the August 19 bombing, I had ordered an investigation into the security measures taken at the UN headquarters and asked Marti Ahtisaari, the former president of Finland and a veteran of multiple UN missions, to lead it. I knew he would take an independent, stringent look at the evidence. He did, and he was furious when he came to me with his assessment.

Basic security measures had not been taken. This was compounded by the fundamental dilemma of our presence in Iraq: if we were going to be effective in playing a role distinct from the occupation, we could not base ourselves in the coalition security area called the "Green Zone," separated from the people of Iraq in the most glaring and dominating manner. At the same time, by basing ourselves outside the zone at the Canal Hotel, we would be exposed to a greater degree to the violence and terror unleashed by the invasion's aftermath. The chaos of postwar Iraq left no way for this dilemma to be resolved other than our departure from the country. I simply could no longer justify the risk to our people of having a permanent mission on the ground. When we did return in 2004, in a diplomatic mission led by Lakhdar Brahimi to help resolve the political standoff between the parties, it was under the strictest security protocols. Once again, the UN was able to play an important role in resolving vital political and governance disputes, but as the deeper forces of a civil war took hold, the violence overwhelmed any diplomatic attempts at bringing Iraq back from the abyss.

Back in New York, the struggle to bring the key member states back into cooperation over an issue as important as Iraq continued. However, my own doubts about the justification for the war, and the wisdom of its prosecution, deepened with every grim day that went by. On September 15, 2004, I had agreed to an interview with the BBC. After some less-than-subtle questions from the journalist about the risk of the United States becoming, in his words, "an unrestrainable, unilateral super-power," he got to the question of whether UN Security Council resolution 1441 had given the war legal authority. I answered: "Well, I'm one of those who believe there should have been a second resolution because the Security Council indicated that if Iraq did not comply there will be consequences. But then it was up to the Security Council to approve or determine what those consequences should be." After some further questioning, the reporter asked if it was "illegal." "Yes," I replied, "I have indicated it is not in conformity with the UN Charter; from our point of view and from the Charter point of view it was illegal."

I had expressed this view, in less direct ways, on other occasions in the past. I had up to that point always sought to retain my ability to engage both sides of this deep global divide by avoiding an outright condemnation of the illegality of the war. But it was no longer possible to sustain this position—even if a television interview was a less than ideal venue for saying that the emperor had no clothes. In Washington and London, the reaction was swift and furious. As the barrage of attacks against me and the United Nations grew in intensity and purpose, I was greatly comforted by a generous and humorous e-mail from my trusted friend Ted Sorensen, former counselor and speechwriter to President John F. Kennedy:

Dear Kofi:

Your BBC statement insures you of: A. a permanent place in history as the most courageous, truthful and independent U.N. Secretary-General, and B. No third term. Congratulations!

Relations with Washington were about to get even worse, however. In October 2004, I received information about an impending assault on the Iraqi city of Fallujah by U.S. forces. My concerns were about the inevitable collateral damage to civilians, the risk of violations of international humanitarian law, and the likely inflammatory effect on the insurgency. I decided to send a letter to Bush, Blair, and Iraqi prime minister Alawi in order to go on the record with them about the risks of further aggravating the situation in the country. Inexplicably, the letter was transmitted by fax by my staff, which ensured that it was promptly leaked. Coming shortly after my statement about the illegal nature of the war, and days before the U.S. presidential election, it provided the UN's enemies in Washington with further ammunition, this time alleging that I was interfering in U.S. domestic politics. Nothing had been further from my mind. My focus was on halting the slide into a deeper conflict, but the reality of our intentions and our actions became increasingly irrelevant as we became the focus of a wider campaign to delegitimize the United Nations. To this end, the Oil-for-Food Programme was the perfect instrument.

The program was established in 1996 to alleviate the suffering of the Iraqi people living under strict sanctions as they bore the brunt of the impact caused by the world's determination to deny Saddam the means to reconstitute his weapons of mass destruction. It mushroomed, however, into a vast multibillion dollar structure involving thousands of contracts from dozens of countries whose companies traded with Saddam's regime. Initially designed as a Band-Aid for the people of Iraq—and for the conscience of those in the West who wished to diminish the impact of sanctions on the civilian population—it was over time manipulated by the Iraqi regime into a scheme involving kickbacks by thousands of international companies. At the same time, and outside the program, extensive smuggling of oil—primarily through Turkey, Jordan, and Syria—took place, providing Iraq with illicit income amounting to some $8.4 billion. To this, members of the Security Council, including the United States and the United Kingdom, turned a blind eye.

For the UN Secretariat tasked with managing this enterprise, the Oil-for-Food program was a persistent source of concern given the magnitude of the sums and trading involved, and the complexity of a system that had been designed as a temporary measure. In early 2004, reports began to emerge from postwar Iraq that numerous individuals—mostly traders and middlemen—had benefited personally from oil allocations under the program. The bombshell was that one of these people was alleged to be Benon Sevan, the long-serving UN official who was overseeing the program as director of the Office of the Iraq Programme. Soon, select corners of the media seized on this charge to allege that the entire program had been a vast, corrupt enterprise. We were stunned by this possibility—and totally unprepared to manage the consequences in a poisonous atmosphere of acrimony, mistrust, and ideologically driven attacks on the institution.

To uncover the truth about the UN's role in a program that over seven years sold some $64 billion worth of Iraqi oil and purchased food and other basic goods for the Iraqi people, I asked Paul Volcker, the former chairman of the Federal Reserve Board of the United States, to lead an independent inquiry. Over the following year, he and his team engaged in a comprehensive effort to establish the role of the UN Secretariat as well as that of the member states in the evolution of the program. Their findings, delivered through a series of reports, were deeply troubling. The UN's management of the program came in for severe criticism, which focused primarily on our procurement, auditing, and supervisory practices. Volcker and his team also identified in excess of two thousand companies from a range of countries which had enriched members of Saddam's regime by paying kickbacks in return for contracts—a fact that was far less reported by the press.

As secretary-general of the United Nations and its chief administrative officer, the findings of the Volcker inquiry were deeply distressing. The incidents of corruption that plagued the program were a great disappointment to me professionally. On a personal level, however, there was the added allegation that my son Kojo had been implicated in the Oil-for-Food matter—and this was far more painful. It also provided the UN's enemies with the means through which to implicate me personally in the malfeasance that had occurred in the management of the program. Beginning in the mid-1990s, Kojo had been employed by Cotecna, a Swiss-based trade inspection company, which in 1998 won a UN contract to inspect humanitarian goods entering Iraq. When this was first raised in the media in 1999, my chef de cabinet, Iqbal Riza, asked the UN's head of management, Joe Connor, a former CEO of Price Waterhouse, to look into the matter and establish whether there was any issue of conflict. He, and our legal counsel, Hans Corell, agreed that since the Contracts Committee had not been aware that Kojo had worked for Cotecna, there was no possibility of a conflict. In addition, Kojo had stopped working for Cotecna in 1998.

The revelation—to me and to the world—that Kojo had continued to receive payments from Cotecna all the way up to February 2004 for work in West Africa, five years later than we first thought they had ended, was deeply painful. I told the press on the day of the revelation that I was surprised and disappointed that my son had not been clearer about his relationship with the company.

The attacks on the UN, and me personally, were growing. In early November, weeks before Senator Norm Coleman of Minnesota published an op-ed article in the *Wall Street Journal* calling for my resignation, my loyal and fearless friend Richard Holbrooke decided to intervene. Knowing Washington as he did, he could see where this was going and suggested a private meeting at his New York apartment overlooking Central Park on Sunday, December 5.

He asked me to come alone, without aides, and said he would be leading a conversation with close and trusted friends who only wished me success, but were prepared to speak candidly about the depth of the challenge and the need for decisive action. He was right. He had carefully assembled a group that included the head of the UN Foundation, Tim Wirth; Les Gelb, President Emeritus of the Council on Foreign Relations; and my former advisors John Ruggie and Nader Mousavizadeh, now at Harvard and Goldman Sachs, respectively. Richard himself played the role of both conductor and soloist—skillfully drawing out even the most difficult questions but always pointing us to solutions. Gelb set the stage by saying that he'd just come back from Washington where he had met with senior members of the administration. It was clear, as he put it, that "they won't push you, but if you stumble, they're not going to catch you either."

Over a long four hours, I mostly listened as close friends looked me in the eye to tell me things they might not have otherwise, but now felt needed to be said. I filled a dozen pages of a yellow legal pad with often bracing statements about the need to address head-on the barrage of accusations—and to do this both as a matter of public engagement as well as substance. If we did not address some of the underlying management and accountability issues raised, as much within the organization as without, by the Oil-for-Food matter, we would not be seen as credible in seeking to turn the page. And if we didn't get a better handle on responding to the media onslaught, nothing we did in practice would get through the din of a twenty-four-hour news cycle feeding on every rumor, allegation, and speculation. I left Richard's home with a sense that changes needed to be made at all levels of the organization, and that transparency in our response was needed more than ever.

During the following week, a range of global leaders began to reach out to express their support. Colin Powell, Rafik Hariri, Nelson Mandela,

Olesegun Obasanjo, and Thabo Mbeki; Paul Martin, Madeleine Albright, and Jimmy Carter; Javier Solana and Tony Blair were among those who reached out to assure me of their friendship and sympathy. Chirac, Schroeder, and Zapatero called me jointly from a meeting to urge me on. And my friend Jim Wolfensohn, the World Bank president, in his inimitable Australian manner offered Nane and me a chance to spend the Christmas holidays at his house in Wyoming as a way of saying "to hell with everybody," as he put it. The Chinese foreign minister called me to say, "China and the Chinese people will always be your good friend, and the Chinese government highly appreciates what you are doing." Tellingly, he concluded by saying that "we support your efforts to protect and defend the sovereignty of the UN."

It is true to say that the Security Council never should have asked us to administer the Oil-for-Food Programme, and that we as an organization never should have agreed to run it. But it is not enough. Once we were engaged in this mission—like any other given to us in a conflict or in poverty-ridden countries—we had a responsibility to manage it competently and scrupulously. In this we failed, through weak and porous procurement practices, incomplete auditing systems, and overall management for which I as secretary-general was ultimately responsible. That the far larger—and more consequential—damage to the Programme came from the oil smuggling implicitly encouraged by Western powers and the thousands of corrupt contracts entered into by companies from countries with seats on the Security Council is a reality that remains underappreciated and underreported.

After the final Volcker report was issued exonerating me of any charges of involvement with Cotecna's contract, I received a call from Bill Clinton. Throughout the ordeal, he had demonstrated his friendship as well as a unique appreciation for the forces that I had been up against. He recounted an extraordinary conversation that he had recently had with George Bush. Clinton had warned him, "You do not want Kofi Annan's blood on your hands." Bush's reply was revealing: "My right-wingers want to destroy the United Nations, but I don't." As much as the ideologues of the Bush administration who took their country and the world into a calamitous war wanted to see the UN shattered in the process, ultimately statesmanship prevailed and Washington slowly realized the need for the organization to regain its indispensable role in international security.

WHEN THE BOMBING STOPS: LESSONS OF IRAQ

"What happens when the bombing stops? What about the day after? What then?" These were the questions that I put to the leaders of the permanent five members of the Security Council—privately and publicly—throughout the long and torturous run-up to the invasion of Iraq. We were all engaged in a contest of resolutions, rights, perceived threats, and imagined opportunities for remaking strategic landscapes, I as interpreter and occasional referee, they as gladiators in a global arena.

The question of the aftermath of war and what would become of Iraq after an invasion of "shock and awe" was given little of the attention that it deserved. Few would argue with this judgment today, with the devastating debris of a decade of civil war barely behind us. A unilateral war that replaced tyranny with anarchy in Iraq holds lessons for every member of the international community: the need for legality and legitimacy when force is used, the vital importance of advance planning for the postconflict environment, the critical condition of security as the basis on which any reconstruction can take place.

It is equally essential that the folly of the Iraq War, with the resulting calamity for the people of the country and the broader region, does not doom forever intervention when action is endorsed by the Security Council, a humanitarian crisis is urgent, and the cause is just and legitimate. In the case of the Iraq War, the Security Council resolution cited by the United States and United Kingdom as basis for their actions could just as easily have been used in the opposite case. The Council itself stated that it would be the judge of whether Saddam was not honoring his obligations and would therefore face serious consequences. And this is why a second resolution was absolutely necessary. It was up to the Council to first determine whether Saddam was in compliance or not. And it was then, separately, up to the Council to determine what the serious consequences would be if he wasn't. It wasn't up to two member states to take the law into their own hands.

When the United States and the United Kingdom recognized that they would not be able to assemble the nine votes necessary for Council authorization, they had a choice: they could have given the inspections more time in order to gain greater evidence for their suspicions, and thereby support for enforcement action. Instead, they proceeded to flout the very authority they so assiduously had sought and in whose defense they claimed to be acting. Their way of defending the authority of the United Nations and the Security Council was to ignore its authority when its judgment didn't suit them. And in an extraordinary line of reasoning for a parliamentarian, Tony Blair decided to argue that since they couldn't receive enough support for their actions in the Council, the Council—and not they—had rendered itself illegitimate.

The Iraq War was neither in accordance with the Charter nor legitimate. For the authors of the war, moreover, the justification kept changing. Was it Iraq's noncompliance with UN Security Council demands? Was it support for terrorism? Was it regime change and democracy promotion? Ultimately, of course, no weapons of mass destruction were found in Iraq; no links to al Qaeda were established; and the idea of regime change, already considered unacceptable by the vast majority of member states, was seen to be an invitation to calamitous consequences for the invader as well as the invaded.

In my address to the General Assembly in 1999, I had observed that the Charter's own words "declare that 'armed force shall not be used, save in the common interest.'" "But what is the common interest?" I asked. "Who shall define it? Who shall defend it? Under whose authority? And with what means of intervention?" I did not expect that my questions would be answered with such a deep divergence of views, and with such dire consequences, as those brought about by the wars of 9/11.

What became known as the war on terror had initially been launched in response to the attacks of 9/11 with broad international support. But as the United States increasingly went its own way—with Iraq and with the way it executed its operations in Afghanistan and elsewhere on a global hunt for al Qaeda cells—a global consensus began to fracture. Among the people of the Muslim world, reeling from the impact of these wars, nothing did more damage than the abuses and crimes that took place at detention centers such as Abu Ghraib. More broadly, many governments began to adopt the principle that a tradeoff between human rights and security was necessary, a deeply damaging regression for human rights and the rule of law. Many would point to the American detention center at Guantanamo Bay as a model for their own flouting of due process.

The wars following 9/11 also became about the very purpose of the United Nations—a clash between those who saw the UN and the multilateral principles it represents as an end in and of themselves and those for whom the UN and its resolutions are seen as a useful means toward ends that may or may not be legal and legitimate in the eyes of the world. In the clash between Saddam Hussein and George W. Bush, a tyrannical master of miscalculation met an ideologically driven leader shocked into unilateral vengeance against all perceived enemies. And for the United Nations, the question came down to two challenges that could not be met at the same time: the defiance by a predatory state of its obligations under the resolutions of the Council, and the decision of the world's sole superpower to ignore the considered judgment of a majority of the members of the Security Council and enter into a war that could not be justified under the Charter.

By behaving the way it did, the United States invited the perception among many in the world—including many long-time allies—that it was becoming a greater threat to global security than anything Saddam could muster. This was a self-inflicted wound of historic proportions—and one that did immense, and possibly lasting, damage to U.S. standing in the world. Abu Ghraib did not come out of a vacuum, and neither did Guantanamo. The way they both ran counter to the principles of the rule of law has done incalculable damage to the global struggle for human rights.

Of course, while the Council opponents of the United States and the United Kingdom claimed to be making a stand on principle, they were also driven by reasons of national interest. They were deeply motivated by a desire to prevent a world in which the United States would be given a license to act how and whenever it wished. It may be Iraq today, but where would it be tomorrow? they would ask.

For them, the urgent need to contain an aggressor state such as Iraq was replaced with the priority of containing the United States, a founding member of the United Nations, one of the permanent five members of the Council, and a pillar of global security. For Washington to allow this evolution in its global position was not only a historic failure of diplomacy but also a tragedy for the rule of law around the world.

Ultimately, there was a deep and irreconcilable tension at the heart of the UN's Iraq policy: Saddam clearly had no intention of ever coming into full and verifiable compliance, and neither the United States nor the UK were willing to bring him in from the cold even if he had. Both sides knew the realities about the other's position and the UN was caught in the middle. And then came 9/11 and a frightened, enraged, and deeply ideological Bush administration set about removing Saddam from power—something no basis in law could justify. The UN is not—and has never been—a pacifist organization. But on the question of war and peace, if it does not stand up for the principles of its Charter, it not only places itself outside the law but also loses its legitimacy around the world.

Epilogue

DREAMS OF A REALIST

A Swahili proverb holds that "You cannot turn the wind, so turn the sail." Turning the sail—from conflict prevention to economic development, peacekeeping, human rights, and climate change—is now more than ever in the hands of each and every one of us. The wind will follow its own unsettled course, but men and women in every society today have the ability to determine their destiny in ways unimaginable in past eras. Tyrants and bigots, warlords and criminals, the exploiters of human capital and destroyers of our natural resources, will always be with us, but their sails are not the only ones that can harness the wind.

Early in the year 2011, a storm of change began to blow across the Arab world. The Arab Awakening saw young people throughout the region step forward as one—desperate for dignity, and demanding the opportunity and the freedom to pursue their aspirations for a better life. This force was of a kind that cannot be resisted—at least not for long. We saw it play out in Africa, in Latin America, and in Asia, and now the Arab world's time had finally come. Nowhere did a regime resist this change more fiercely, or more doggedly, than in the Syrian capital of Damascus. Over the course of a bloody year that began in March 2011, the world witnessed the youth of Syria take to the streets week after week pleading for a better, more just, more accountable form of government. With the protests escalating, armed resistance growing, and security forces continuing with a crackdown that, as of this writing, is estimated to have cost some 10,000 civilian lives, Syria's spring has been transformed into a nascent civil war.

In February 2012, while I was reviewing the final drafts of this book at my home in Geneva, I received a call from my successor Secretary-General Ban Ki-moon. He wanted to know if I would accept a request, conveyed to him by a group of foreign ministers, to take on the role of the international community's envoy for the crisis in Syria. They needed a mediator who could engage with the internal, regional, and international divisions that accompanied the Syrian conflict, and who would seek to resolve them peacefully. I accepted, knowing how difficult it would be to bridge the hostilities and to create the context for a negotiated transition to a free and representative government in Syria. I also knew that the alternative, an armed civil conflict drawing in global and regional powers and spilling over into fragile neighboring countries, could have far wider—and more lasting—ramifications. This was a conflict as complex, and as virulent, as any that I had encountered in my fifty years of international diplomacy.

The crisis in Syria was not only one of street protest movements and rebel groups pitted against a decades-old regime, but a maelstrom in which also swirled the jealously guarded interests of dozens of regional players, including Turkey, Israel, Jordan, Saudi Arabia, Qatar, and Iran. These divisions were compounded by the diverging interests of Russia, China, the United States, and the EU. Furthermore, Syria is as complex as any society one might care to name in the region. Its cleavages are rapidly becoming as deep and bitter as those of Lebanon and on a scale that threatens a clash of sectarian animosities that could dwarf even those that shook Iraq after 2003. It is a conflict that threatens the disintegration of a state at the crossroads of numerous regional and international forces, of religious and sectarian rivalries, and in a region stalked by extremism. Furthermore, Syria holds one of the world's largest stockpiles of chemical weapons.

In this light, it is perhaps understandable that, when I accepted the job, the dominant—indeed, it seemed, the only—message in the media was that this was "mission impossible." How, in such a crisis, could there even be the possibility of a peaceful transformation of Syrian society? I knew this would be an intervention that would tread the most delicate of tightropes, woven in a dozen divided strands. I focused first on bridging the intense divisions in the Security Council, and after receiving support from all sides for my six-point plan, I began to engage with the regime with strong international support. Initially, in March 2012, the Syrian government and the Syrian opposition accepted the peace plan. At the time of this writing, in May 2012, the violence had resumed at a terrible cost to the civilian population of Syria. To the members of the Security Council and those countries with influence on Syria, my message was clear: if Syria was to see an end to the violence and a transition to a legitimate government, they had to exert the necessary joint pressure for diplomacy to succeed.

The period ahead for Syria is as fraught and uncertain as any facing the countries of the Arab world today. Change must come to Damascus—the regime knows this, the region knows this, and the world knows this. The question is whether it will be achieved through a bloody and immensely destructive civil war, or whether the people of Syria will see their aspirations for genuine freedom and individual rights realized through a transitional process to representative government.

Just as each of us can look to Syria and see the price its citizens are paying to achieve a measure of freedom and dignity, we as a global community should learn the hard-won lessons of the past, and seek to prevent injustices and inequities from taking root before they lead to crisis and conflict. A culture of prevention can be far more effective than a slogan. We know that the three pillars of security, development, rule of law and human rights are indispensable in and of themselves, and need each other to ensure that one is not threatened by the weakness of the other. The lesson of the crises of public trust and governance sweeping the world from the Arab Spring to Europe and Asia is that without the rule of law and human rights, unequal development or narrow forms of security are not sustainable. For governments, NGOs, corporations, and individuals alike, this is a lesson with the power to transform the lives of states as well as peoples.

The promise of agricultural development is one area where innovative science and investment, rightly applied, can make a difference to millions. I am now involved in an effort to transform food production in Africa—and create true food and nutrition security—through the Alliance for a Green Revolution in Africa (AGRA). Our mission is to empower smallholder farmers throughout the continent to create food security from the bottom up, farm by individual farm. With projects in more than a dozen countries in Africa, we aim to double the income of smallholders through the use of improved seeds, increased productivity, and adequate storage facilities, assisting the farmer all along the value chain.

AGRA aims to address one of the principal objectives of the Millennium Development Goals; namely, to reduce hunger and poverty by 50 percent. Agriculture will continue to play a critical role in the development of my continent of Africa, and if it is allowed to sustain broader social and economic progress, Africa can truly enter a new period of prosperity. As the crisis in Kenya demonstrated—and conflicts elsewhere in Africa continue to remind us—honest, accountable, and legitimate leadership remains the critical difference between a better future and a descent into new periods of crisis and underdevelopment. The Arab Awakening that has galvanized the politics of so many of the countries of

North Africa is inspiring youth throughout the continent to ask for more, and better, from their leaders, and to take their rightful place in the global wave of economic integration that has transformed societies, from China to Brazil and India.

If the MDGs have succeeded in creating a universally accepted template for addressing the sources of social and economic development, R2P—the Responsibility to Protect—has changed the global understanding of sovereignty, such that no state should be allowed to violate the rights of its citizens with impunity—and allow no leader to imagine that his standing will be unaffected by the way he treats his people. In any such ambition, where the aim is to alter the balance of power between state and citizen, progress will be slow and fitful. None of us behind the development of this emerging international norm imagined that states everywhere suddenly would respect the rights of their peoples, or that the answer when they failed was necessarily military action in the name of human rights. What we sought—and still seek—is a consciousness on the part of leaders and governments everywhere that their integration into global society cannot progress without respect for human rights.

The MDGs and R2P each represent, in their own way, attempts to renew the structures of global governance for a purpose beyond the privilege of states, and to empower individuals to turn their sails toward realizing their potential. In a world undergoing dramatic shifts in the balance of power—between the West and the East; the state and the private sector; an economy designed for the benefit of a few and one reimagined toward sustainable inclusive growth—the United Nations can still play a vital, convening role and be an agent for progress.

The UN Charter was written in the name of "We the Peoples," and if it renews itself for a new era of people power, the organization can aspire to making a far greater impact in the lives of those who need it most. From the farmer in Africa to the girl being educated in Afghanistan to the Chinese family buying their first home to the Sudanese village enjoying peace, security, and self-rule, new dreams are being realized in every part of the world.

A United Nations that serves not only states but also peoples—and becomes the forum where governments are held accountable for their behavior toward their own citizens—will earn its place in the twenty-first century.

INDEX